The Shape of Change

AND

The Shape of Change: Stocks and Flows

This book is a combined edition of two books, *The Shape of Change* and *The Shape of Change: Stocks and Flows.* We have found that over the two years that *The Shape of Change: Stocks and Flows* has been available, more and more people are buying both books. This was to be expected, since the necessary pre-requisites for using the lessons in *The Shape of Change: Stocks and Flows* are the games and lessons presented in *The Shape of Change.* Having them printed in one volume is not only more convenient, but also more cost effective, both for the publisher and the purchaser. This edition is literally the two books put together in the same volume with nothing added or subtracted. As such, the lessons in the original book *The Shape of Change* still can be used as stand-alone lessons without their follow-up in *The Shape of Change: Stocks and Flows.*

The Shape of Change: Stocks and Flows begins immediately following page 146 in *The Shape of Change.*

The Shape of Change and The Shape of Change: Stocks and Flows

Graphic Design/Layout: Amanda Wait, www.MiceSentiments.com
Illustrations: Nathan Walker, www.NathanWalker.net

ISBN: 978-0-9753169-7-9

Additional copies are available from:
The Creative Learning Exchange
www.clexchange.org
milleras@clexchange.org
978-635-9797 in Acton, Massachusetts

Printed in USA by InstantPublisher.com

THE Shape OF Change

Rob Quaden, Alan Ticotsky
and Debra Lyneis

Illustrated by Nathan Walker

Revised Edition

Creative Learning Exchange
Acton, Massachusetts
2008

To Carol, Adam, and Rachel
To Becky and Charlie
With much love

Graphic Design/Layout: Amanda Wait, www.MiceSentiments.com
Illustrations: Nathan Walker, www.NathanWalker.net

ISBN: 978-0-9753169-5-5

Additional copies are available from:
The Creative Learning Exchange
www.clexchange.org
milleras@clexchange.org
978-635-9797 in Acton, Massachusetts

Printed in USA by InstantPublisher.com

Table of Contents: The Shape of Change

Acknowledgements

With grateful appreciation to:

- *Davida Fox-Melanson, for giving us freedom and encouragement to "do what is good for kids"*
- *Jim and Faith Waters, for their willingness to invest in teachers*
- *Mary Scheetz, for believing in first-class treatment for us and fellow educators*

Over the years, the Waters Foundation has generously provided training, technology, encouragement, and especially time for us to work in the classroom mentoring our colleagues and developing lessons using system dynamics. We treasure the professional atmosphere, intellectual stimulation, and valuable friendships we have found. None of this would have happened without the Waters Foundation support.

Many members of the professional system dynamics community have given us their time and expertise. Jay W. Forrester, the founder of the field, has shown us high standards of quality and perseverance. The late Barry Richmond taught us systems thinking skills and the goal of using them to foster "systems citizenship." Carlisle resident Jim Lyneis has been a valuable resource for system dynamics expertise for many years. We thank them all for their help and hope that our attempt to give teachers a basic, non-technical introduction to system dynamics holds true to all that they have taught us.

In Carlisle, in addition to Superintendent Davida Fox-Melanson's strong support, many teachers have been steady partners in our work. Their willingness to field test lessons and provide feedback has been indispensable. As teachers, we are particularly grateful to our students whose insights and enthusiasm continue to inspire us.

We thank Lees Stuntz of the Creative Learning Exchange for her leadership and organization, and for reviewing our work. We would also like to thank the Gordon Stanley Brown Fund for backing the editing and publishing of these lessons.

We appreciate the efforts of Jane Sutton who reviewed much of the manuscript.

Finally, we thank Deb Lyneis. Deb's high expectations combined with unending patience have made her a valuable partner. Her enthusiasm has inspired us to do our best. Deb's attention to detail comes through in every lesson in the book.

The Shape of Change

Nothing is constant except change.

Change is all around us.

But understanding change is certainly not a trivial task. Nearly everything students study in school concerns change.

- Daily temperatures and hours of daylight change with the seasons.
- Money accumulates in a bank account with interest.
- Populations of New World settlers increase, while the numbers of Native Americans decrease.
- Populations of endangered species dwindle. Populations of yeast cells in a test tube explode and collapse.
- Tensions escalate and result in disagreements, revolutions, and wars.
- Social movements grow in acceptance or fade away.
- Excitement builds as a plot unfolds.
- Fictional characters grow in courage, self-esteem, and honor.

One way to grasp how something is changing is to trace how it grows or declines over time. Is there a pattern? Are there turning points? Can you get a better understanding of what is happening by standing back and taking a wider view? Tracking changes in a clear and graphic way can spark insightful thinking.

The activities in ***The Shape of Change*** are designed to help students observe and understand how and why things change over time. Students participate in a game, experiment, or other hands-on activity. Then they draw simple line graphs of the changing behavior over time or they draw a connection circle. As they refine and share their work, students also consider causes and broader implications, honing a keener awareness of the changes all around them.

By generalizing from their classroom experiences with the activities in this book, students gain a deeper appreciation for the way things work.

- How did the population of wooly mammoths change over time and finally become extinct?
- How does the temperature of a cup of hot water cool to reach room temperature?
- How does an epidemic spread, whether it is smallpox in the New World, this year's flu, a computer virus, or a rumor?
- How does friendly behavior grow in a classroom?
- How can we manage renewable resources to achieve sustainability?

In this edition of ***The Shape of Change***, the connection circle explanations in Lessons 10 and 11 are revised to sharpen students' focus on the underlying causes of change.

? Frequently Asked Questions

Will this be fun?

Students love this approach. It is fun to play hands-on games and learn through experience. Students work in teams, share ideas, and listen to each other, not just the teacher. Often, something surprising happens, and discovering the reason is eye-opening.

When students are active, cooperating, and building their own meaning, their level of engagement is high and the learning sticks with them. Also, students who have struggled with typical academic tasks often have a new opportunity to "show what they know" using new learning tools.

Each chapter approaches the lesson with an eye toward three simple yet profound questions:

- What is changing?
- So what?
- Now what? [1]

? Will this be on the test?

The activities take on big ideas that are central to the curriculum in Grades 3–8 and that are transferable to other topics. For example, students construct their own understanding of sophisticated and important topics like sustainability and exponential growth and decay.

The lessons in ***The Shape of Change*** *align with National Council of Teachers of Mathematics (NCTM) standards:*

> *Students solve problems in various contexts, organize their thinking through various forms of communication and learn to express their thinking concisely.*

The lessons also address the concepts and processes in the standards of the National Science Teachers Association (NSTA):

- *Systems, order, and organization*
- *Evidence, modes, and explanation*
- *Change, constancy, and measurement*

? Will this be complicated?

Each chapter begins with a short summary and a list of materials so that teachers can see at a glance what is covered and what materials are necessary. Background information is succinct, and procedures are laid out step by step. Student worksheets are at the end of each lesson, ready to photocopy.

? What do students do?

Students acquire new learning tools and work together to apply them in team learning situations. Teamwork gives rise to better thinking through dialogue, motivation to tackle tougher problems together, mutual respect, and fun. All the lessons in the book are structured to build cooperative learning.

"Hands on with heads on": students are actively engaged with the purpose of improving their thinking and communication skills.

? Can my students do these lessons?

Although the activities in this book are written for Grades 3–8, they have all been used in a range of classrooms. For example, the In and Out Game and Making Friends have been played by Kindergartners and first graders, while the Mammoth Game has been played even in college classes!

? How much time do the lessons take?

Our classroom experience has shown that it takes 45 to 60 minutes to complete each activity. Allow more time if you want students to do more extensive writing. Of course, the age of the students will make a big difference. For example, the Mammoth Game takes 45 minutes in Grade 7 while third graders need two periods of 45 minutes each.

? Do I have to do the lessons in order?

Each lesson can stand alone. Chapters 1–8 may be done in any order, and the connection circle technique in Chapters 9–11 will be useful in many contexts. Lessons 6–8 can be taught as a unit on renewable resources.

? Can we do more lessons like these?

If you enjoy these activities and want to try more, see the references listed after each lesson. For more information, contact us through the Creative Learning Exchange, or visit the Creative Learning Exchange website at www.clexchange.org. We would appreciate your feedback on these lessons as well as suggestions for other classroom resources. Also, take a look at the Waters Foundation website at www.watersfoundation.org.

? How can I assess what students are learning?

Every lesson concludes with guiding questions designed "to bring the lesson home." Student responses to these questions will reveal their level of understanding. In many cases, individual student worksheets can be used to monitor performance.

After any of the lessons, asking students to write a short answer to these four open-ended questions will provide insight into their thinking and reinforce writing skills:

- *What is changing?*
- *How is it changing?*
- *Why is it changing?*[2]
- *What else changes in this way?*

Teachers and students will be happy that thinking, not memorizing, is the key to learning from these activities. Try these lessons and watch your students start paying attention to the shape of change.

? What is the next step?

To take a closer look at the underlying structures causing the changes students observe in these lessons, see our next book, ***The Shape of Change: Stocks and Flows*** *(2007), also available from The Creative Learning Exchange.*

The Shape of Change

- Hands-on activities
- Teamwork
- Reflection
- Dialogue among students
- Constructivism and inquiry
- High student engagement
- Accommodation to different ability levels
- Sophisticated content
- High-level critical thinking
- Agreement with goals of national standards, e.g., NCTM, NSTA
- No prerequisites for teachers or students
- Simple preparation and easy directions

Curriculum Connections

All of the lessons in ***The Shape of Change*** are interdisciplinary. Students use math as a foundation to explore questions across the curriculum. As they use graphs to understand how things change over time, they also find that similar patterns of behavior arise in diverse places: the mammoth population declines in a pattern much like the cooling of a cup of hot water. The debriefing questions at the end of each lesson encourage students to make their own broader connections.

The following table suggests ways that each lesson can fit into your curriculum. For example, your class may not study mammoths or the Ice Age, but chances are endangered species or population changes come up as topics of concern.

NOTES

1 The Waters Foundation uses these questions in its teacher training workshops—a good way to maintain focus on the central purpose of system dynamics in education. Students delve beyond surface events to question their causes and broader implications.

2 Gayle Richardson framed these questions as a way to help students understand and graph change. For more information, see "Getting Started with Behavior Over Time Graphs: Four Curriculum Examples," 1998, available from the Creative Learning Exchange at www.clexchange.org.

Lesson	Math	Science	Social Studies
The In and Out Game	Graphing from tables, function rules	A way to view change over time in any context	
Making Friends	Graphing from tables, function rules, linear and exponential growth		Social competency, defining and using friendship skills, inclusion
The Mammoth Game	Graphing from tables, exponential decay, probability	Ice Age, population dynamics, extinction, endangered species	Ice Age, population dynamics
The Infection Game	Exponential growth, S-shaped growth, bell-shaped growth, interpreting graphs	Contagious diseases	Spread of smallpox in Americas, rumors, fads, and social movements
It's Cool	Predicting, collecting data, graphing from tables, interpreting graphs, exponential decay	Movement of heat, insulation, using a thermometer, Celsius scale	
The Tree Game	Graphing from tables, interpreting graphs	Renewable resource management, sustainability	
The Tree Game Puzzle	Graphing from tables, function rules, interpreting graphs	Renewable resource management, sustainability, supply and demand	
The Rainforest Game	Graphing from tables, linear growth, equilibrium,	Renewable resource management, economics, sustainability, effect of delays	
The Connection Game		Activity to raise awareness of complexity in any context	
Fries Connection Circle		Comprehension strategy for understanding complexity	
Keystone Connection Circle			

Lesson 1

The In and Out Game

The In and Out Game is a simple activity that introduces and reinforces the understanding of change over time. Players physically move into and out of a designated area of the classroom to observe how the total number of students in the area changes as students enter and leave. By looking at a table and a graph of the action in the game, students learn concepts that will be applied to other activities in this book. The In and Out Game reinforces math skills such as recording, graphing, and predicting.[1]

MATERIALS

- Large display area (easel pad, display board, or chalkboard)
- Large easel graph pad
- Colored markers and chalk
- Rope or tape to mark an area of the classroom floor

How It Works

The number of students in the designated game area changes over time as some players enter the area and other players leave during each round. Students count the total number of players in the area after each round and record their observations on a class graph. In the first game, the rule is: 2 students "In" and 1 student "Out" each round. In the second game, students play with different rules, make predictions and compare the results. They learn through experience that the change in the total number of students in the area depends on the number of students flowing in and out over time.

One way to view the accumulation of players in the area is to think of them as a "stock," like a stock, or quantity, of goods on a store shelf. The stock of goods is increased by restocking and depleted by customer purchases over time. Other changes over time can be viewed in the same way:

- The accumulation of water in a bathtub increases as water flows in through the faucet and decreases as water flows out through the drain.
- Money in a bank account increases with deposits and decreases with withdrawals.
- Populations of people and other species change over time through births and deaths.
- The number of passengers on a bus or train varies as people get on and off.
- Your weight depends on the calories you consume and burn off.

If you are wondering why something is changing over time, it is useful to think of it as an accumulation (or stock) and ask what is flowing In and Out over time to cause the change.

In this game, students are playing with the very basic structure of change as they examine and document what happens to the total number of students in the stock as some students "flow" in and out. Students begin to notice patterns of behavior over time and their causes. In the process, they have fun building math skills—counting, computing, graphing, and predicting.

Procedure

1. Ahead of time, prepare a large blank table and graph on the easel or board.

Round	Players In the Stock	Players Going In	Players Going Out
Start			
1			
2			
3			
4			
5			
6			
7			
8			
9			
10			

Prepare the table and graph on an easel pad before playing.

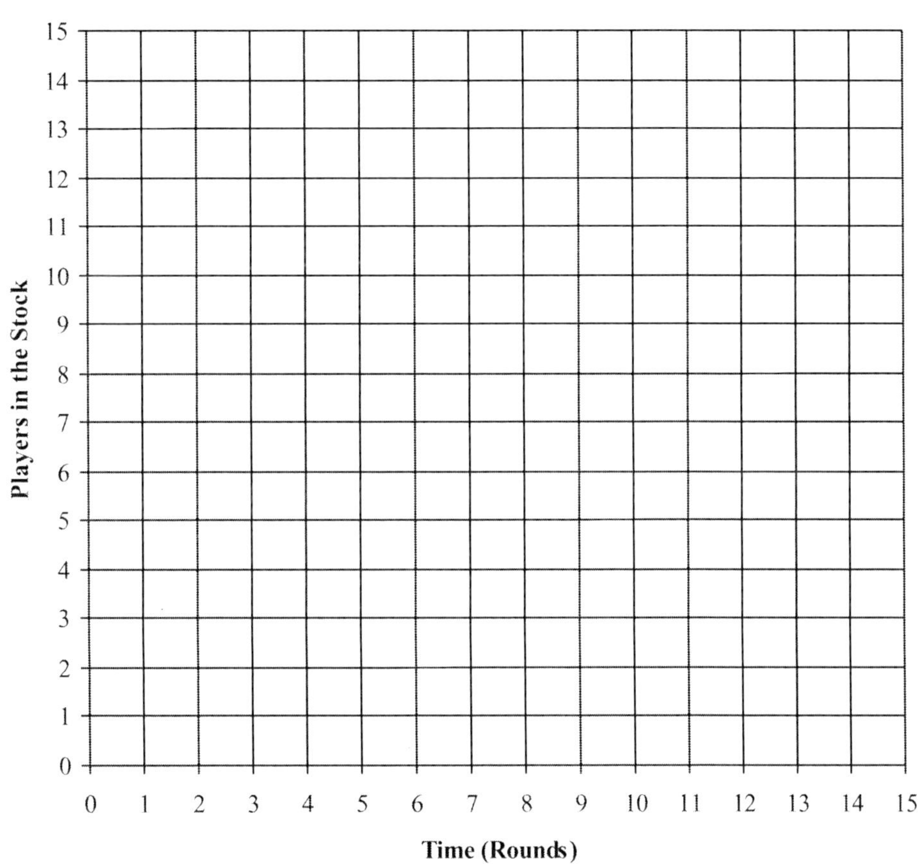

(Label the vertical axis with the number of students in the class.)

Also, designate a place in the room for the players to stand and be counted—this is called the "stock." Delineate the stock area with rope or masking tape on the floor and create pathways to be used as the "flows" through which players enter and exit the stock, again using rope or tape.

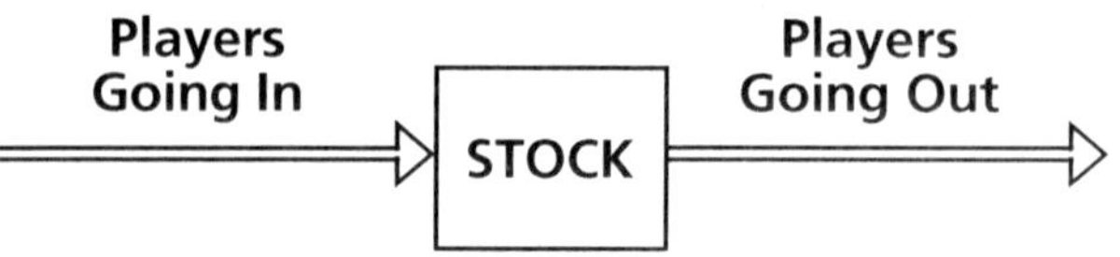

2. Explain to the students that they will be playing a game and keeping track of the number of players in the stock area. As they play, students will take turns entering and leaving the stock through the flow pathways.

3. Announce the rules for **Game 1**. Record these initial values on the first line of the chart.

A. In the stock to start: 0 players
B. Inflow each round: 2 players going In
C. Outflow each round: 1 player going Out

4. Ask two volunteers to walk through the In flow and enter the stock. Ask one of them to exit through the Out flow. Count how many players now remain in the stock—one player. Record that number on the next line in the column for "Players in the Stock" to begin Round 1.

What causes a quantity to change over time? Students learn by acting it out.

Round	Players In the Stock	Players Going In	Players Going Out
Start	0	2	1
1	1		
2			
3			

5. Choose two new volunteers and play another round.

- Record 2 Players Going In and 1 Player Going Out.
- Count how many players remain in the stock (2) and enter this number to begin Round 2.
- Repeat this process, recording the new numbers on the table. Students will soon be able to make predictions as they see patterns emerge. Guide their predictions with questions, after playing several rounds.

? What will the values on the table be after the next round?

? What would the values be after 15 rounds? 32 rounds?
The number of players in the stock will continue to increase by one each round. There will be 15 students in the stock in Round 15.

Round	Players In the Stock	Players Going In	Players Going Out
Start	0	2	1
1	1	2	1
2	2	2	1
3	3	2	1
4	4	2	1
5	5	2	1
6	6	2	1
7	7		
8			
9			
10			

6. After playing and recording several rounds, begin drawing the graph, as shown on the next page. Create a line graph by plotting the data points for the people in the stock and connecting the points. Point out that the vertical axis is labeled "Players in the Stock." The horizontal axis measures time, counted in rounds played. The graph shows how the stock behaves during the time that the game is played. We call this a *behavior over time graph.*

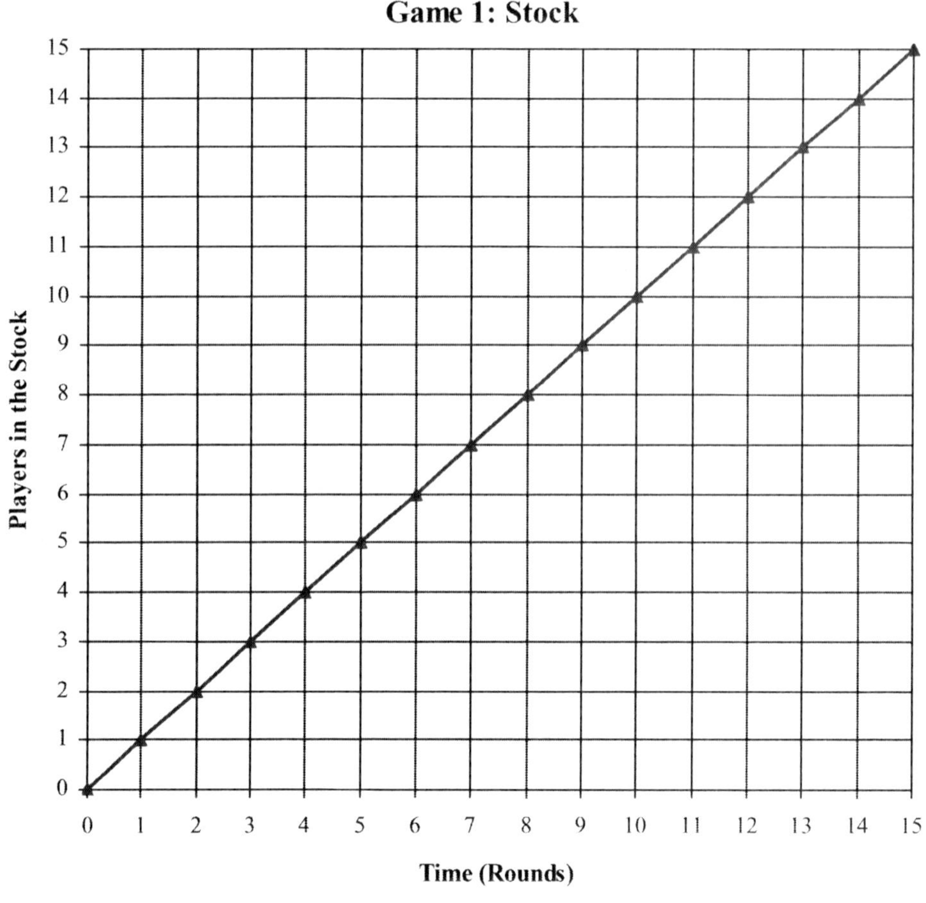

The game is a discrete activity. We connect the dots to help students see the patterns more clearly.

Be sure to differentiate between the students in the designated area each round (the stock) and the players entering and leaving each round (the flows). First plot the stock as shown above, then plot the flows. Plotting the flows will produce horizontal lines because the flows are constant, as shown on page 13.

Again, ask students to make predictions about the stock.

? What will the line look like after the next round? 15 rounds?
The line will continue with the same diagonal slope.

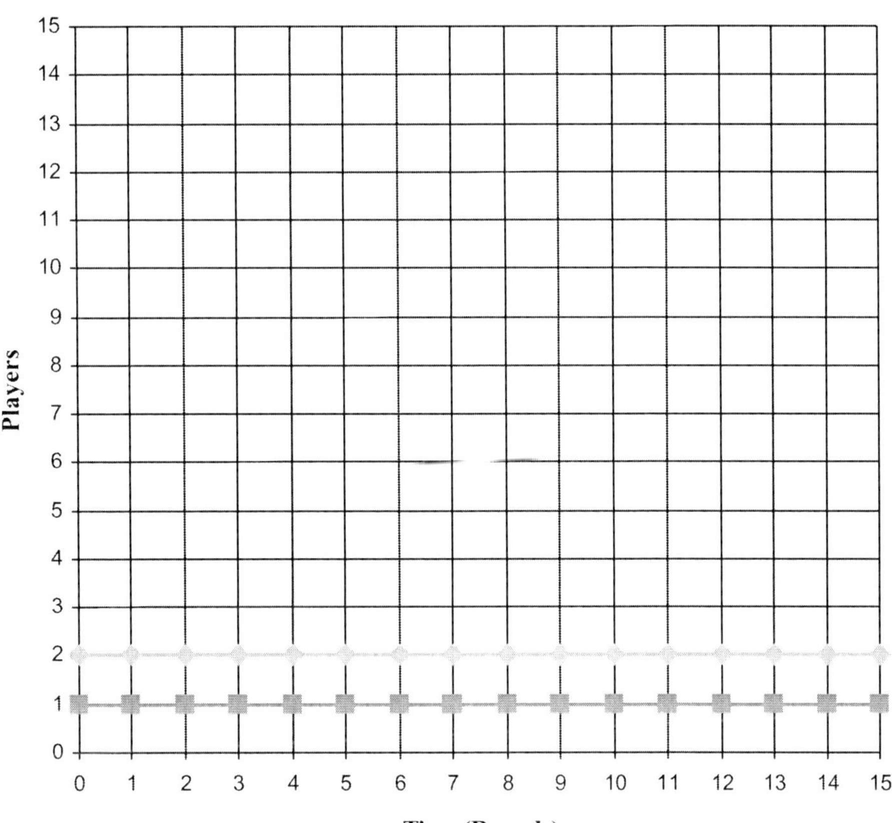

7. Prepare students to play **Game 2**, this time with a different set of rules.

There are three rule choices to make for each game:

A. How many players are in the stock to start the game.
B. Inflow: how many go In each round
C. Outflow: how many go Out each round.

Once the rules are established, they cannot be changed until you end the game and begin another.

Use the following rules for Game 2:

A. In the stock to start: 0
B. Inflow each turn: 5
C. Outflow each turn: 2

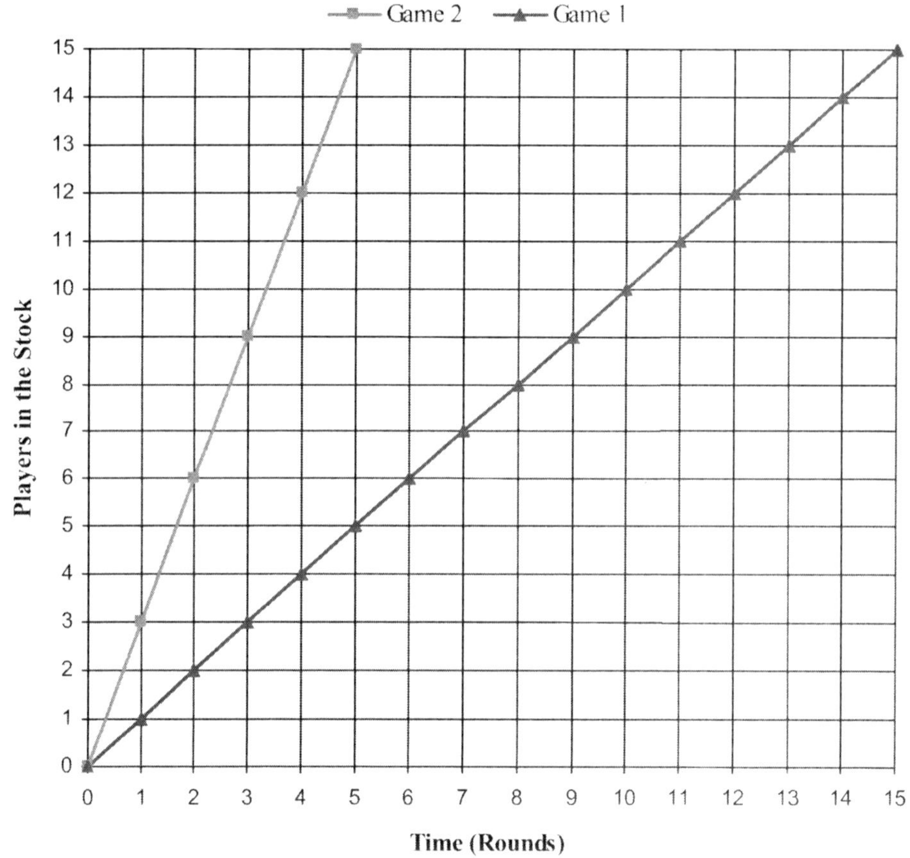

Enter these initial values on a new table and follow the same procedure as the first game. Walk through a few rounds of the game and record the data on a new table. However, graph the stock in Game 2 on the *same graph* as Game 1 in a *different color* so that students can compare the two lines.

Bringing the Lesson Home

Use the graph to focus a discussion on what happened in the game using questions like these:

? How does the graph show us what happened to the number of players in the stock in Game 1 and Game 2?

In both games, the number of players in the stock grew over time because more players were going in than going out each round.

? How are the lines for Game 1 and Game 2 similar?

Encourage answers such as: Both lines are straight; both show that the stock is increasing at a steady rate; they both start at 0; etc.

? How are they different?

While older students can talk in terms of slope, younger students may use words like "steeper" and "flatter" to describe the different rates of change.

? Which line is steeper? Why?

The graph for Game 2 is steeper, because more players stayed in the stock each round. The difference between inflow and outflow was greater than in the first game.

Students learn to use graphs to consider and communicate their ideas about change over time.

Encourage students to deepen their thinking.

? What makes a stock change?

Inflows and outflows cause a stock to change—in this case, students going in and out make the number of students in the stock change over time.

? How can we make the behavior over time graph of the stock steeper?

Increase the inflow or decrease the outflow so that the stock accumulates at a faster rate.

? How would the graph be different if there were some players in the stock at the start of the game?

The line would not begin at zero at the beginning of the game. (Graph A)

? What happens when an outflow is larger than the inflow?

The stock decreases. The line will go down and might reach zero. (Graph B)

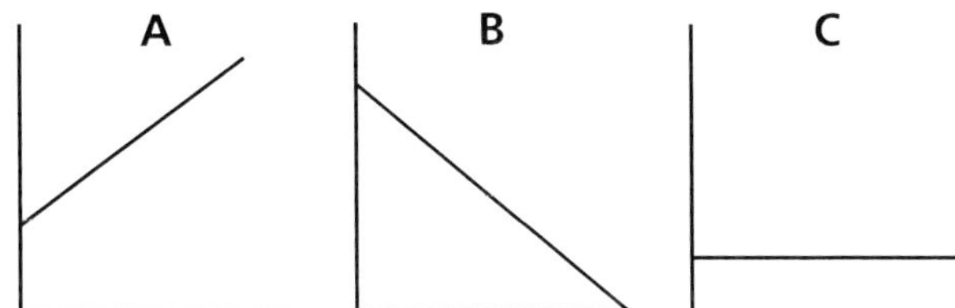

Alternatively, present students with these three graphs and ask them to define the game rules that produce them.

? What happens when the inflow and outflow are equal, say, 3 In and 3 Out each round?

The graph of the stock is a horizontal line, because the stock remains constant. (Graph C on previous page)

? Ask students if they can think of any experiences in life that resemble the In and Out Game. What makes the stock increase or decrease over time?

Encourage students to apply the lesson to a range of examples.

- *Money in a bank, piggy bank or pocket over a week or month*
- *Populations of humans and others species over years*
- *Water in a bathtub over minutes, or a pond over a year*
- *Passengers on a train or bus over a day*
- *People in a store, in the school, or in the lunchroom over an hour or day*
- *The weight of their book bags throughout the day*
- *Their hunger, fatigue or happiness over the course of a day or week*

The In and Out Game is a simulation for any stock with flows in and out. Any change over time can be viewed as an accumulation, or stock, that is increased by its inflows and decreased by its outflows.

NOTES

1 An expanded version of this game, "The In and Out Game: A Preliminary System Dynamics Modeling Lesson" by Ticotsky, Quaden and Lyneis, 1999, is available from the Creative Learning Exchange at www.clexchange.org. It includes adaptations for primary, upper elementary and middle school students, plus complete instructions to help students build their own system dynamics computer models of the game.

Lesson 2

Making Friends

After reviewing why making friends is important, students play a non-competitive tagging game. They track the rate of growth of friendships in the class when students employ their friendship skills and behave in friendly ways. By changing the rules of the game each time it is played, students discover the effect of rates of growth. Math skills such as graphing, comparing, and computation reinforce affective skills including cooperation and inclusion, in this adaptation of the "Friendship Game" by P. Clemans.[1]

MATERIALS

- Large display area (easel pad, display board, or chalkboard)
- Large easel graph pad
- Markers, chalk
- Set of name cards of class members in a paper bag or container

How It Works

Creating a sense of community within a classroom does not happen automatically. Teachers devote significant amounts of time and energy to ensuring that learning flourishes in a supportive, caring environment. Many schools include a social competency program in their curriculum. In Making Friends, students follow up work on cooperation and civility. They investigate the rates of growth possible in building friendships when students behave in friendly ways and everyone is included.

The Making Friends Game allows students to try different scenarios non-competitively and compare the results. Choosing members of the class to build a "Friendship Team" reinforces the goal of including everyone. Students benefit greatly when they approach cooperative learning with a positive attitude.

Students play and graph two versions of the game.

- In the first game, two students are added to the friendship team each round. Adding a constant number each time produces a straight line on the graph, or linear growth. It takes a long time to get everyone on the team.
- In the second game, each student already on the friendship team recruits a new member each round. As the team grows larger, the number of new members also grows larger each round. It takes only a few rounds to include everyone. This accelerating growth produces a curved line because the size of the team determines the number of new players. This pattern is called *exponential growth.*
- In both games, the shape of the line on the graph represents the nature of the growth—an important and non-trivial concept for students.

Generating and posting a list of Friendship Skills before playing is very important. Tagging a player represents practicing the behaviors designed to create a caring, cooperative classroom.

Procedure

1. Prepare a large graph before playing as illustrated on the following page. The horizontal axis represents time in rounds of the game. The vertical axis records the number of Friends and is labeled with the number of students in the class. Also prepare a table. You will graph two or three games on the same graph for comparison, but you will use a new table for each game.

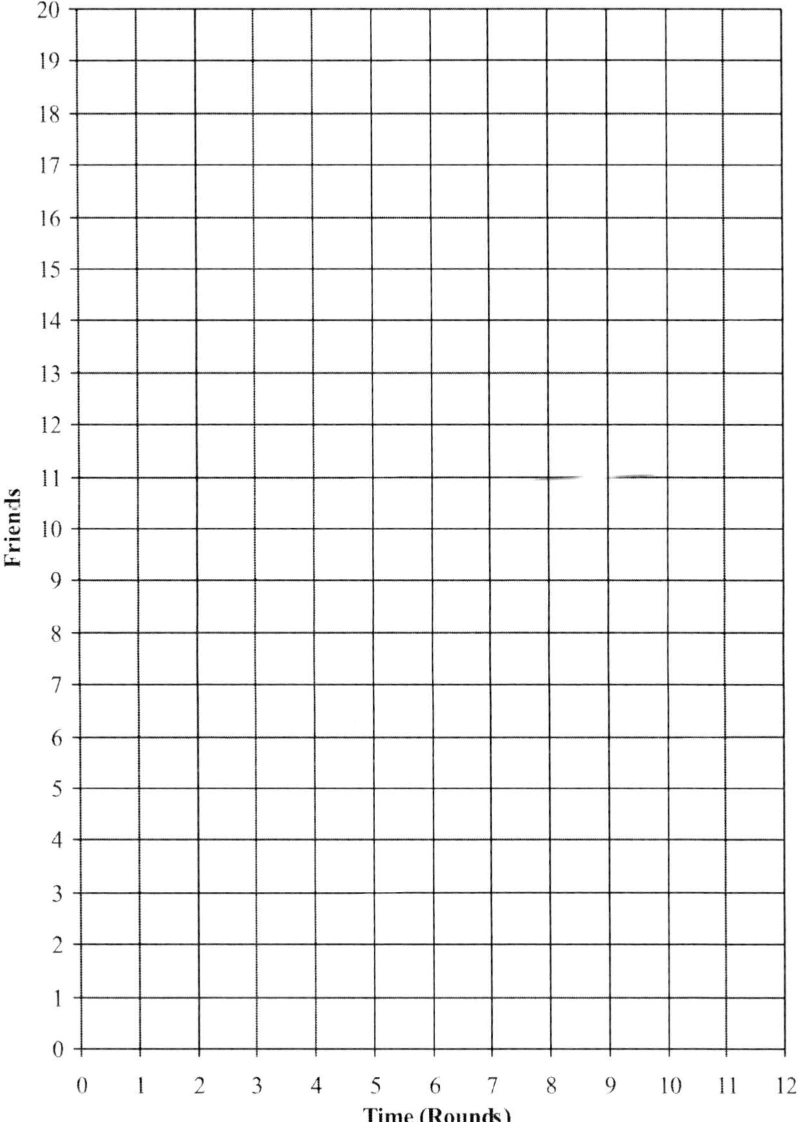

Round	Friends
Start	
1	
2	
3	
4	
5	
6	
7	
8	
9	
10	

2. Ask students how they make friends. What qualities define a good friend? Can you have more than one friend at a time? What are the behaviors and skills that they can practice to be good friends? This conversation can be very rich and earnest, especially if the class has already been engaged in team building activities.

3. Explain that students are going to play a simulation game in which players pretend to make friends. They will play *Making Friends* until all the members of the class are on the Friends Team.

FRIENDSHIP SKILLS

Be a good listener

Respect differences

Include everyone

Share

Be helpful

Smile

Game 1

4. Choose two or three students to begin the game on the Friends Team and remove their names from the container of name cards. (Choosing three works well if the total number of players is a multiple of three; otherwise choose two.) Move the chosen players to a designated area of the classroom where the Friends Team will meet. Record the data on the table as shown.

Game 1

Round	Friends
Start	2
1	
2	
3	
4	
5	
6	
7	
8	
9	
10	

5. On a signal from the teacher, the rest of the students close their eyes. The first Friends Team players each randomly draw one student name card from the container. They silently tag those students gently, implying that they have employed their friendship skills. The tagged students open their eyes and join their taggers in the Friends Team area. When the turn is completed, everybody opens their eyes and helps record the data for that round.

6. The original Friends Team players stay in the Friends Team area and the newly chosen players prepare for their turn. Students close their eyes, while the new players draw name cards and bring one more person each back to the Friends Team area. Again, count and record the number of friends on the team.

Game 1

Round	Friends
Start	2
1	4
2	6
3	8
4	10
5	12
6	14
7	16
8	18
9	20
10	22

After a round or two, students will be able to predict the pattern of growth. As the game progresses, continue to keep track of the size of the Friends Team using the table. Play the game until everyone is included. If numbers are uneven and the last turn does not end with everyone getting to choose, include the teacher or imagine there is an extra player or two.

Before playing each round, ask students to predict what will happen to the number of friends in the next round. Is a pattern emerging?

7. When the game is over, use the data to make a line graph as a class, tracking the number of players on the Friends Team. Help students locate points on the graph and connect them, as shown below. Ask students to analyze what happened.

A line graph helps students see the pattern of change over time. We call this a *behavior over time graph*.

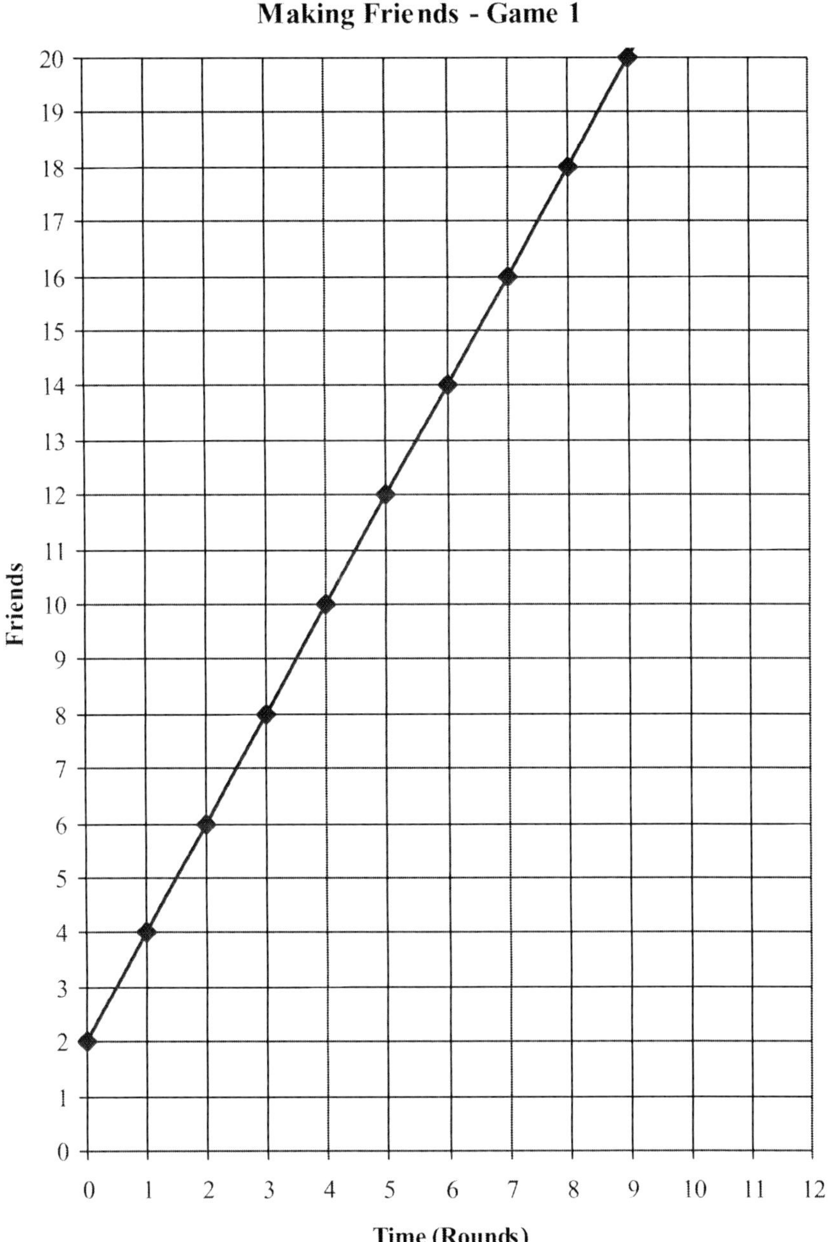

The game is a discrete activity. We connect the dots to help students see the patterns more clearly.

? What do you notice? What happened to the number of friends? Why is the line straight?

The team grew by the same number of players each round.

? Why does it slant upwards diagonally?

The number of players increased each turn.

? What would happen if you had another class join and you kept playing for 5 more rounds? 10 more?

The straight line would be extended, slanting diagonally at the same angle and rate.

Game 2

Game 2

Round	Friends
Start	2
1	4
2	8
3	16
4	32
5	64
6	
7	
8	
9	
10	

8. Tell students that they will play another game. The rules will change. This time, instead of simply sitting in the Friends Team area after choosing a new friend once, every friend will now be able to choose a new friend every round. After all, people are not restricted to one friend! People can use their friendship skills over and over.

What do the students predict will happen? Ask for opinions and record the predictions on the board. Predictions are just best guesses for now—they help students think about the results as they unfold.

Play the game and record the results on a data table similar to the table used for Game 1. Before each round, ask students to predict what will happen to the number of friends in that round and in future rounds. Is a pattern emerging?

9. Graph Game 2 on the same graph as Game 1, but use a different color marker for the line, as shown on the next page.

Bringing the Lesson Home

Use the graph and questions like these to focus the discussion on what happened to the number of friends in the game. Then, relate the lesson to the students' own experience.

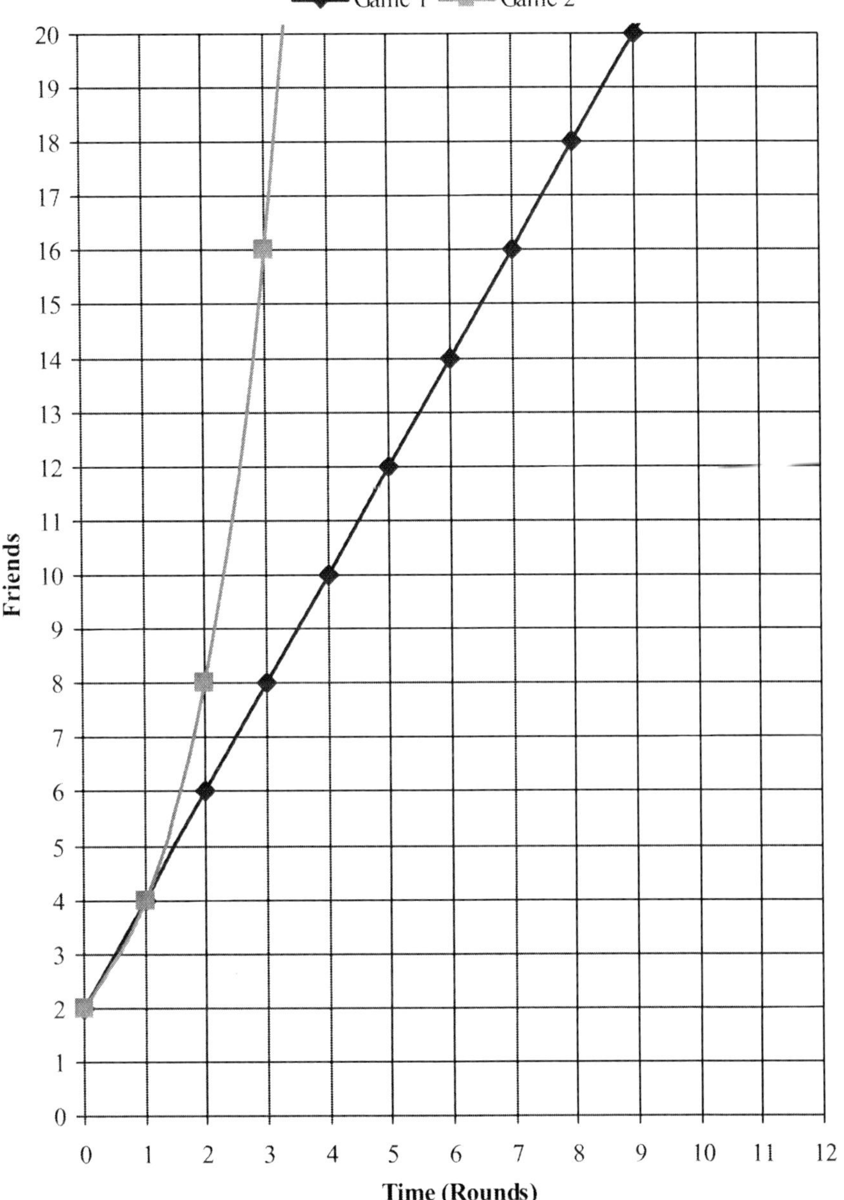

Allowing players on the Friends team to choose new friends every time in Game 2 causes doubling. The line curves and grows faster than the line in Game 1.

? What does the graph tell us about what happened to the number of friends in Game 1 and Game 2?

In both games the number of friends increased, but the Friends Team grew much faster in Game 2.

Save enough time for this important lesson wrap-up. Help students use the game to build critical thinking skills and an understanding of their own friendship behavior.

? How are the lines different? How are they similar?

Both lines go up, indicating an increase in the size of teams, but the line in Game 2 curves, getting steeper with each round. Older students can explore the concept of slope when comparing the lines. Younger students can use terms like "steeper" and "flatter."

? Did the rate of making new friends change in Game 2 compared to Game 1? Why?

Yes. In Game 2, players on the Friends Team were allowed to choose a friend every round rather than choosing only once.

? Why does Game 1 produce a straight line and Game 2 produce a curved line?

In Game 1, the same number of friends joined the team each turn. Therefore, the graph showed a steady increase represented by a straight line. In Game 2, the number of players joining increased each turn, so the slope of the graph became steeper as the game progressed. The more members there were on the team, the more new players got chosen each round, making the team even bigger for the next round of choices, and so on. This pattern is called compounding or exponential growth.

? What would happen in Game 2 if another class joined the game?

Even though the number of players would be much greater, only one more round would be required to complete the game because the Friends Team doubles each round.

? Which set of rules creates a fully inclusive Friends Team faster?

Allowing players to choose a friend each turn is much faster than allowing them only one choice per game.

? How can this relate to our class?

If students use their friendship skills often with all their classmates, friendships spread quickly. The atmosphere in the class is much friendlier when everyone is included.

Feedback

Feedback occurs when the size of the existing team affects the number of new arrivals, which in turn affects the size of the team, and so on. This process reinforces growth and produces a curved line on the graph. For example, if the team doubles each time, it can grow from 1 to 2, to 4, to 8, etc.

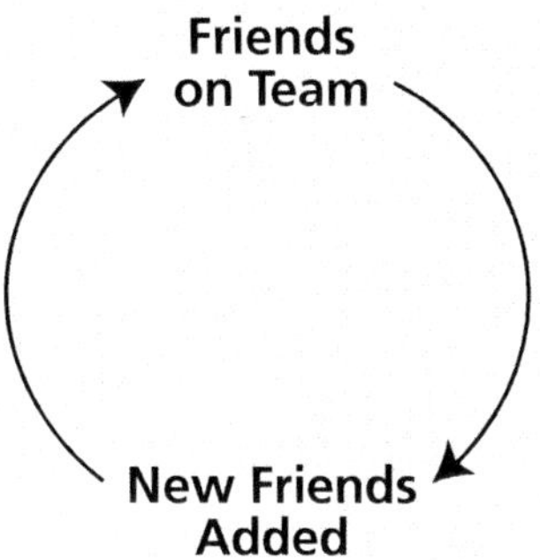

Variations and Extensions

New Rules

The next time students play Making Friends, they can try out rules of their choice. Encourage them to change variables, such as the original number of friends at turn zero or the number of friends one person may choose. Remember to reinforce the connection to what the simulation represents: using friendship skills to grow a cooperative, supportive classroom environment.

Unfriendly Behaviors

In the Making Friends game, friendships spread through positive behaviors and interactions. Unfortunately, negative behaviors can also spread by the same growth mechanism. Teasing can spiral out of control on the playground, for example, if students begin to join in. Peer pressure can lead to other negative behaviors. If students are confronting issues like these, use Making Friends to point out objectively each person's responsibility in determining the pattern of spread. They can use their friendship skills to turn things around.

NOTES

1 For an earlier version of this lesson see "Graphing the Friendship Game: A Preliminary System Dynamics Lesson" by Ticotsky and Lyneis, 2000, available from the Creative Learning Exchange at www.clexchange.org.

Both "Making Friends" and "Graphing the Friendship Game" are adaptations of the original "Friendship Game" by Peg Clemans, Catalina Foothills School District, Tucson, 1996, also available at www.clexchange.org.

Lesson 3

The Mammoth Game

Teams of students play a dice and graphing game to track the population growth and decline of a herd of twenty mammoths. By changing probabilities with the dice, students can explore theories of extinction and speculate about which factors contributed to the wooly mammoth's demise. Interdisciplinary links include science topics such as extinctions and population rates, and social studies investigation of Ice Age cultures. Math concepts include graphing, probability, percentages, fractions and exponential decay. [1]

How It Works

Scientists believe wooly mammoths were once plentiful on the North American continent but became extinct about 11,000

MATERIALS

- 20 dice per team
- Cardboard boxes for dice rolling
- Markers of the same two colors for each student
- One copy of the *Mammoth Game Rules* (page 36) per team
- Copies of two worksheets for each student (see pages 37–38)

  1. *Keeping Track of Your Herd*
  2. *Graph of Your Mammoth Population*

This is a simulation. We want to understand why mammoths went extinct, but because we cannot study real mammoths in the classroom, we will use dice to represent them.

years ago. Opinions vary as to the cause of their demise. Was the warming climate responsible, or was an as yet undiscovered disease the primary culprit? Did predators hunt mammoths to extinction?

Although scientists have not reached consensus, most agree that the arrival of a significant number of humans put more pressure on a mammoth population already stressed by a warming climate. Skillful human hunters may have reduced the already vulnerable mammoths to numbers that spiraled to extinction.

Students simulate the effect of human hunting upon a declining population by playing two versions of the Mammoth Game. One version will track the mammoth population without human hunting and graph the extinction curve. The second game will add hunters as a factor and students will see the rate of extinction increase. Displaying and comparing the graphs helps students see the patterns of behavior more clearly.

Procedure

1. Generate a list of mammoth extinction theories with students. This conversation in class can be very rich.

2. Tell students that they will pretend to track the population of a herd of twenty mammoths over time. Then, they will graph the population.

3. Distribute 20 dice per team of students. Each die represents one mammoth, so the starting population is 20. Students record this on the *Keeping Track of Your Herd* worksheet (page 37), under Game 1. (Keep a few extra dice available in case a herd population rises above 20 during the game.)

Game 1		Game 2	
Year	**MAMMOTHS**	**Year**	**MAMMOTHS**
Start	20	Start	
1		1	
2		2	

4. Give one copy of the *Mammoth Game Rules* (page 36) to each team or use an overhead projector to explain the rules. Each time the set of dice is rolled, one simulated year goes by. The number on each die determines the fate of the individual mammoth it represents. To begin play, shake and roll all the dice into the cardboard box. Sort the dice using the rules in the box below.

Because they want their mammoths to survive, younger students may be tempted to cheat and change the dice results. Explain that this is a simulation, not a contest. The object is similar to a science experiment —if you create certain conditions, what is the result?

Rules for Game 1

1 = a calf is born

2 = the mammoth is killed by a predator

3 = the mammoth dies of starvation

4 = the mammoth keeps living another year

5 = the mammoth keeps living another year

6 = the mammoth keeps living another year

Post these rules for easy reference.

5. Accuracy is very important, so spend enough time establishing procedures. Each student should track the population on his or her own table, but all team members should agree on the numbers.

- Sort, count, and record the number of mammoths remaining after the first year.
- For the second year, roll the dice again, using only those mammoths that survived the first year plus any new calves. Record the results.
- Play and record for 20 "years" or until the mammoths become extinct.

Cooperative team learning works best when students understand what their roles are.

6. Depending on the age of the students and your classroom routines, you can either assign jobs to team members or let them choose tasks among themselves. For example, one student might remove dead mammoths, another adds new calves, a third is the official counter, and so on. Rotate jobs to involve everyone.

Students draw line graphs so that they can more easily discern patterns of behavior over time.

7. After students finish playing the game, ask each student to plot the results on the *Graph of Your Mammoth Population* worksheet (page 38).
   - Each student should graph the data using the *same color* marker.
   - Graphing can be difficult for younger students, so be sure they are plotting points correctly before connecting them to make a line graph.
   - It works best to play the game *first* and then draw the graph.

Here is an example of a student graph. Expect student graphs to vary somewhat.

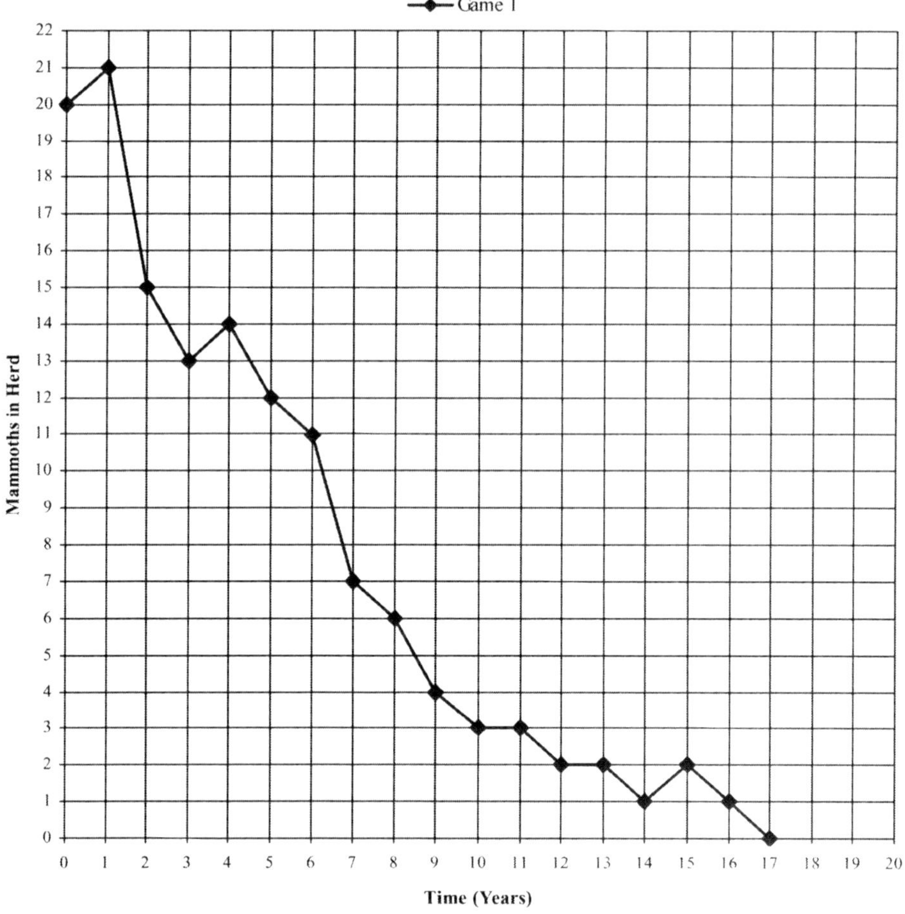

Bringing the Lesson Home

Game 1

Post one graph from each team on the wall for easy comparison and discussion. Questions like these will arise. Help students use the game to build critical thinking skills and deeper understanding.

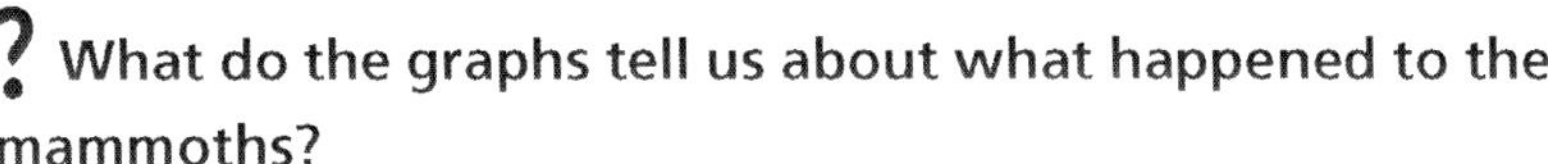

? What do the graphs tell us about what happened to the mammoths?

All of the herds went extinct.

? When did your mammoths go extinct? Why did that happen?

These are brainstorming questions that stimulate student thinking. In Game 1, predators and starvation caused deaths. There could have been other causes too, such as disease.

? If some baby mammoths were born each year, why did the population still decline?

The population declined because more mammoths were dying than being born each year.

? What is the general pattern of the graphs? Depending on the level of the students: What is the rate of change? What is the slope?

The graphs show a steep downward curve at first that levels out as the mammoths approach extinction.

? What is similar about all the graphs? What is different? Why?

All the graphs decline in the same general pattern. The lines vary somewhat because the dice rolled differently for different teams; in real life, different herds would have different luck too—bad weather, less food, illness, etc.

Older students can discuss slope. Younger students use descriptions like "steeper" and "flatter" to describe the rates of change.

? Why is the line curved? What does the curved line say about what was happening to the population? Why is the line steeper in some places than in others?

The line is steeper at first because there were more mammoths to die at the beginning. As the herd shrank, the death rate applied to fewer and fewer animals until there were none left. This pattern is called exponential decay. *The line is curved because the number of deaths varied, depending on the number of mammoths left.*

? At what point was the herd half its original size?

The half-life is about 4 years.

? Would the animals still become extinct if you started with a bigger herd, say 100 mammoths?

The size of the herd would not affect the general pattern. Under the same death rate, the herd would be half its size by the same time and extinct by the same time. This idea surprises students.

Playing Game 2

1. Change one of the "the mammoth keeps living another year" fates to "the mammoth is killed by a hunter." Introducing human hunters into the game allows players to compare what happens to the mammoth population when hunting pressure is applied.

Rules for Game 2

1 = a calf is born

2 = the mammoth is killed by a predator

3 = the mammoth dies of starvation

4 = the mammoth is killed by a hunter

5 = the mammoth keeps living another year

6 = the mammoth keeps living another year

It does not matter if a prediction is wrong or right. Predictions help students reflect on their thinking as the game progresses.

2. Ask students to predict what might happen in Game 2 and explain their reasoning.

? How many dice numbers represent deaths in Game 2?

The death fraction in Game 2 is 3/6, or 1/2. In Game 1 it was 2/6, or 1/3. On average, when the dice are rolled, a larger fraction of the herd will die each year in Game 2.

3. Play Game 2 following the new rules. Then, let students graph the results in a *second color* on the *same graph* used for Game 1.

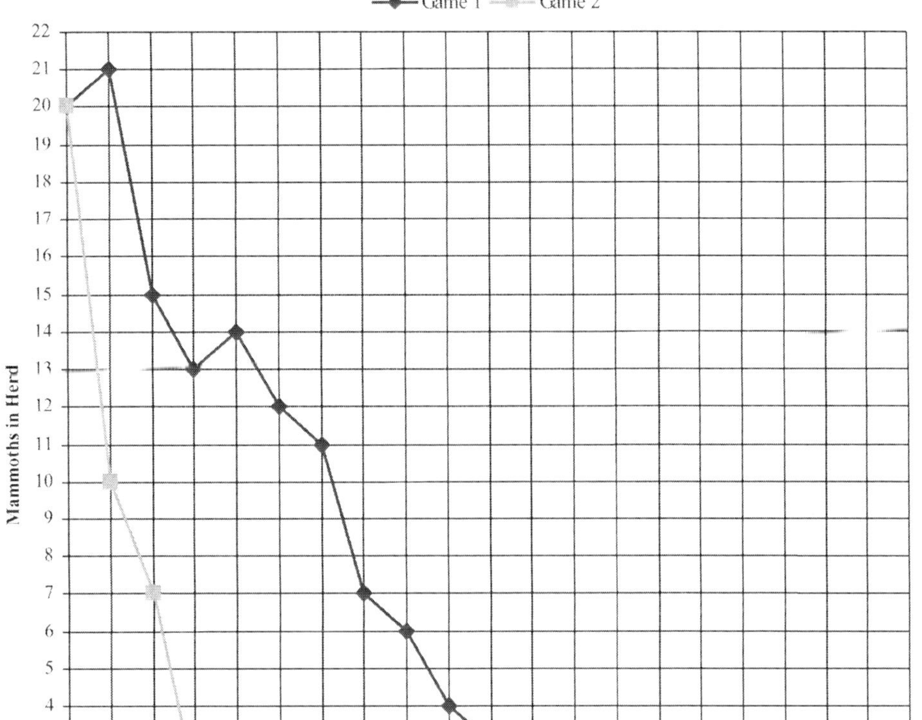

Bringing the Lesson Home

Game 2

Again, post the student graphs for easy comparison and discussion prompted by questions like these.

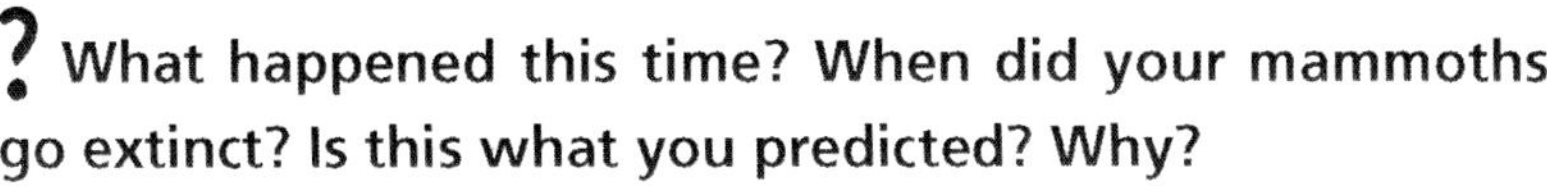

? What happened this time? When did your mammoths go extinct? Is this what you predicted? Why?

> *Mammoths went extinct even more quickly than before because more mammoths were dying each year and not enough babies were being born.*

Be sure to reserve enough time for this last step. Let students think about what they have learned.

? Is there a general pattern again? Why is it steeper in some places than others?

Again, the graphs show a steep downward curve that levels off as the mammoths approach extinction. The population decreased at a faster rate at the beginning because the death rate applied to more mammoths at first. By the end, there were fewer mammoths left to die.

? Why is the line curved? Why isn't the line straight?

The line is curved because the number of deaths varied depending on how many mammoths were left. The line would be straight if a constant number of mammoths were born and died every year.

? How are the lines for Game 1 and Game 2 alike? How are they different?

Students may use words such as steep, flat, and slope to describe the lines. Explore these concepts. Be sure to relate the shape of the line to the rate of population decline. Both lines show exponential decay, but Game 2 had a higher death rate, so the mammoths died off more quickly.

? What difference did the hunters make?

Broaden the discussion to explore extinction theories. Why might one herd survive somewhat longer than another? It is likely that herds faced different conditions. In earlier times, mammoths were able to rebound after various disasters. Could the new human hunters have been enough of a threat to mammoths to push them to extinction?

Encourage students to step back and take a broader look.

? What makes a population decline?

Deaths exceed births.

? What makes a population grow?

Births exceed deaths.

? Can a population stay the same?

Yes, if births and deaths are equal.

? Does this happen only to mammoths? Can you think of other cases?

The same principles apply to all populations.

- *Populations of bacteria in a test tube*
- *Populations of fish in a pond or deer in a forest*
- *Populations of people in the world, or in a country or town (including migration).*

Births cause a population to grow larger. A larger population results in even more births, causing the population to grow even larger, and so on. At the same time, deaths cause a population to decrease, and a smaller population results in fewer deaths. These are called *feedback loops.*

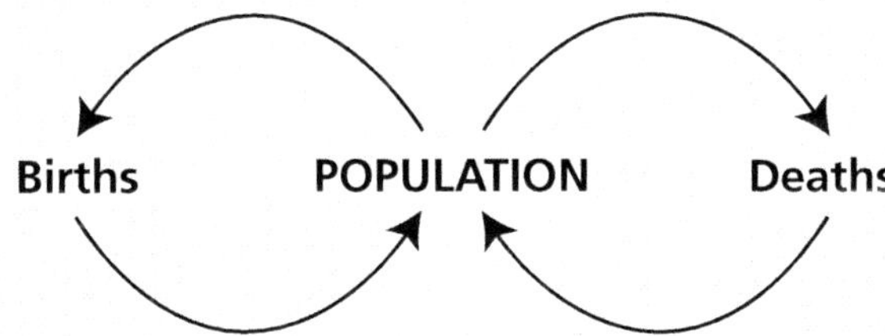

NOTES

1 The Mammoth Game was adapted from the teacher's guide to Newton's Apple, Show Number 1509, Twin Cities Public Television, St Paul, MN, 1997.

For a simple system dynamics computer model of the Mammoth Game with complete instructions for using it with students in the classroom, see "The Mammoth Extinction Game" by Stamell, Ticotsky, Quaden and Lyneis, 1999, available through the Creative Learning Exchange at www.clexchange.org.

"What It's Like to Be a Pioneer: Let the Children Surprise You" by Lyneis, 1999, at www.clexchange.org, relates an anecdote about children playing the Mammoth Game.

The Call of Distant Mammoths, by Peter D. Ward (Copernicus, 1997) explores theories of mammoth extinction and relates them to modern species—an excellent resource for adults.

Mammoth Game Rules

1. Each die represents *one mammoth.*

2. Each roll of the dice represents *one year.*

3. Roll all the dice at once into the box. The numbers on the dice will tell you what happened to each mammoth.

GAME 1
1 = A calf is born
2 = The mammoth is killed by a predator
3 = The mammoth dies of starvation
4 = The mammoth keeps living another year
5 = The mammoth keeps living another year
6 = The mammoth keeps living another year

4. Do what the numbers tell you to do:
If a calf is born, add one die to the herd.
If a mammoth dies, remove that die from the herd.
If a mammoth keeps living, just leave that die in the game for the next round.

5. Continue to play for 20 years (20 rounds.) Record how many mammoths are in your herd at the end of each year on your *Keeping Track of Your Herd* worksheet.

6. Change the rules for Game 2.

GAME 2
1 = A calf is born
2 = The mammoth is killed by a predator
3 = The mammoth dies of starvation
4 = The mammoth is killed by a human hunter
5 = The mammoth keeps living another year
6 = The mammoth keeps living another year

Name____

Keeping Track of Your Herd

Record the number of mammoths remaining in your herd after each year.

Game 1		Game 2	
Year	**MAMMOTHS**	**Year**	**MAMMOTHS**
Start		Start	
1		1	
2		2	
3		3	
4		4	
5		5	
6		6	
7		7	
8		8	
9		9	
10		10	
11		11	
12		12	
13		13	
14		14	
15		15	
16		16	
17		17	
18		18	
19		19	
20		20	

Name____

Graph of Your Mammoth Population

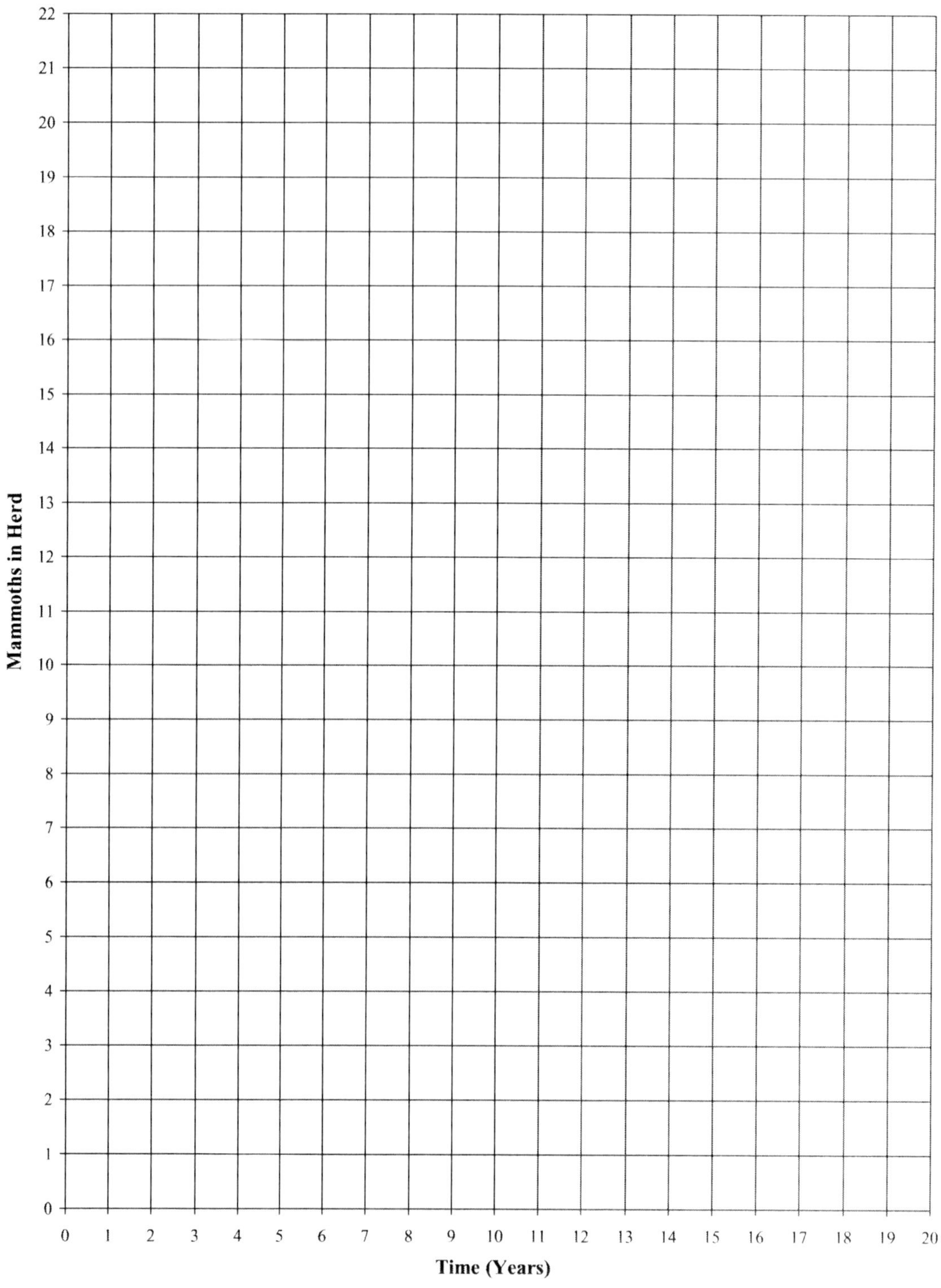

Lesson 4

It's Cool

In this lesson, students engage in the scientific method as they measure, record, and graph the changing temperature of a cooling cup of boiling water. They look for patterns of behavior over time and form hypotheses. The lesson reinforces science concepts including energy transfer, the Centigrade scale, laboratory technique and measurement skills. Math skills and concepts include measuring, gathering data, making graphs, and working with rates of change. [1]

How It Works

There is a difference between heat and temperature. Heat is a form of energy which makes molecules in water move around very rapidly. When water is heated in the kettle, it gains more

MATERIALS

- Electric tea kettle to boil water
- A lab thermometer and a cup for hot liquids for each team
- A stopwatch or timer
- Copies of three worksheets for each student (see pages 48–50):

  1. *Cooling Prediction Graph*

  2. *Cooling Data Table*

  3. *Cooling Experiment Graph*

heat energy. When the water cools, energy flows out of the water and into the air.

Heat always flows from an area of higher temperature to an area of lower temperature.

Temperature is one measure of how much heat energy an object has, and it is measured on a thermometer in degrees. Heat is the amount of energy needed to bring the water to a certain temperature. Two different objects can have the same temperature but contain different amounts of heat energy. Two different amounts of water at the same temperature hold different amounts of heat energy. Various items baked in an oven together contain different amounts of heat energy. Heat energy is measured in calories or BTUs. Heat energy always travels from a region with high temperature to a region with low temperature.

In the classroom experiment, heat from the boiling water flows into the air, the water cools, and the temperature drops. The temperature drops rapidly at first, but the rate of change slows as the water approaches room temperature.

SAFETY FIRST!!!

Make sure to use thermometers and cups that are designed for hot liquids. Standard air temperature thermometers may burst in hot water.

Procedure

1. Explain to students that they will be conducting a scientific experiment. They will be measuring the temperature of hot water as it cools and they will record and graph their data.

2. Emphasize that the experiment will work only if students follow the guidelines.

- Boiling water is very hot and dangerous, so they must be very careful with it.
- They must record their data very accurately.
- They must cooperate in teams in order to accomplish this task.

3. To familiarize students with the Celsius scale, discuss some of the following measures:

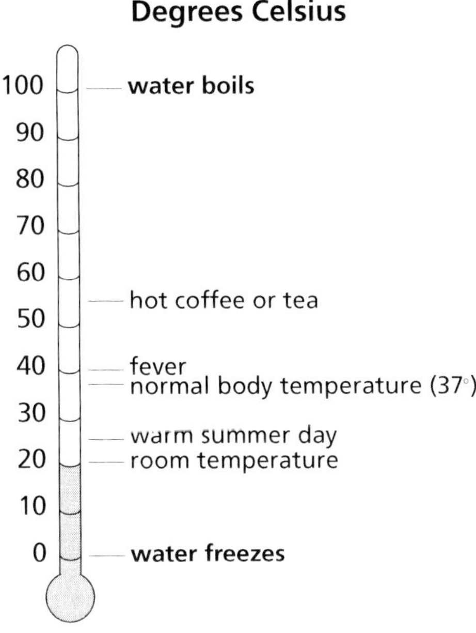

4. Draw a set of axes on the board. Label the horizontal axis "Time (Minutes)." Label the vertical axis "Temperature (Degrees Celsius)," with a minimum value of 0 degrees Celsius and a maximum value of 100 degrees Celsius.

Choose students to come to the board to draw behavior over time graphs of the following:

- The temperature of water in a pot on the stove starts at 50 degrees and rises at a constant rate to 90 degrees.

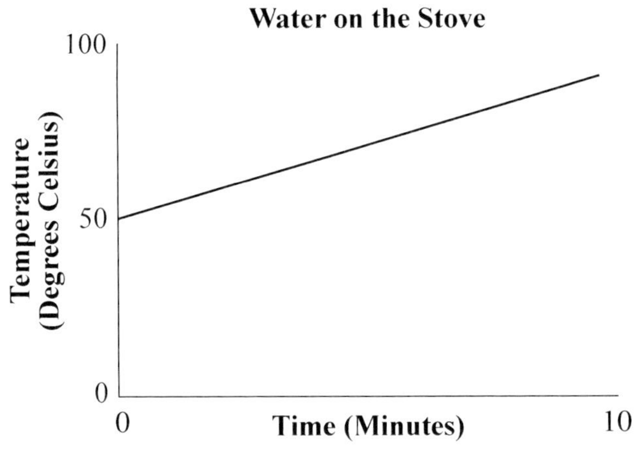

A *behavior over time graph* is a line graph sketching how something changes over time.

- The temperature in a room is 20 degrees and does not change.

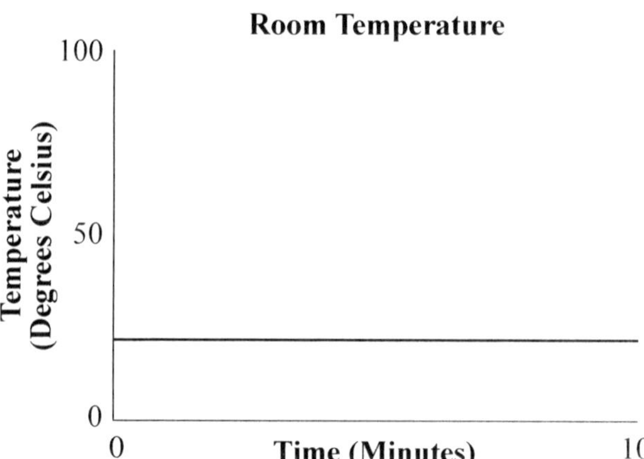

A prediction is what they think will happen—it does not matter if it is wrong or right. Making predictions helps students think about the experiment when they see how closely the results match their predictions.

5. Ask students to think about what will happen to the temperature of boiling water in a cup over time. Ask them to sketch a behavior over time graph of their predictions on the *Cooling Prediction Graph* worksheet (page 48).

6. Give each team one cup and fill it with boiling water. Have students measure the initial temperature immediately and record it on the *Cooling Data Table* worksheet (page 49). Note that the initial temperature is less than 100 degrees because the heat source has been removed.

7. Using the stopwatch, announce each subsequent minute with a ten second warning and tell the students to "measure and record" their water temperature.

Make sure that more than one student reads the thermometer. This increases the learning and the accuracy of the measurements.

While teams gather and check their data, each individual student completes his or her own data chart.

8. After about five minutes, when all teams are on track, have each student graph the data on the *Cooling Experiment Graph* worksheet (page 50). Plot the first few points together, checking that students mark the initial temperature on the vertical axis and a dot on each subsequent minute line. This can be confusing for young students. Suggest that students use a straightedge to

follow each minute line accurately up from the bottom to where it intersects the current temperature line.

Meanwhile, continue to announce each minute with instructions to "measure and record." Continue graphing for at least twenty minutes.

9. Finally, ask students to connect the dots on their graphs. This should be a smooth curved line, so it is best if students do this without using a straight edge.The graph below shows typical behavior.

Cooling Experiment

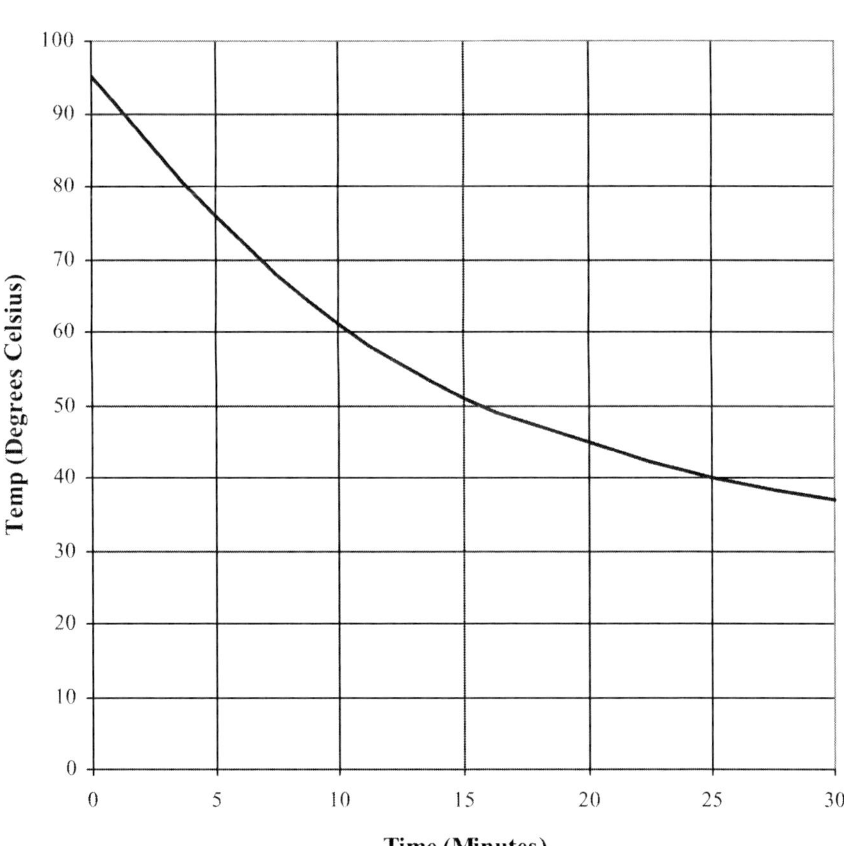

Bringing the Lesson Home

Students have made predictions and conducted an experiment. Now, to come full circle, they make sense of what they have observed and draw conclusions.

For comparison, collect several of the prediction graphs and the experiment graphs from the students and post them on the wall. As students look at the experiment graphs, lead a class discussion with questions like these.

? How do the graphs show what happened to the temperature of the water?

The temperature dropped rapidly at first, then more slowly. The graphs show a steep downward curve that started to level off as the water approached room temperature.

? What was the temperature of the water at the start of the experiment?

The water was boiling in the pot (100°), but cooled slightly when poured into the cups. Students can report their initial readings.

? What was the temperature of the water after 1 minute? 5 minutes? 15 minutes? Did every team get the same results?

? Did the water cool at a constant rate? What do you notice about the shape of the line?

The line is not straight because the water did not cool at a constant rate.

? When did the water cool the most?

The cooling rate was highest at the beginning where the curve is steepest. At this point, the difference between the water temperature and room temperature was greatest, so the heat energy flowed quickly.

? When did it cool the least?

The cooling rate was lowest at the end as the water slowly approached room temperature. When the temperature difference is small, heat flows more slowly.

? The graphs show the temperature during a period of 20 minutes. Predict the temperature after 30 minutes. Explain your logic.

The temperature will continue to go down, but at a slower and slower rate. Once the water reaches room temperature, it will stay there.

? Predict the temperature after 60 minutes, 100 minutes.

The temperature will remain constant at room temperature.

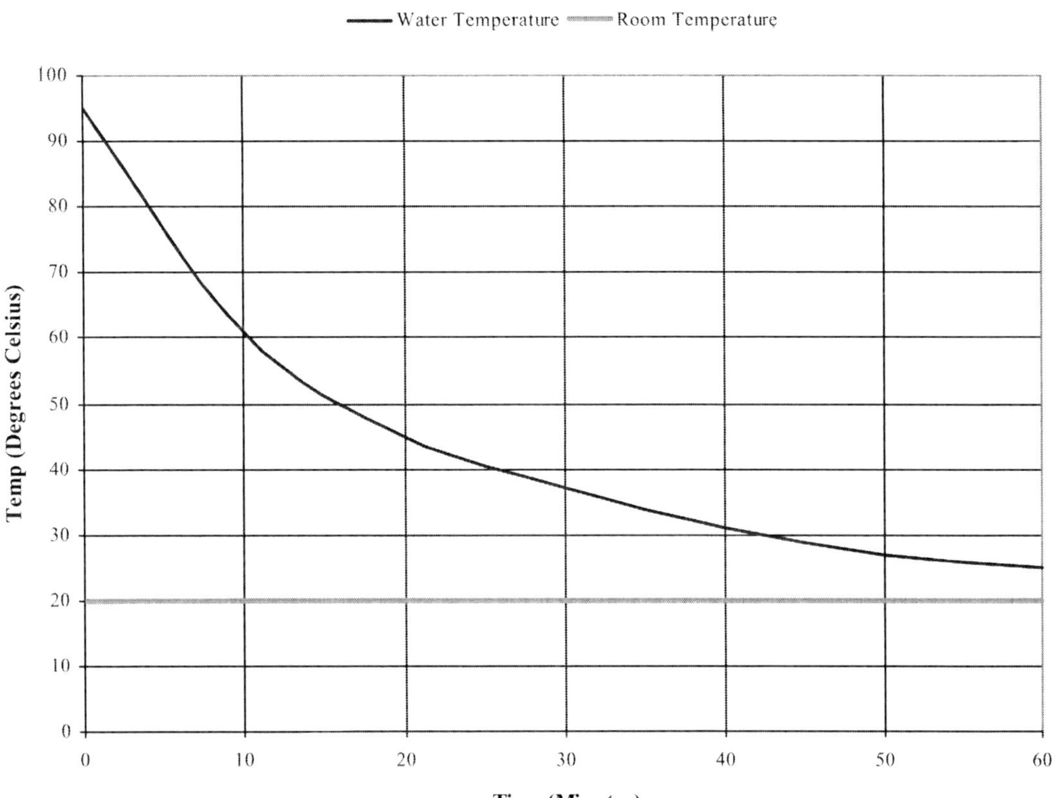

This graph shows how the water temperature would approach room temperature if students ran the experiment for a longer time.

? How does your experiment graph compare with the prediction graph?

- **Do any of the graphs look alike?**
- **In what ways were the predictions correct?**
- **How were the actual results different from the predictions?**

Students need to know that it does not matter if their original predictions were correct or not. What is important is that they made a prediction. It is also important to have students share what they were thinking prior to the experiment and to compare those thoughts with their thinking after the experiment.

What Happened to the Heat?

- The water started off hot (heat energy was added in the kettle).
- The temperature of the water was much higher than the surrounding air temperature, so heat energy started to flow out of the water at a fast rate.
- This loss of heat made the water cooler, so temperature difference between the water and the air was a little smaller. Therefore, the heat energy started to flow out of the cup at a slower rate.
- This process went on and on, until the temperature of the water was the same as the temperature of the room. This is the reason that the graph curved a lot at the start and then got flatter as time went by. This pattern of change is called exponential decay.

? Can you think of other examples of heat transfer that fit the pattern we observed?

- *An ice cream cone melts much faster on a hot day than in winter. The heat energy flows more quickly when there is a bigger gap between the temperature of the ice cream and the temperature of the air.*
- *A house loses heat more rapidly on a cold winter day. If the furnace does not come back on, the house will eventually cool down to the outside temperature as the heat escapes. The same principle works for an air conditioned house on a very hot day, only the heat transfers into the house rather than out of it.*

? Can you think of other examples of exponential decay?

- *Excitement about some toys: When the toy is new, you are very interested in it, but as time goes by, you use the toy less and less, until it sits on the shelf with all the other toys.*
- *The value of a car as it ages: The value drops rapidly at first and more slowly in later years.*
- *Exponential decay is common in many other systems. Students who play the Mammoth Game (Lesson 3) will recognize the same pattern in a declining population.*

NOTES

1 For a simple system dynamics computer model of this cooling experiment with complete instructions for using it with students in the classroom, see "It's Cool: An Experiment and Modeling Lesson" by Ticotsky, Quaden and Lyneis, 1999, available through the Creative Learning Exchange at www.clexchange.org.

For more advanced lessons and background on cooling experiments and computer modeling see the "Cooling Cup Packet" by Celeste Chung and Albert Powers, 1993, also at www.clexchange.org.

Name______________________________________

Cooling Prediction

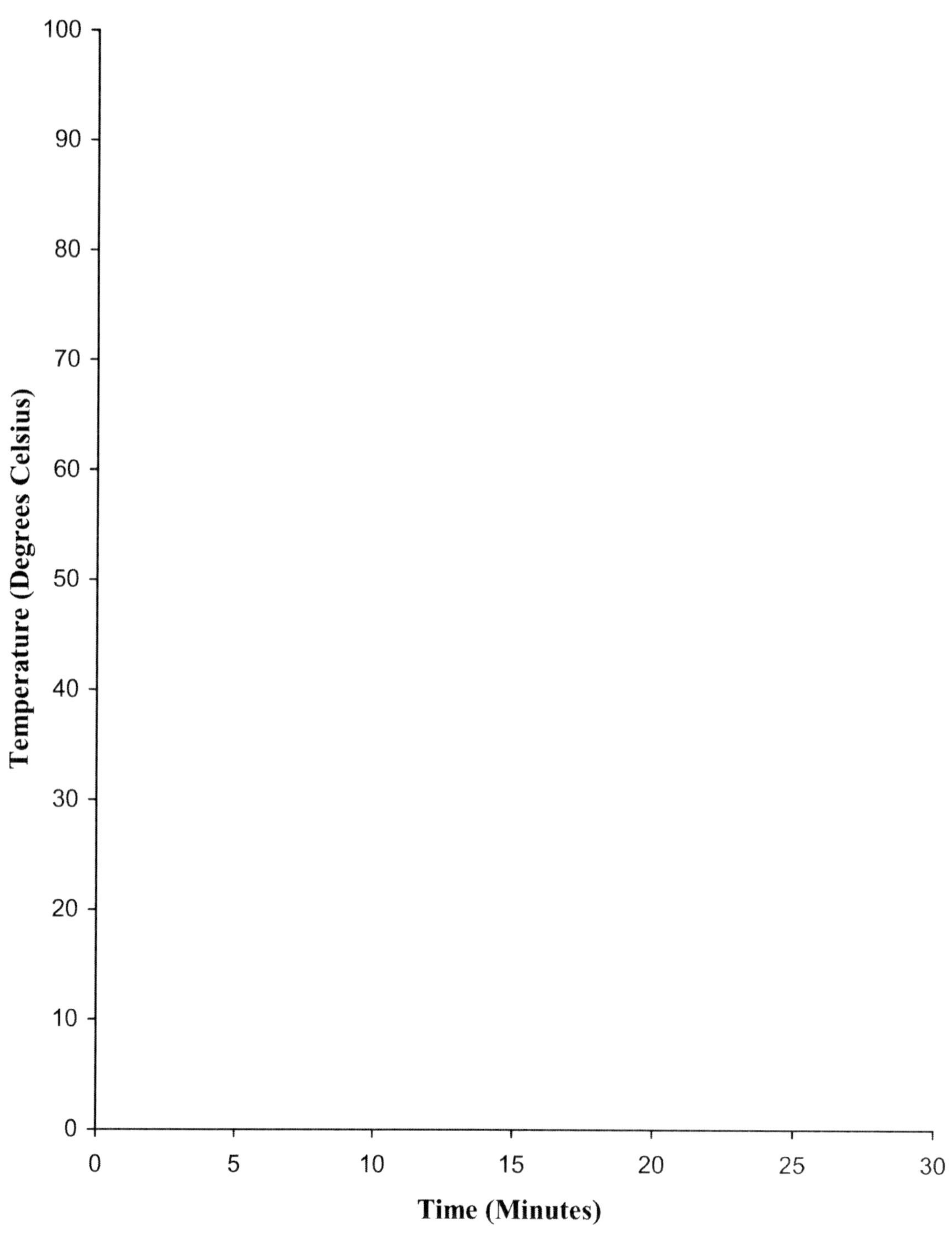

Name______________________________

Cooling Data

TIME (Minutes)	TEMPERATURE (Degrees Celsius)
Start	
1	
2	
3	
4	
5	
6	
7	
8	
9	
10	
11	
12	
13	
14	
15	
16	
17	
18	
19	
20	
21	
22	
23	
24	
25	
26	
27	
28	
29	
30	

Name____

Cooling Experiment Graph

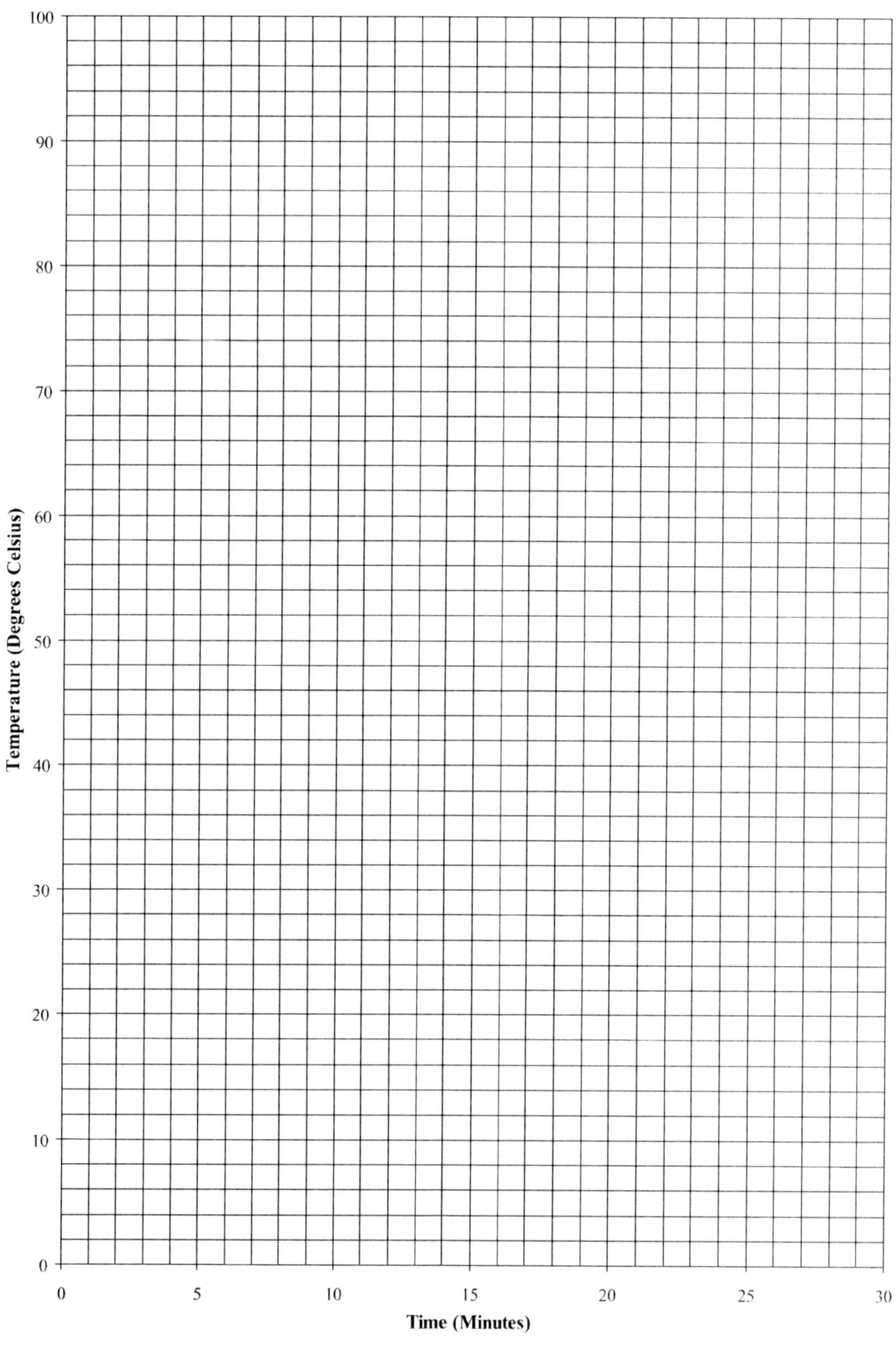

Lesson 5

The Infection Game

Students play a game that simulates the spread of an epidemic. The behavior we see in the game could represent bacteria spreading through an animal population, a virus spreading through a computer network, a rumor spreading through a school, the adoption of a fad in a country, or any other type of contagious agent.[1]

Social studies concepts could include the spread of diseases, ideas, social movements, or revolutions. The spread of disease can also be discussed from the science point of view. The disease in question might be a cold virus, the flu, smallpox, or AIDS. Math skills include drawing and interpreting graphs, fitting a curve through data, and looking at patterns of behavior over time.

Combine two classes to play this game. It takes at least 35 players to generate clear patterns of behavior.

MATERIALS

(See pages 60–64)

- Copies of four student worksheets:
  1. *Individual Record Sheet A*, for *one* student
  2. *Individual Record Sheet B*, for all remaining students
  3. *Spread It Around*, for each student
  4. *Spread It Around Again*, for each student
- One copy of the *Teacher's Class Record Sheet*

How It Works

Do not divulge this background information to students. Their motivation and learning is much more effective when they discover the structure for themselves.

In this game the interaction that drives the spread of an epidemic is represented by the multiplication of numbers. One student will be assigned the number zero, while the rest will be assigned the number one. As they multiply their numbers together in pairs, the repeated multiplication process will cause more and more products to result in zero. In other words, the number zero simulates the infective agent spreading through the population.

A similar pattern in different situations is called a *generic structure*. This game simulates the generic structure of the spread of contagious activity, or infection. Once students understand the spread of an epidemic they also understand the spread of a rumor, a fad, a social movement, or a computer virus. The basic structure is the same.

Procedure

1. Explain the rules without telling the name of the game.

Rules for Students

- You will each receive a sheet to track the results of the game.
- You will each be given a secret number which will be already filled in on your record sheet.
- Secrecy and accuracy are very important.
- You will play the game for several rounds. In the first round, find any other student, and quietly tell each other your numbers. Then, on your own, secretly multiply your two numbers together and record the product on the next line of your sheet. This will be your new number for the next round.
- **Example:** If you have a 2 and the other student has a 3, you will both get 2 X 3 = 6 for your new number on the next line.
- **Second round:** Find any other student, tell each other your number, secretly multiply them together, and record the new product for the next round.
- Continue to do this until the teacher ends the game.

By using the numbers 2 and 3, instead of 0 and 1, you deliberately mislead the students a little. This adds to the surprise element.

2. Give one *unknowing* student *Individual Record Sheet–Form A* (page 60) and give the rest of the students *Individual Record Sheet–Form B* (page 61). Give *Form A* with the starting number 0 to a student who is reliable about following directions and who is likely to exchange numbers with a variety of boys and girls. Re-emphasize the importance of secrecy, and let students play the game for about 4 minutes.

You do not need to interrupt play to announce rounds. It works best if you just let students mingle freely for about 4 minutes.

3. When time is up, ask students to notice the last product on their sheets. Most, if not all of the students should have the number zero. Ask who *started* with the number zero. Tell students that they will be asked to think about this later.

4. Gather data from the students now for later debriefing.

- Ask students who had their FIRST entry of zero in the beginning to raise their hands. (This should be only *one* student.) Record this information on the first column of the *Teacher's Class Record Sheet* (page 64).
- Ask for hands to count how many students had their FIRST entry of zero in the second round. Repeat this for all subsequent rounds and record the information until there are no new "infections" with zero. Do not discuss the results with students yet.
- It is essential to record *only* the number of *new* students infected each round in the first column.
- You will also need the *total* number of infected students as the game progressed. Record this in the second column of the *Teacher's Class Record Sheet*, by keeping a running tally and adding the number of new students each round, as below.

Do not be overly concerned about accuracy in counting. Small errors will not affect the overall outcome.

Round	Number of NEW Zeros	TOTAL Number of Zeros
Start	1	1
1	1	2
2	2	4
3	4	8
4		

A *behavior over time graph* is a line graph sketch showing how the number of infections changed over time during the game. It reveals a pattern of behavior.

5. Provide some individual reflection time for students to think about the *total* number of students with a product of zero as the game progressed. *Without revealing the actual data*, ask students to draw *behavior over time graphs* representing what they think happened to the *total* number of students with a product of zero during the game using the *Spread It Around* worksheet (page 62).

6. Students share their predictions with their teammates, reach a consensus and draw the team graphs on their worksheets. Ask each team to send a representative to the board to sketch the team's graph and explain the reasoning behind it. At this point, it is more important for students to explain their thinking than to produce the "correct" graph.

7. Compare the student predictions with a graph of the actual results of the game. Using data previously collected on the *Teacher's Class Record Sheet*, use the values in the Total Number of Zeros column to plot a graph on the board.

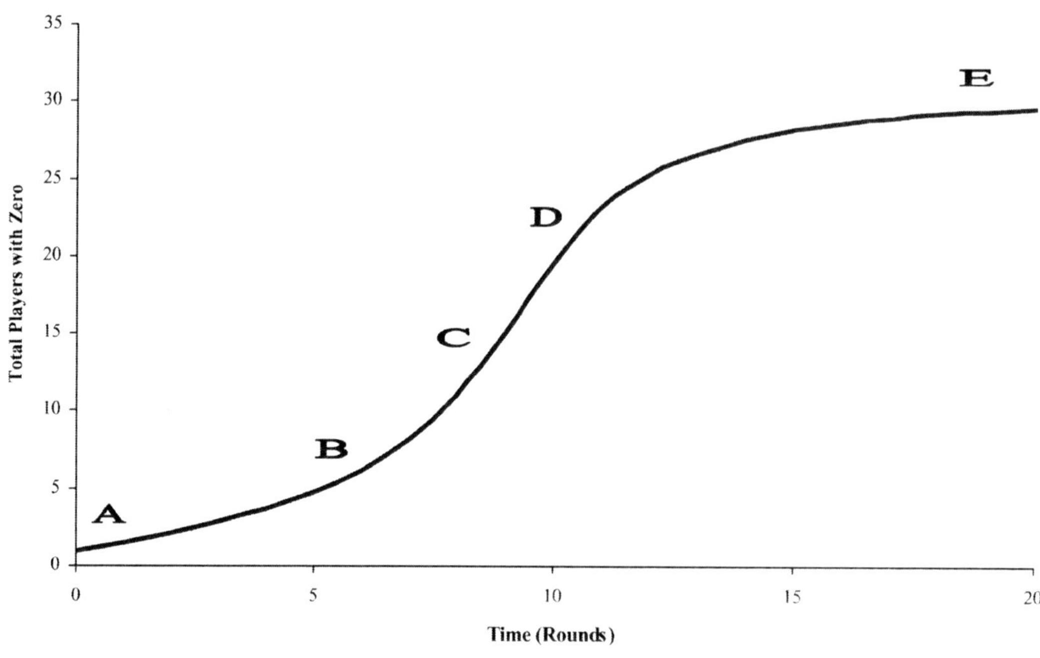

Bringing the Lesson Home

Use the class graph (shown on the previous page) to help students understand the progress of the "infection" and its real-world implications. Devote ample time to this step. Let students use their experience to construct a deeper understanding of the world around them.

? What does the graph tell us? What happened to the number of students "infected" with zero during the game?

At first only one student was infected, but the infection eventually spread to everyone in the class in a general pattern called "S-shaped growth."

? Why does the line have an S shape? How does this relate to what was happening during the game?

Engage students in a dialogue about the shape of the graph and relate the different sections of the graph to different phases in the game. If the students have difficulties, ask questions rather than giving them answers to get them to think about the different phases.

- **What was happening at region A? Why is the line flatter?**
  This is the initial spread. Very few people had the infection, so it spread very slowly at first.
- **What was happening at region B? Why is the line steeper?**
  Growth was increasing. As more and more people were infected and they interacted with others, the disease spread at an increasing rate.
- **What happened at C? Does the curve change its shape?**
  At this point the curve changes its direction, like an "S."
- **What was happening at region D?**
  Now growth was decreasing. When most people already had the illness, there were fewer healthy people to infect, so the disease spread more slowly. The number of infected people was still increasing, but at a slower rate.
- **What was happening at region E? Why is the line flat?**
  There was no further growth. Everyone was infected.

How does the class graph compare to the team prediction graphs? By evaluating their earlier predictions, students reflect on their own thinking.

Focus on the general pattern. Your graph will be different from our example, but the general shape will be similar.

Now, broaden the lesson with questions like these.

? How is this like something else we are studying?

Explore links to the curriculum. For example, in a history class, ask students to predict the effect of Europeans carrying the smallpox virus to native people in the Americas. In economics, ask students to list some fads or products that spread rapidly through society.

? Can students think of other examples of this infection behavior? Without intervention, the "infection" starts out slowly and spreads more rapidly until it approaches saturation.

- *Other infectious diseases like the flu or medical problems like head lice*
- *Rumors spreading through a school*
- *Computer viruses*
- *A fad like a style of clothing, a new toy, a popular song or movie*
- *The adoption of a new technology like cell phones or DVD players*
- *A social movement or political idea like the American Revolution, abolition of slavery or women's suffrage*

? In what way is this simulation NOT realistic? What are limitations of the simulation?

This simulation shows a disease from which there is no recovery. That is, once you are infected, it is not possible to revert back to "uninfected." In the real world this almost never happens. Usually there are some individuals who recover. Other individuals might be resistant and not get the disease at all. Depending on the ability of the students, you might ask them how the rules of the game would need to change to make the game more realistic.

The game is a simplified version of reality. This makes it easier to understand the "structure" of reality. However, be aware that the game includes a number of assumptions that make it different from real life.

The simulation also implies that contact with a carrier will always result in getting the disease. Again this is highly unlikely —the probability that a contact will result in actual infection is almost always less than 100%.

While it is possible to change the rules of the game to reflect these issues, doing so will not significantly alter the shape of the graph.

Take Another Look

It is also interesting to explore the *rate* of the spread of the infection. In student terms: how many *new* people were infected in each round of the game (rather than the *total* number of people infected)?

The *total* number of infected students is a *stock*, or an accumulation over time. It is increased by the number of *new* infections that *flow* in each round.

Students can now analyze the data of the number of *new infections* each round. Lead a discussion similar to the debriefing of "the *total* number of students with a zero", but this time focus on "*new* students with a product of zero."

- As before, ask students to draw *behavior over time graphs* of what they think happened to the number of *new* infections over the course of the game using the worksheet *Spread It Around Again* (page 63).
- After discussing their predictions, use the teacher's data for the "Number of New Zeros" to draw and analyze the actual graph of the game. Again, the class graph may differ somewhat from our example below, but the general shape should be similar.
- Focus on the general pattern of behavior, not the details.
- Carefully lead a dialogue to elicit student understanding.

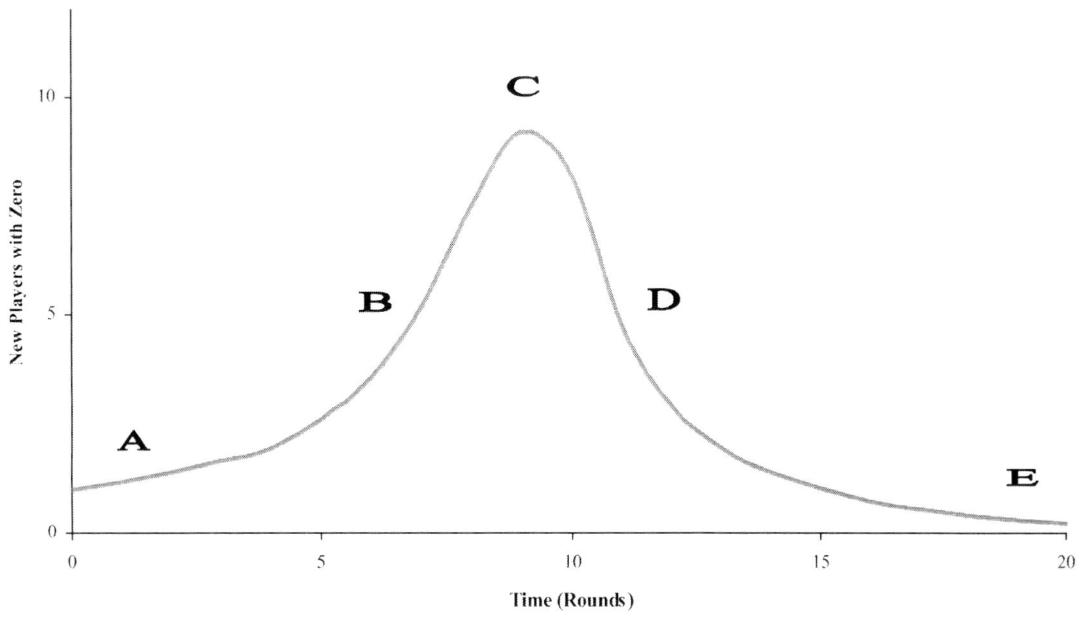

? What happened to the number of new infections?

There were only a few new infections at first. Then there were many. By the end there were no new infections. This pattern is called a "bell-shaped" curve.

? How is the class graph (on the previous page) different from the team predictions? How is it similar? What does the shape of the curve say about what was happening in the game?

As before, ask questions to elicit understanding of the phases of the game.

- **What was happening at region A?**
  The infection started off slowly, but then grew at an increasing rate as more and more people transmitted the infection.

- **What was happening at region B? Why is the shape of the curve changing?**
  When fewer contacts resulted in new infections, the number of new infections slowed down, but the total was still increasing.

- **What happened at C?**
  The number of new infections reached its peak. This corresponds to point C on the previous graph where the line changed direction like an "S." (All of the letters on the graphs correspond. This point is particularly noteworthy because it is a turning point.)

- **What was happening at region D?**
  The number of new infections was declining. The total number of infections was still increasing, just at a slower rate.

- **What was happening at region E?**
  There were no new infections because everyone was already infected. The epidemic had run its course.

? How does the graph of the *new* infections relate to the graph of *total* infections? If these graphs are drawn on the same time scale, what will they look like?

The rate of new infections starts off slowly, but increases at an increasing rate. When the rate reaches its maximum (top of bell

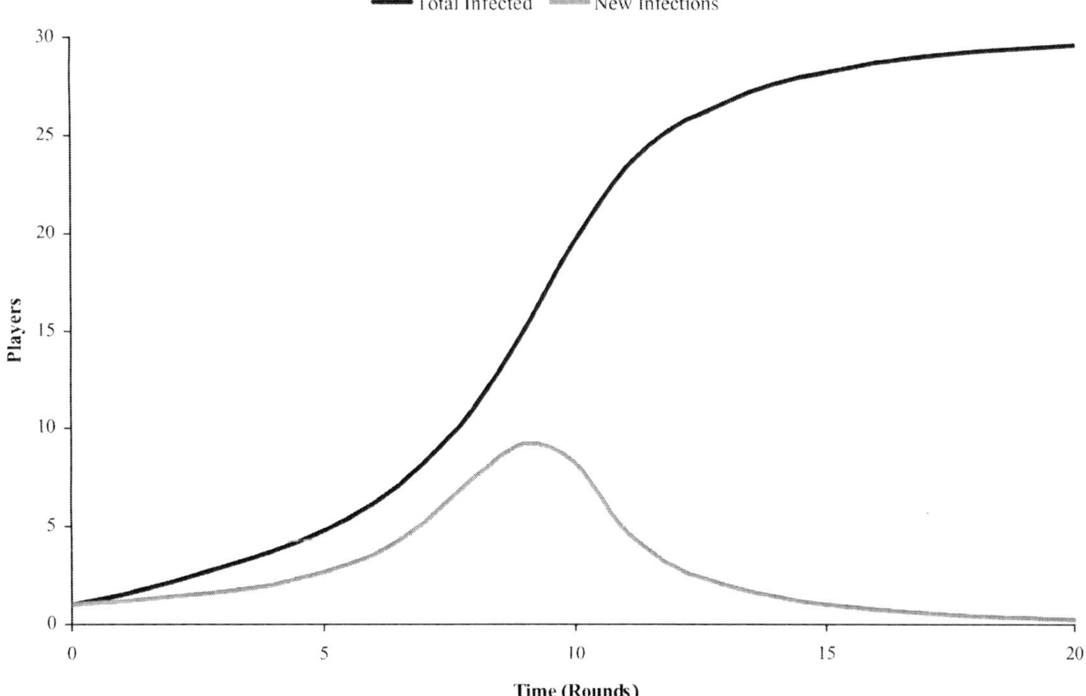

curve), the total number of infections continues to increase, but at a slower rate. So, while the number of NEW infections is DECREASING, the TOTAL number of infections is still INCREASING. When the number of new infections is zero, the total number of infections has reached its maximum—everyone is infected.

? How does this pattern relate to the other curriculum and real world examples of "infections" discussed earlier?

As before, discuss the spread of other diseases, rumors, computer viruses, fads, social movements and other contagions.

NOTES

1 The Infection Game is adapted from the Epidemic Game developed by Will Glass at the Catalina Foothills School District, Tucson, Arizona, 1993. The "Epidemics Game Packet" includes the original game, a system dynamics model and student exercises for older students. It is available from the Creative Learning Exchange at www.clexchange.org

Thanks to Jan Mons of the GIST Project in Brunswick, Georgia for her suggestions.

Name____

Individual Record Sheet • Form A

1. You start out with a number given to you by the teacher, written next to **Start** below. *Do not share this number with anybody, except as explained below.*

2. Once the game starts, select another student and tell each other your numbers. On your own, secretly MULTIPLY the two numbers and write the product on the next line. Now this is your new number.

3. Select another student and repeat the process until time is called.

ROUND	NUMBER
Start	0
1	
2	
3	
4	
5	
6	
7	
8	
9	
10	
11	
12	
13	
14	
15	
16	
17	
18	
19	
20	

Name____

Individual Record Sheet • Form B

1. You start out with a number given to you by the teacher, written next to **Start** below. *Do not share this number with anybody, except as explained below.*

2. Once the game starts, select another student and tell each other your numbers. On your own, secretly MULTIPLY the two numbers and write the product on the next line. Now this is your new number.

3. Select another student and repeat the process until time is called.

ROUND	NUMBER
Start	1
1	
2	
3	
4	
5	
6	
7	
8	
9	
10	
11	
12	
13	
14	
15	
16	
17	
18	
19	
20	

Name____

Spread It Around
Total Students with Zero

1. Sketch what you think happened to the *total* number of students who had a product of 0 as the Infection Game progressed.

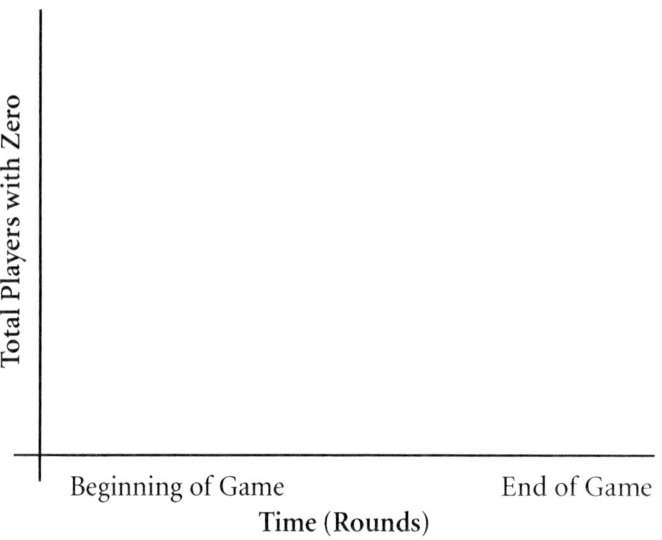

2. Compare your graph with the graphs of your teammates. Explain your thinking to your teammates and listen carefully to their explanations. Come to an agreement with your teammates and sketch your team's graph below. Be prepared to explain your thinking to the class.

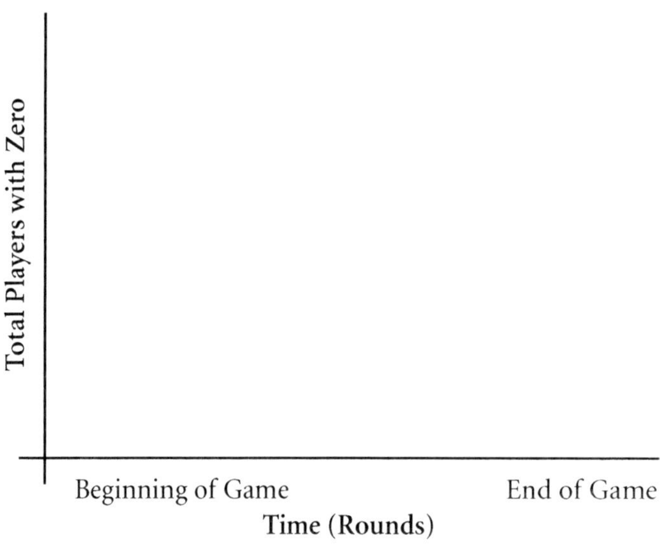

Name____

Spread It Around Again

New Students with Zero Each Round

1. Sketch what you think happened to the number of students *newly infected* each round as the Infection Game progressed.

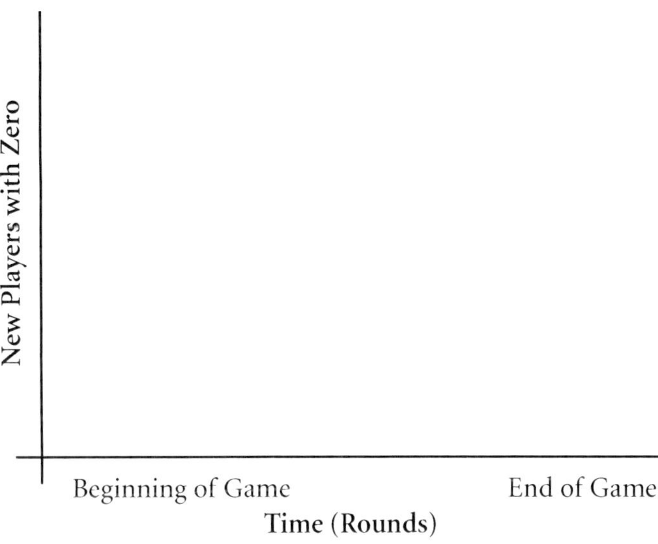

2. Compare your graph with the graphs of your teammates. Explain your thinking to your teammates and listen carefully to their explanations. Come to an agreement with your teammates and sketch your team's graph below. Be prepared to explain your thinking to the class.

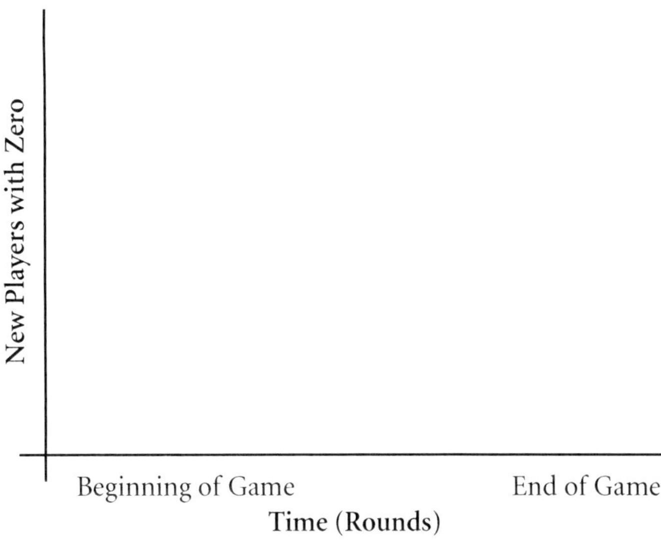

Teacher's Class Record Sheet

Round	Number of NEW Zeros	TOTAL Number of Zeros
Start		
1		
2		
3		
4		
5		
6		
7		
8		
9		
10		
11		
12		
13		
14		
15		
16		
17		
18		
19		
20		

Lesson 6

The Tree Game

Students explore what happens to the number of trees in a forest over time as a forester plants and harvests a certain number of trees each year. Playing the game, students experience resource management and the need for long term planning. The Tree Game complements science, social studies, economics and ecology units on renewable resources and sustainability. Math skills include computation, graphing from tables, and understanding the causes of patterns of change over time.[1]

How It Works

Students play a game that simulates the growing and harvesting of trees. The game is set up so that the company's stock of trees

MATERIALS

- Approximately 150 wooden craft sticks (Popsicle® sticks) for each team of students
- One container for each team to hold the sticks
- One copy of two worksheets for each student (see pages 71–72):

  1. *Forest Inventory Table*

  2. *Forest Inventory Graph*

This is a simulation. Since we have neither the time nor the resources to experiment on a real forest, we use sticks to play out our forest management policies in class.

increases at a constant rate: the forester plants the same number of new trees each year. However, the trees are harvested at an increasing rate: the forester doubles his cutting rate each year. In addition to giving students an intuitive understanding of linear and exponential change, the game illustrates the difficulties of supplying a natural resource product in an environment with rapidly growing demand.

Procedure

1. Ask each team of 3 or 4 students to count 120 sticks into their container. The remaining sticks should be put aside in a neat pile on the table.

2. Explain to the class that the container of sticks represents a forest which will undergo some changes.
   - Each year trees will be added and removed according to a certain rule.
   - The sticks that are added represent new trees planted; the sticks that are removed represent trees that are cut down to provide lumber for housing, production of paper, etc.

3. Explain that each person on the team will have a job. Post the job descriptions on the board for quick reference.
   - The Forest Managers will plant new trees each year. (The manager starts with a small pile of sticks to add in.)
   - Lumberjacks will cut trees down each year. (They will remove sticks.)
   - Record Keepers will keep track of the inventory data in a table.

4. Explain the rules of the game to students.

Rules for Students

- You start with a forest of 120 trees.
- Each year plant 4 new trees.
- The first year, cut 1 tree. This represents the wood that is used for building houses, making paper etc.
- The second year, cut 2 trees; the third year, cut 4 trees, and so on. In other words, the number of trees you remove from the forest *doubles each year*.
- Each year, the managers add sticks, the lumberjacks take away sticks, and the record keepers record the data on the *Forest Inventory Table*.
- Be as accurate as possible.

Although data is collected in teams, each student completes an individual worksheet.

5. Students record their data on the *Forest Inventory Table* (page 71). Point out that part of the table has already been filled in on the worksheet. Ask students to play the first round (the first year) to confirm the results. Starting with 120 trees, students plant 4 trees and cut 1, leaving them with 123 trees to begin Year 2, as shown below.

Year	Number of Trees in the Forest	Number of Trees Planted	Number of Trees Cut Down
Start	120	4	1
1	123		

6. Teams can then continue to play and record their results. Help any teams that need clarification. Here is a completed table.

Often students will start to see patterns and fill in the table based on that pattern, rather than actually counting sticks. Depending on the age of the students, it helps their understanding if they can force themselves to keep using the sticks for a while.

Year	Number of Trees in the Forest	Number of Trees Planted	Number of Trees Cut Down
Start	120	4	1
1	123	4	2
2	125	4	4
3	125	4	8
4	121	4	16
5	109	4	32
6	81	4	64
7	21	4	not enough left

7. By Round 7 of the game, students will report that they have no trees left.

? Why did students run out of trees to cut?

The increasing demand outstripped the supply. There were not enough trees left to cut in Year 7. The forest is gone.

8. Ask each student to use the data from the *Forest Inventory Table* to plot the *Forest Inventory Graph* (page 72). Students connect the points with a smooth line to show what happened to the stock of trees over time.

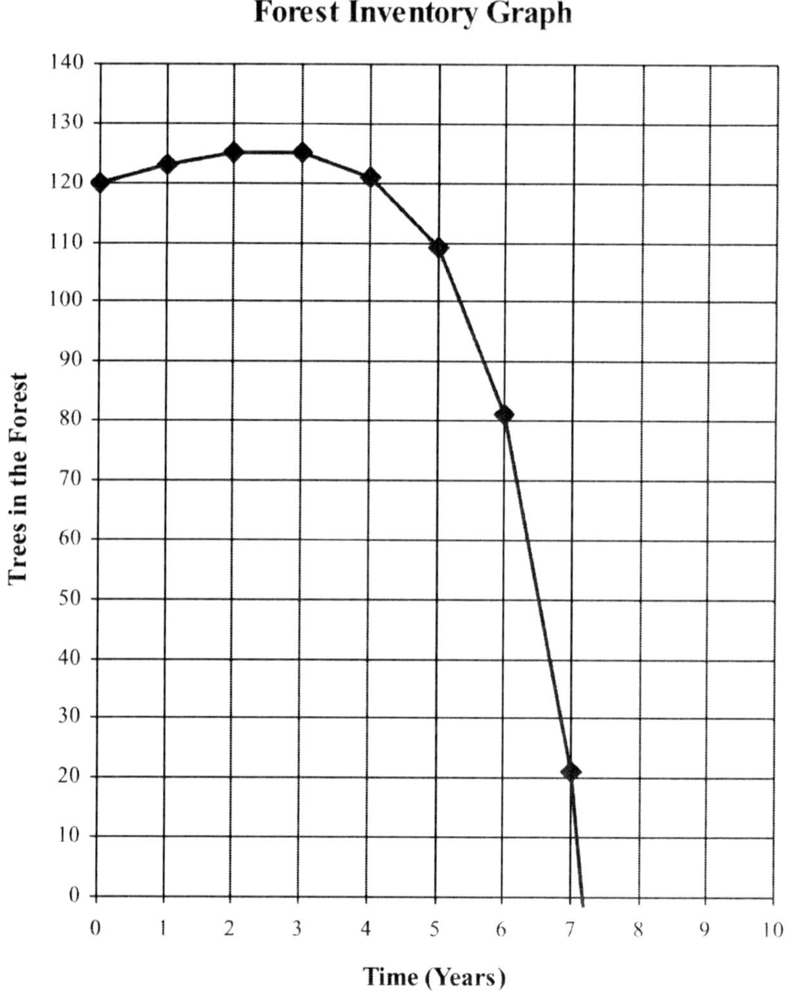

Bringing the Lesson Home

Post several student graphs and use them to focus the discussion on what happened in the game. The following questions should arise, often raised by the students themselves.

? How does the graph show what happened to the stock of trees in the forest over time?

The stock of trees grew slightly at first but then rapidly decreased until there were no trees left by the seventh year.

? When did the forest grow? Why?

The forest grew for the first two years because students were planting more trees than they were cutting down each year.

? When did the forest decline? Why?

The forest began to decline in the fourth year because students were cutting down more trees than they were planting each year.

? Did the forest ever stay the same? Why?

The forest stayed at 125 for Year 3 because students planted 4 trees and cut 4 trees. There was no change in the total number of trees that year.

? Why did the forest grow in size for a while and then start to decline?

At first the planting rate exceeded the cutting rate so the forest grew. However, because the cutting rate doubled each year, it soon overtook the planting rate. Then the forest declined.

? Why did the rate of decline increase as time went on?

The number of trees cut doubled every year to meet the rising demand for lumber. As more and more trees were cut, the decline steepened.

? What caused the changes in the stock of trees?

The total number of trees in the forest was determined by BOTH the planting and the cutting of trees over time. This is an important concept.

What happened to the forest? Students use line graphs to reveal and examine patterns of change. We call these *behavior over time graphs.*

There is a stock, or quantity, of trees in the forest. It is increased by the number of new trees that flow in through planting. It is decreased by the number of trees that flow out through harvesting. Like water filling and draining a bathtub at the same time, they can happen simultaneously.

? In our game the cutting rate increased to satisfy a rising demand for goods, while the planting rate remained constant. In real life, would the owner of the forest have planted more trees?

Encourage students to think about what they would do.

? In real life, can a forester harvest trees a year or two after planting as we did? If a tree actually takes more than 20 years to mature, how would this delay affect the forester's long term planning and planting rates?

Again, this is a brainstorming question with many possible responses. In general, the delay from planting to harvesting makes the real-world system much more complex than the game. If there is a rise in demand, the forester will have to wait 20 years to harvest his new trees, so he must always try to plan ahead. (The Rainforest Game, Lesson 8, addresses this issue.)

After playing the Tree Game, students are ready for the Tree Game Puzzle (Lesson 7). *In Grade 5, we usually do both lessons in about an hour.*

? Does the *Tree Game* remind you of other similar situations?

- *Christmas tree farming—harvesting and planting to meet projected demand*
- *Rainforest cutting—clearing forests faster than they can grow back*
- *Managing other renewable resources or agricultural products —balancing how much is produced and how much is used*
- *Managing your money—balancing what you earn and what you spend so you won't run out*

NOTES

1 The Tree Game was adapted from Activity 27 "Timber," in *Counting on People: Elementary Population and Environmental Activities*. Zero Population Growth, 1994.

Name______________________________

Forest Inventory Table

Record the number of trees you plant and cut each year.
Then count how many trees remain in the forest to start the next year.

Year	Number of Trees in the Forest	Number of Trees Planted	Number of Trees Cut Down
Start	120	4	1
1	123		
2			
3			
4			
5			
6			
7			
8			
9			
10			

Name____

Forest Inventory Graph

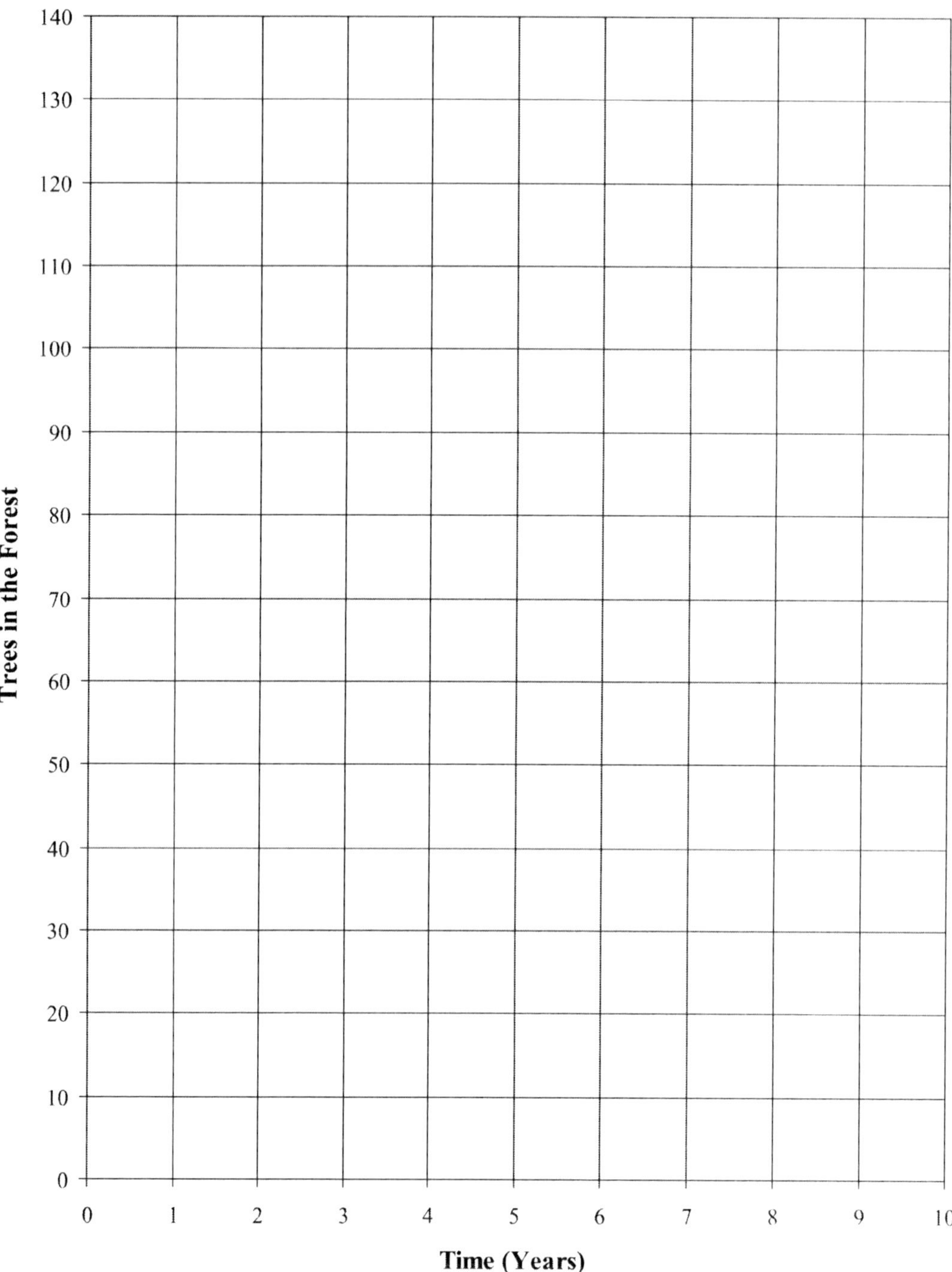

How many years did it take for the forest to disappear?

Was the forest always shrinking? Explain.

Lesson 7

The Tree Game Puzzle

This puzzle is an extension of the Tree Game. After playing the Tree Game, students explore what happens to the number of trees in a forest following a variety of planting and harvesting policies. Math skills include computation, making and interpreting graphs, problem solving, and communication.

How It Works

As teams of students experiment with their simulated forests, they invent their own planting and harvesting rules, collect data based on those rules, graph the results, and see what those graphs reveal about the rules. All of the rules and graphs are posted separately. Students match them up, explain their reasoning, and think about the long-term consequences of various resource management policies.

MATERIALS

- Approximately 150 wooden craft sticks (Popsicle® sticks) for each team of students
- One container to hold the sticks for each team
- One copy of three worksheets for each team (pages 78–80)
  1. *Tree Puzzle Rules*
  2. *Tree Puzzle Inventory*
  3. *Tree Puzzle Graph*

Procedure

Give students the option of using sticks to count their trees. If they have just played the Tree Game, some students may not need this concrete step.

1. In the Tree Game, teams of students started with:
   - 120 trees in the original forest
   - An "In" rule of 4 (the planting rate for new trees each year)
   - An "Out" rule that followed the pattern 1, 2, 4, 8, etc. (a cutting rate that doubled each year)

2. This time, teams will make up their own rules and see if other students can guess the rules from the graphs. They will be changing the planting and cutting rates.

3. Give each team one copy of the *Tree Puzzle Rules* worksheet (page 78) and explain the rules as outlined below. Remind students that accuracy is important.

Rules for Students

1. Decide how many trees are in your forest to start. Write that on your *Tree Puzzle Rules* worksheet in LARGE numbers.
2. Make up a rule for the number of trees planted each year. Write the rule on the worksheet. Write LARGE.
3. Make up a rule for the number of trees cut each year and write it on the worksheet. Write LARGE.
4. The rules can be stated in words, with formulas, or by listing numbers to describe a pattern. For example:
   - "Start by cutting one tree, then double the number of trees cut each year."
   - "Cut 1, 2, 4, 8, ..."
   - "Newly cut trees = 2 * old number of cut trees"
5. Use your rules to complete the table on the *Tree Puzzle Inventory* worksheet.
6. After you have completed the table, use it to make a graph of the number of trees in the forest over time on the *Tree Puzzle Graph* worksheet.
7. When you are done, hand in all worksheets to the teacher.

The rules are easier to guess when different teams start with a different number of trees, so you may want to require that each team start with the *same* number of trees. If you leave the starting number of trees somewhat ambiguous, most teams will start with 120 trees, because that is what happened in the previous game.

4. As teams finish, collect their two worksheets.
   - Take the *Tree Puzzle Rules* and *Tree Puzzle Inventory* worksheet from the first team and write a large numeral "1" on each sheet.
   - Take the same team's *Tree Puzzle Graph* and write a large letter on that sheet.
   - Do this for all of the team rules and graphs.
   - Once all groups have handed in their worksheets, the students will be asked to match the rules with the graphs, so make sure not to match the labels in an obvious manner—instead, assign random letters to the graphs. It is helpful if you keep a list of the matching sheets: 1-J, 2-A, 3-Y, etc.
   - Keep the inventory table worksheets aside for reference or checking if necessary.

5. Different teams of students will be working at different rates. If some of the teams finish early, ask them to produce another set of rules. Perhaps give these groups a challenge, such as, "Can you come up with a set of rules that produce a graph that goes up and down over time?"

6. Post all the rule sheets on one section of a wall and all the graphs on another section. Give teams a few minutes to examine the sheets and challenge them to match rules with their graphs.

Bringing the Lesson Home

Ask each team to explain how a rule could be matched with a graph. (Teams are not allowed to match their own rule and graph.)

? How did your team determine the match?

If students have difficulties explaining their thinking, have them focus on the simultaneous effect of the inflow and outflow on the stock of trees.

Students have to predict how the quantity of trees in the forest changes over time when trees are continuously planted and cut at certain rates. This game is a natural way for students to think about the effect of inflows and outflows on the stock of trees.

Once a team has proposed a match, ask other students to verify the logic and assumptions of the presenting team. As students present different arguments, the class will come to a consensus on the matches in a non-threatening manner.

After all the graphs and rules have been matched, expand the debriefing to include an economic context.

Our open-ended matching approach is easier than it may seem. Students actually enjoy making guesses, explaining their reasoning and defending their team's arguments before the class.

? What stories do these graphs tell? What was happening from the forester's point of view? Is the graph realistic?

- *Select a few graphs for class discussion. What do the graphs tell us?*
- *For example, an "out" rule of 8 could mean that there is only a demand for 8 trees per year, or that there has been a restriction on cutting trees for some reason.*
- *An increased planting rate may suggest that the forester expects a rise in house building because the economy is improving or the population is growing.*
- *Some graphs may show a depletion of the forest; others may show growth. What could be the causes and implications?*

? Does the Tree Game Puzzle remind you of other real world situations?

- *Renewable resource management for sustainability*
- *Agricultural planning for planting and harvesting to meet demand*
- *Money management to balance income and spending*

The change in any stock depends on what flows in and what flows out over time, usually simultaneously and following different rules.

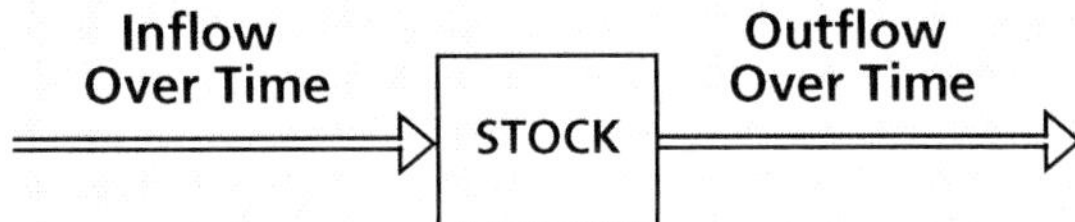

Tree Puzzle Rules

Write LARGE.

Starting number of trees:

Rule for planting trees:

Rule for cutting trees:

Tree Puzzle Inventory

Year	Number of Trees in the Forest	Number of Trees Planted	Number of Trees Cut Down
Start			
1			
2			
3			
4			
5			
6			
7			
8			
9			
10			

Tree Puzzle Graph

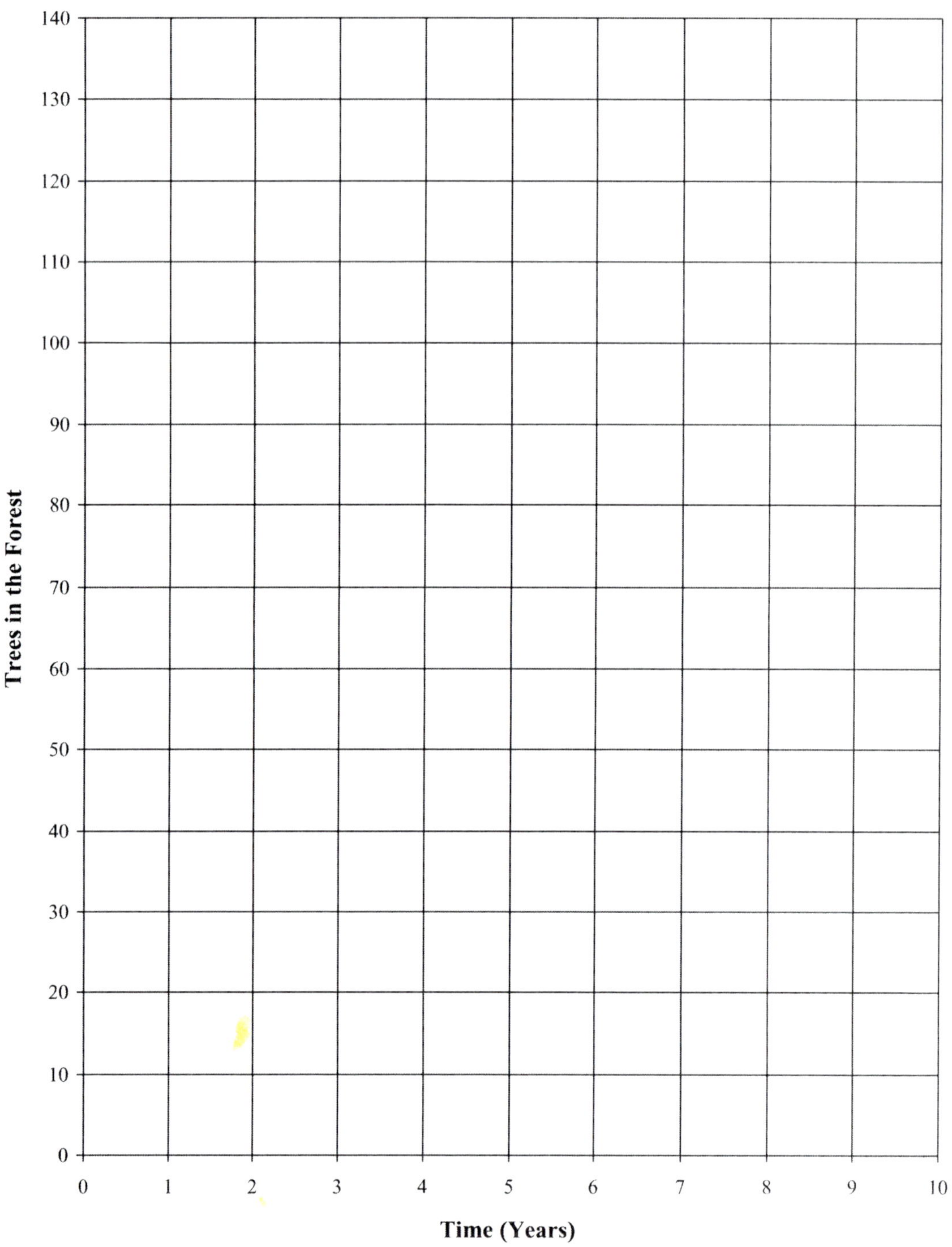

Lesson 8

The Rainforest Game

In this simulation game students act out the lives of trees. Following different planting and harvesting policies, they learn about delays in managing a renewable resource. Math skills include recording data in tables, graphing, predicting outcomes and describing patterns of behavior over time. The Rainforest Game can be part of an interdisciplinary unit on rainforest resources and inhabitants. It can also complement other science, social studies, economics and ecology units on the sustainable use of any renewable resource.

The logistics of the Rainforest Game are somewhat more involved than others in this book. You may find it helpful to review or play The In and Out Game (Lesson 1) and The Tree Game (Lesson 6) first.

MATERIALS

- Large display board or overhead projector
- Markers or chalk
- One copy of three worksheets for each student (pages 93–95)

  1. *What Happened to the Trees?*

  2. *Yearly Forest Inventory*

  3. *Mature Trees in the Forest* graph

What is Happening to the Rainforest?

The rainforest is disappearing at an alarming rate, exploited by people for its bounty of natural resources. The myriad of species living there, many as yet undiscovered by humans, are under severe pressure. Animals and plants may be headed for extinction or continued existence only in zoos and other micromanaged environments.

What can be done? This question has no simple answer. Raising awareness of the problem is a first step. People must realize that when an area is cleared, it may take many years to return to forest, if indeed it ever will.

Students generally recognize that the rainforests are threatened, but they may suggest a simplistic solution—stop cutting down the trees. However, many people depend on the rainforest for their livelihood and basic necessities of life. Because the resources of the rainforest provide so many products and opportunities, there will always be incentive to exploit them. When the removal rate is higher than the rate of renewal, the forests will inevitably decline over time.

First play the game, and then complete the table. That way, students' attention will remain on the game. Completing the table may be difficult for some students and doing it after the game avoids distractions.

Playing the rainforest game gives students a chance to experiment with different planting and harvesting scenarios and to establish equilibrium. The game applies to the sustainability of any forest or other renewable resource.

How It Works

Students play a simulation game in which they pretend to be trees that grow from seeds to mature trees in four "years." Over the course of the game, students enact three different sets of planting and harvesting policies. After playing, they use a table and a graph to analyze what happened.

Overview of Lesson Sequence

1. **Policy 1:** Play Years 1–5 of the simulation to demonstrate linear growth. The number of mature trees remains constant at zero until Year 3; then it grows at a constant rate.
2. **Policy 2:** Play Years 6–8 to demonstrate equilibrium. The number of mature trees remains the same when the planting and harvesting rates are equal.
3. **Policy 3:** Play Years 9–12 to test increased planting and harvesting. Delays produce surprising results.
4. Students reflect on the game, complete tables, plot graphs, and draw conclusions.

Do not announce the purpose of each policy to students—let them learn it from experience.

Important: Students complete the table *after* they have played the complete game. We have inserted tables within the text so that you can anticipate what will happen, but *do not* share this information or interrupt the flow of the game with these details. Just let the students play and build their own intuitive understanding.

Procedure

1. After discussing the current condition of the rainforest, tell students that they are going to play a simulation game to examine what happens to a forest when trees are planted and cut down over time. Since real trees cannot grow in the classroom, students will act out the growth of trees in an imaginary forest. They will be told how many trees to plant and harvest each year.

2. Point out that it takes time for trees to grow, but this game will speed things up. They will pretend that a tree takes only four years to reach maturity: seeds are planted in year one, sprout and grow a little in year two, become taller in year three, and mature to full grown in year four. Students will pantomime these stages.

3. At first, all the students in the class represent seeds stored in a warehouse. At the beginning of the game, there are no trees in the forest and many seeds in the warehouse.

Students as Trees

Year 1 Seed—curled up or sitting on the floor

Year 2 Sprout—kneeling

Year 3 Sapling—standing, hands at sides.

Year 4 Mature Tree—standing, hands clasped behind head, elbows out

4. **Policy 1.** Select one student in the class to be the Forest Manager. The responsibility of the manager is to count the number of mature trees and report that number to the class at the end of each year.

- To start the forest, select three students to be "planted" as seeds in the forest area of the classroom.
- For the first year, choose three different students to be "planted" while the original seeds "sprout."
- For the second year, plant three new seeds while the earlier plantings grow into sprouts and saplings.
- Continue planting three new seeds and growing the forest for a total of 5 years.
- At the end of the 5th year, ask the Forest Manager to count the stock of mature trees once again and report the results to the class.

This discussion should be very brief. It is intended to encourage students to start thinking about the issues. A more complete discussion and understanding will come at the end of the lesson.

Pause for a minute. Help students understand the behavior of the system by asking for a *brief* recap of what they have observed. It took four years for the first seeds to become mature trees. After that, adding three seeds per year caused the mature forest to increase by three trees per year. Although there is a delay between planting and maturity, the forest has a steady supply of trees at each stage of growth.

For your information only, below is a table showing the number of trees at each stage of growth each year. Notice that the first seeds planted (in bold font) move diagonally down the table as they become sprouts, saplings and, finally, mature trees in four years. *Again, do not share this table with students or interrupt the flow of the game with this information.*

Just let students play the game. They will stop and think about it later. It is OK to clarify the rules of the game, but resist every urge to step in and explain what is happening to the forest.

Policy 1: Linear Growth

Year	Seeds in Ground	Sprouts	Saplings	Mature Trees	Trees Harvested
Start	**3**	0	0	0	0
1	3	**3**	0	0	0
2	3	3	**3**	0	0
3	3	3	3	**3**	0
4	3	3	3	**6**	0
5	3	3	3	**9**	0

5. **Policy 2.** Next, change the policy and try the following scenario:
   - Beginning in Year 6, while continuing to plant three new seeds each year, *harvest* three mature trees per year to sell. (Remove three mature trees from the forest and return them to the warehouse as seeds.)
   - Ask the Manager to count and report the number of mature trees now remaining at the end of Year 6. (There will be nine trees left.)
   - Continue planting three seeds and harvesting three trees per year in Years 7 and 8.
   - Ask the Forest Managers to count the number of mature trees and again announce the results to the class.

Pause briefly again. Ask students to predict the results of this policy. Continuing to plant three seeds and remove three trees each turn will produce equilibrium, or a stable situation in which numbers remain constant. Every year, three saplings grow into mature trees to replace the three harvested mature trees. The number of new seeds in the ground matches the number of mature trees harvested, and everything is in balance (as shown below for your information only).

Policy 2: Equilibrium

Year	Seeds in Ground	Sprouts	Saplings	Mature Trees	Trees Harvested
6	3	3	3	9	3
7	3	3	3	9	3
8	3	3	3	9	3

6. **Policy 3.** Suggest that you have an opportunity to make more money by selling more trees. The forest area in the classroom has a surplus of mature trees, and since you have more seeds in the warehouse, you can also plant more trees per year.

- In Year 9, increase the harvesting number to five, and match that by planting five new seeds each year as well.
- Ask students to predict the outcome of that strategy.
- Play four rounds to see what happens.
- Once again ask the Forest Managers to count the number of mature trees. It may surprise the class that the number of mature trees has declined.

Policy 3: Increased Planting and Harvesting

Year	Seeds in Ground	Sprouts	Saplings	Mature Trees	Trees Harvested
9	5	3	3	7	5
10	5	5	3	5	5
11	5	5	5	3	5
12	5	5	5	3	5

7. After playing the game, ask students to reflect upon the events of the simulation using the worksheet, *What Happened to the Trees?* (page 93)

- Students write a few sentences about the game.
- They draw a *behavior over time graph* of the number of mature trees in the forest as the game progressed. This is a *line graph* with time on the horizontal axis that sketches what they think happened to the number of mature trees over the course of the whole game.

Writing a short, one paragraph summary serves two purposes: students settle down after an active game, and they organize their thoughts, preparing to analyze what happened.

8. Now students are ready to tabulate the results of the game on their *Yearly Forest Inventory* worksheets (page 94). Use an overhead projector or the board to help students complete the table by asking guiding questions.

? How many plants did we have to start?

We planted three seeds and there were no other plants, so we have the number 3 in the first column and zeros in all other columns. See below.

? What happened in Year 1?

The three seeds grew into sprouts and we planted 3 new seeds as shown in the table below.

Year	Seeds in Ground	Sprouts	Saplings	Mature Trees	Trees Harvested
Start	3	0	0	0	0
1	3	3	0	0	0

? Where do the sprouts come from?

One year's seeds are the next year's sprouts. Then the sprouts become the saplings in the table for the following year. The year after that, they become mature trees. Therefore, a number entered in the seed column will move diagonally down to the right through the table until reaching the mature trees column.

? Why did the first mature trees appear in Year 3?

Trees take four years to mature from seeds. We had seeds in the ground to start. Review Years 0–3 as you enter the numbers of trees at each stage.

? In Years 4 and 5, the number of mature trees increased each year. Why?

Three seeds were being planted each year and no trees were being harvested so the forest grew steadily.

Year	Seeds in Ground	Sprouts	Saplings	Mature Trees	Trees Harvested
Start	3	0	0	0	0
1	3	3	0	0	0
2	3	3	3	0	0
3	3	3	3	3	0
4	3	3	3	6	0
5	3	3	3	9	0

? Harvesting three trees/year began in Year 6 and continued in 7 and 8. What happened to the number of mature trees?

It remained steady, in equilibrium, at nine trees because the harvesting rate equaled the planting rate. (Note: To compute these, the number of mature trees increases to twelve trees but is reduced to nine after three trees are cut.)

Year	Seeds in Ground	Sprouts	Saplings	Mature Trees	Trees Harvested
6	3	3	3	9	3
7	3	3	3	9	3
8	3	3	3	9	3

? In Year 9, harvesting and planting were increased. What was the result?

The number of mature trees declined for three years. This is because of the delay in the growth of the five new seeds. At first, only three saplings were still maturing, but five trees were cut down each year.

Year	Seeds in Ground	Sprouts	Saplings	Mature Trees	Trees Harvested
9	5	3	3	7	5
10	5	5	3	5	5
11	5	5	5	3	5
12	5	5	5	3	5

Students need to think and talk about their experience in the game to build understanding.

? What happened in Years 10–12?

The forest reached a new lower equilibrium at three trees.

9. When the table is completed, students use it to graph the number of mature trees on the *Mature Trees in the Forest* worksheet (page 95). The horizontal axis measures Time in years and the vertical axis represents the number of Mature Trees in the forest each year.

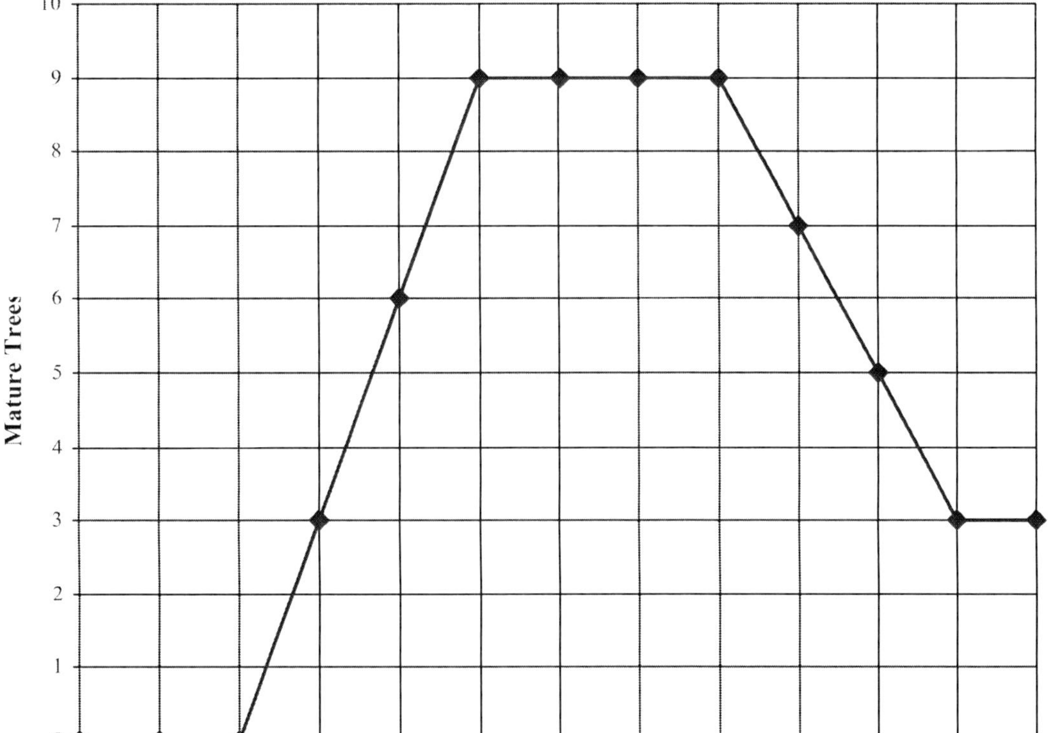

- Some students may need close guidance plotting the first few points.
- After students have plotted the points, ask them to connect the points to produce a *behavior over time graph* like the one on the previous page.

Bringing the Lesson Home

Use the graph and the table to focus a discussion on the game and its implications.

? What happened to the forest in this game?

Use a question like this to start a class discussion. Some students will be quite articulate, but others may be confused about the exact nature of the dynamics in this game. The questions below help to bring home the important points.

? What happened to the forest during the first 5 years?

Once the first seeds had matured, the forest grew at a steady rate.

Students are surprised by the effect of delays on the number of trees in the forest. By acting out the growth of trees and thinking about it together, students develop a good understanding of this important and sometimes elusive concept.

? How did the graph show the stock of mature trees in Years 1 and 2?

The line stayed at zero because there were no mature trees yet.

? When did the stock of mature trees remain constant?

It was constant when the number of saplings that became mature trees was the same as the number of mature trees cut. At that point, the number of mature trees was represented by a flat horizontal line on the graph.

? What happened when the number of trees harvested was increased and the number of seeds planted was increased to match the larger harvest?

The number of mature trees declined steadily, reaching equilibrium at a lower number of trees than before the increased harvest.

? Was this a surprise? Why doesn't the forest maintain equilibrium when you increase planting and harvesting at the same time?

Even though planting was increased to match an increase in harvesting, there were three years when the forest suffered a net decline in mature trees. The delay in trees reaching maturity caused the outflow to be greater than the inflow.

? Having a sustainable yield means having enough of a resource in the pipeline to replace what is removed from the system. How can a forest manager be assured of having enough trees year after year?

The forester must plan ahead to have a steady flow of new trees to replace those that are cut down.

How does your final graph compare to your original sketch? Help students reflect on their thinking. How have their mental models changed during the lesson?

? Summarize in your own words what happened in this game.

The supply, or stock, of mature trees was at zero for three years; then it rose by three trees each year. When harvesting began in Year 6, the number leveled off, or reached equilibrium, at nine trees. In Year 9, after harvesting and planting rates went up, the stock of mature trees went down. It leveled off at three trees, a lower level than the first equilibrium period.

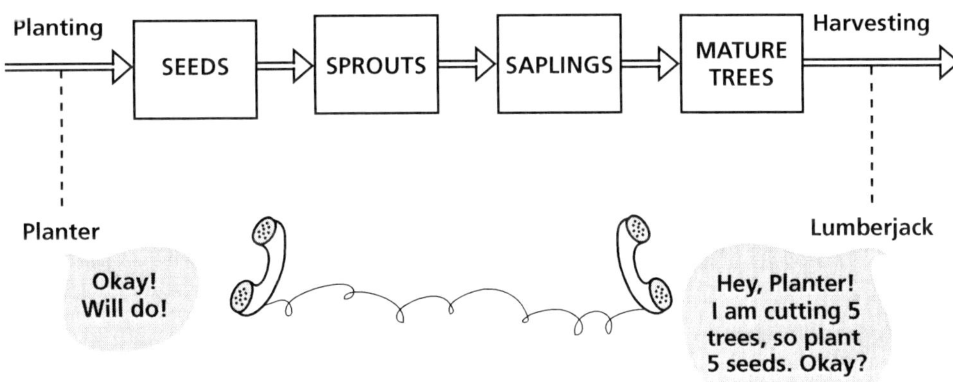

? What would happen if we decided to harvest more than 5 trees in Year 9 (while also planting more seeds)?

The delay, along with the more aggressive cutting policies could result in the ELIMINATION of the mature forest. For example, cutting nine trees in Year 9 would leave only three mature trees in Year 10, which then would all need to be cut in an attempt to maintain the more aggressive policy.

? Are there other situations in which maintaining a steady supply of some resource is necessary?

- *Other renewable resources such as livestock, fisheries, and aquifers experience similar delays.*
- *Stock in a warehouse, factory, or retail store follows a similar pattern.*
- *Veteran members of a sports team or organization also need to be developed over time.*

NOTE

This game was inspired by the classic system dynamics brain teaser described by Barry Richmond in An Introduction to Systems Thinking, STELLA, High Performance Systems, Inc., Hanover, NH, 2001 (p.26)

(High Performance Systems is now isee systems. For information, visit www.iseesystems.com <http://www.iseesystems.com> .)

Name_______________________________________

What Happened to the Trees?

Write a brief paragraph about what happened in our "forest." What happened to the number of mature trees over the years?

On this graph, sketch a line for the number of mature trees over time.

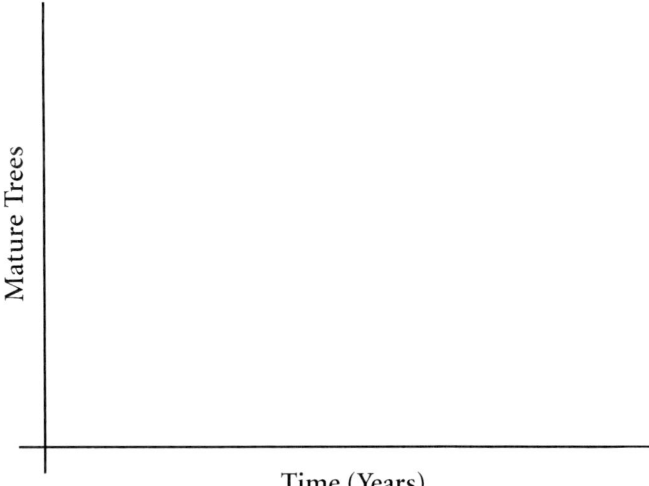

Name____

Yearly Forest Inventory

Year	Seeds in Ground	Sprouts	Saplings	Mature Trees	Trees Harvested
Start					
1					
2					
3					
4					
5					
6					
7					
8					
9					
10					
11					
12					
13					
14					

Name_______________________________________

Mature Trees in the Forest

Use your Forest Inventory data to plot the number of *mature trees* in the forest over time.

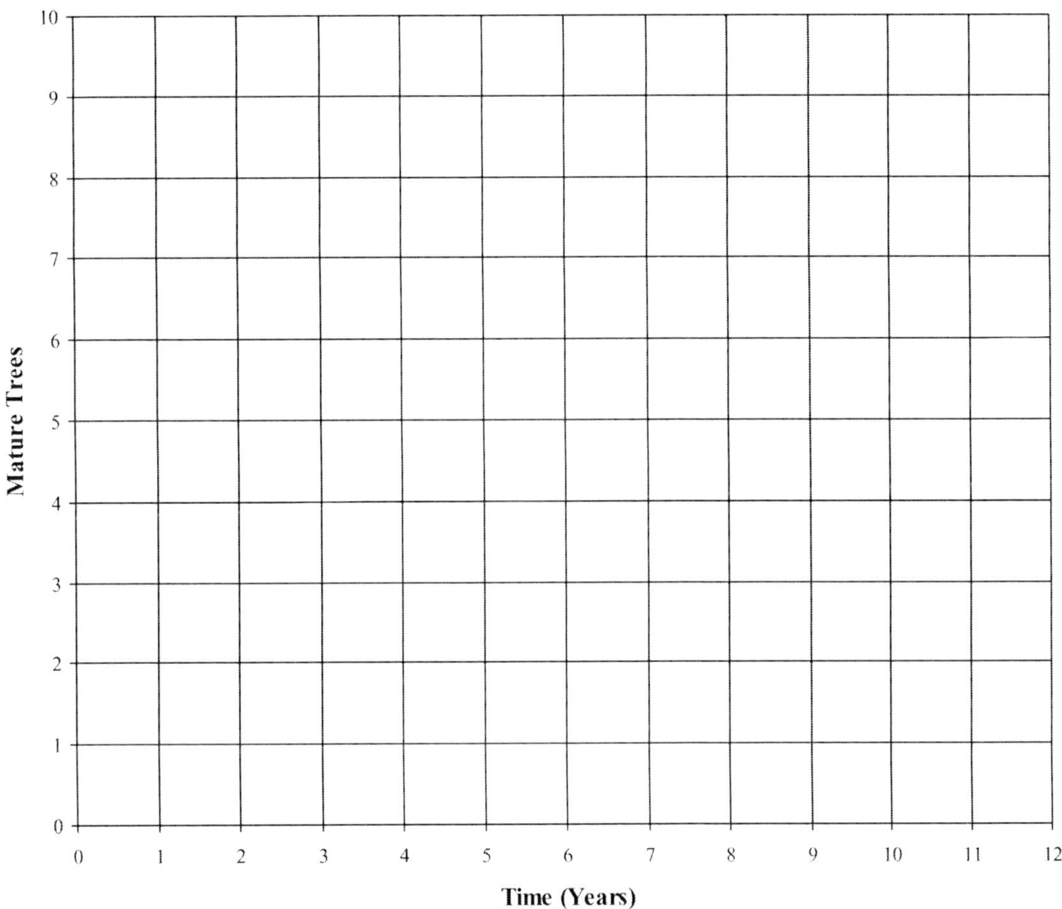

How does this differ from your original sketch? Why?

Lesson 9

The Connection Game

In this activity, students play a game in which their movements around the room depend on the movements of other players. Even a small change in position by one person can cause the whole team to move about. Diagramming the game afterwards introduces the concept that parts of a system are interconnected and changes to one element can cause far reaching effects. Through their own actions, students become aware of the concept of complexity in an apparently simple game.

The Connection Game is based on the *Triangle Game* developed by Meadows and Booth-Sweeney.[1]

MATERIALS

- Large open space in which to play the game
- Easel pad or display board
- A large number card for each student

How It Works

Most things are not as simple as they seem. For example, many times we think in terms of simple cause and effect: if we do action A, then consequence B will result. In reality, causes and effects are interrelated in a complex manner, which can make them difficult to understand. So, action A will probably have a range of consequences, causing C and D as well as B. B creates its own set of consequences also, some of which may be delayed and some of which will be unintended. Now, instead of a simple linear cause and effect chain, we see an intricate web of connections.

Life is full of webs of connections. The Connection Game gives students direct experience with complexity.

Here's an example. Removing a "pest" from the environment may seem like a good idea. But what are the effects on other organisms? What will happen to the predators and prey of the removed pest, and what populations will increase to fill the niche left empty?

Procedure

1. Define "equidistant." Demonstrate by asking two student volunteers to stand about 8 feet apart. Ask the class to suggest where the teacher should stand to be equidistant, or equally distant, from the two students. Using student suggestions, move to a point where the teacher is equidistant from the two students—students usually suggest the midpoint on the line between them. Ask the class for other suggestions for places to stand equidistant from the two students. Repeat this until students understand the concept clearly.

Equidistant

For students A and B, the teacher may stand anywhere along a line to be equidistant from them.

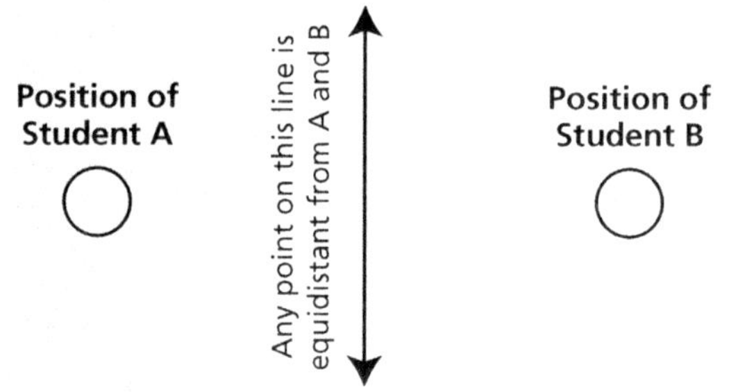

Position of Student A

Any point on this line is equidistant from A and B

Position of Student B

2. Ask students to stand in a large circle, leaving two or three feet of space between them. The game works best with 10–15 players but can be played with more or fewer. Space can become a problem indoors if the team is too large. In that case, split up the class and play multiple games with different teams.

3. Distribute number cards to students in order around the circle. The cards should be visible to all players.

4. Tell students they are going to play a game. They are all on the same team and have a common goal. Explain the rules of the game to students as outlined in the box below:

Rules for Students

- Look around the circle and randomly choose the numbers of two other players. *This is secret! Do not tell anyone what numbers you have chosen.* Remember your position in the circle and the positions of your chosen numbers.
- When the teacher gives a signal, move to a point equidistant from the other two players whose numbers you have chosen. Do this with no talking.
- The game continues until all players are equidistant from the two others they are watching, and movement stops—a state of equilibrium.
- The goal is to achieve equilibrium as quickly as possible.

Avoid having students concentrate on who chooses whom. The emphasis in the game should be on the way a change or disturbance to a web of connected elements causes ripples of disruption to spread through the system. Urge students to choose randomly when they select players to track during the game. You may suggest everyone choose a boy and a girl, or choose based on numbers held by players, or even choose someone who may not be a best friend. Otherwise, if one of the players in the game is not chosen to be observed by anyone, his or her feelings might be hurt.

5. It takes only a few minutes for the students to find equilibrium. After they do, draw a large circle on the board or easel with numbers around the edge for all the students, as shown below.

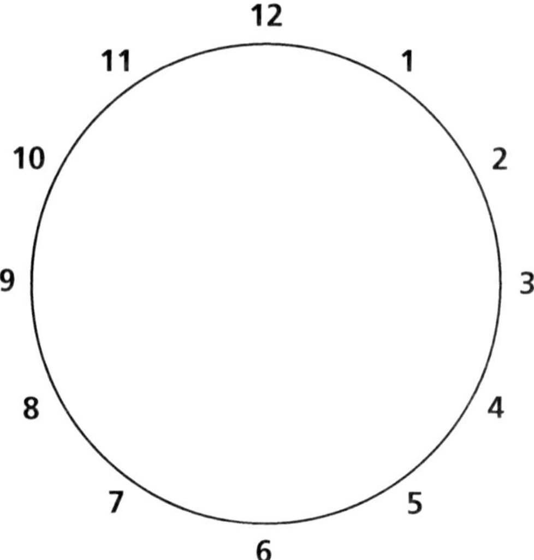

6. Using different colors for each student (until you have to repeat colors), have players draw arrows FROM the numbers they watched TO their own number on the diagram. This will indicate which numbers caused other numbers to move. Here is a sample circle.

Students are surprised to see the complexity when all their connection arrows are drawn.

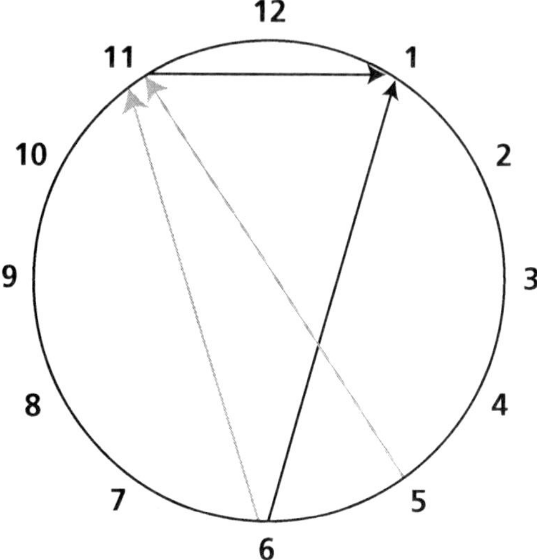

Notice that Student 1 tried to stay equidistant from 11 and 6, while Student 11 tried to stay equidistant from 5 and 6. Therefore, during the game, movement by 5 caused 11 to move, which then caused 1 to move, even though 5 was not a marker for 1. And, this is only a partial diagram! (Don't worry! This concept becomes obvious as the game is played.)

7. After all students have drawn their arrows, choose two or three students to trace the connections that caused them to move during the game. Students follow a trail of arrows from their number and tell the story: "I moved when 8 moved, who moved when 12 moved, who moved when 3 moved, etc."

Bringing the Lesson Home

Use the diagram to focus a discussion on what happened in the game.

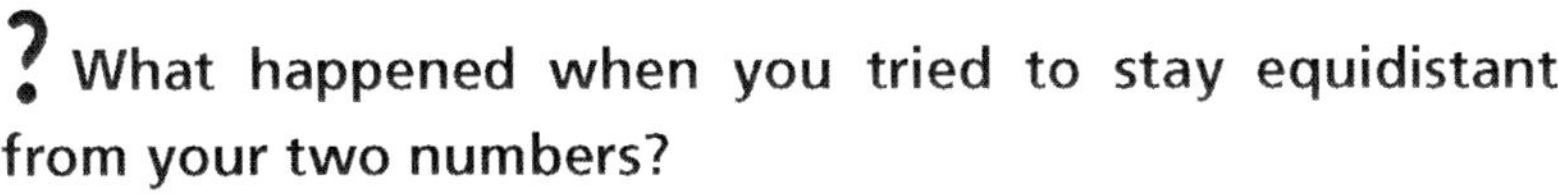

? What happened when you tried to stay equidistant from your two numbers?

Everyone started moving at once. Just when students thought they were in the right spot, one of their numbers would move and they would have to move again. Finally the movement settled down.[2]

? Was it difficult to achieve the goal of equilibrium? Why or why not?

Most students express surprise that they were able to reach equilibrium. The movement is so chaotic and complex that it seems impossible. Groups are generally able to settle down in a few minutes.

? What strategy did you find most effective? If you played again, what would you do differently?

Some players find staying back helps. If the circle collapses, there isn't much space to maneuver. Other players may mention moving slowly. This is a case where answers truly will vary.

? How did one person's change in position affect others in the group?

The arrows create a complicated picture but you can trace connections by following the lines with a finger or pointer. When someone moved to be equidistant from two other players, that caused other players to adjust their positions. Change rippled through the group.

The Connection Game **is fun. Students enjoy playing it and talking about it.**

? More arrows are clustered at some numbers. What effect did that have on the game?

Some numbers will have more connections than others. Those players would have caused more movement when they moved since many players were tracking them. Some numbers might have no arrows out. That means those players could move without affecting the movement of others. All the players in the game are connected in some way.

? Can you think of an example of one behavior causing many other unexpected things to change?

- *Eradicating a pest upsets the balance between predators and prey, affecting other animals and plants in the system, causing new problems.*
- *You stay up late to finish homework, but the next day you are tired, so you don't do very well on the test, so you have to stay for extra help, so you miss the bus, so you get home late, so you don't have enough time to finish homework again.*

NOTES

1 Linda Booth Sweeney and Dennis Meadows, 2001, The New Systems Thinking Playbook, Institute for Policy and Social Science Research, UNH, Durham. This book presents 30 engaging activities demonstrating principles of systems. Players learn by doing.

2 The Connection Game is a fun classroom activity that lets students play with complexity and change within a system. It is an example of agent-based simulation: the behavior is caused by individual agents following a simple rule. This approach is different from system dynamics which traces behavior changes to the underlying feedback structure of the system. Many problems can be studied in either way.

Lesson 10

Do You Want Fries With That?
Learning About Connection Circles

Connection circles are thinking tools designed to help students understand complexity. Using connection circles as graphic organizers, students focus their attention on a problem and generate ideas about its causes and possible solutions. As in previous lessons, students identify *what* is changing and describe *how* it is changing. In this lesson, they begin to think about *why* it is changing. They trace cause and effect relationships to uncover feedback loops that underlie the problem.[1]

In this lesson, students use connection circles to examine an article about the health risks associated with rising French fry consumption. Any story about something that changes over time, fiction or nonfiction, can be analyzed with a connection circle. The topics students study are complex and often difficult to

MATERIALS

- Overhead projector or display board
- Several different colored pens or markers for each student
- Connection Circle template for each student (page 133)
- Posted copy of Connection Circle Rules (page 134)
- Copies of article, "Eyes on the Fries" (page 135)

understand; seldom is an issue as simple as it appears on the surface. Connection circles help students delve into a problem and manage a number of different ideas at once.[2]

How It Works

The purpose of a connection circle is to help students focus on the problem presented by the author and to uncover its causes. Here is a quick overview:

- First, students briefly define the problem: What is the author concerned about? What is the main point or problem? *What* is changing over time?
- Next, *how* is it changing? In a few words, or using a quick behavior over time graph sketch, students describe how the problem is increasing or decreasing over time.
- Finally, students look for elements in the story that contribute to the problem. They use a connection circle to organize their thoughts, find cause and effect relationships, and trace the feedback loops that tie them together to explain *why* the problem occurs.

Procedure

1. Choose a story to read with students. The piece may be a newspaper or magazine article, a book chapter, or a work of fiction. It should address an issue that is increasing or decreasing over time. For this lesson, we will examine the article "Eyes on the Fries" by Rene Ebersole, which is reproduced for your convenience beginning on page 131.[3]

It may help you to also read Lesson 11 for another connection circle example.

2. Create teams of four students each. Although this structure is not necessary for the steps of the lesson, we have found that collaborative conversations improve student thinking. Ask students to read the article—independently, shared orally in groups, or aloud as a class.

3. **What's the problem?** *What* is changing over time? As a class, briefly identify the main problem the author is presenting. Stu-

dents may say, "People are worried that cardiovascular disease is rising;" or "People are getting fatter and fatter eating too many French fries." Help students distinguish the central problem from other details like the recipe for French fries or the characteristics of oils, factors that do not increase or decrease over time.

Students further sharpen their focus on the problem by defining it in terms of *change over time.*

4. After quickly identifying the problem, ask students to think about *how* it is changing. The author says that the number of people with cardiovascular disease is rapidly growing over time. So are the number of obese people, the number of McDonald's restaurants and the consumption of French fries. If students are familiar with behavior over time graphs, ask them to sketch how the problem is changing—just as they did in the Infection Game and the Tree Game.

Students might suggest graphs like these:

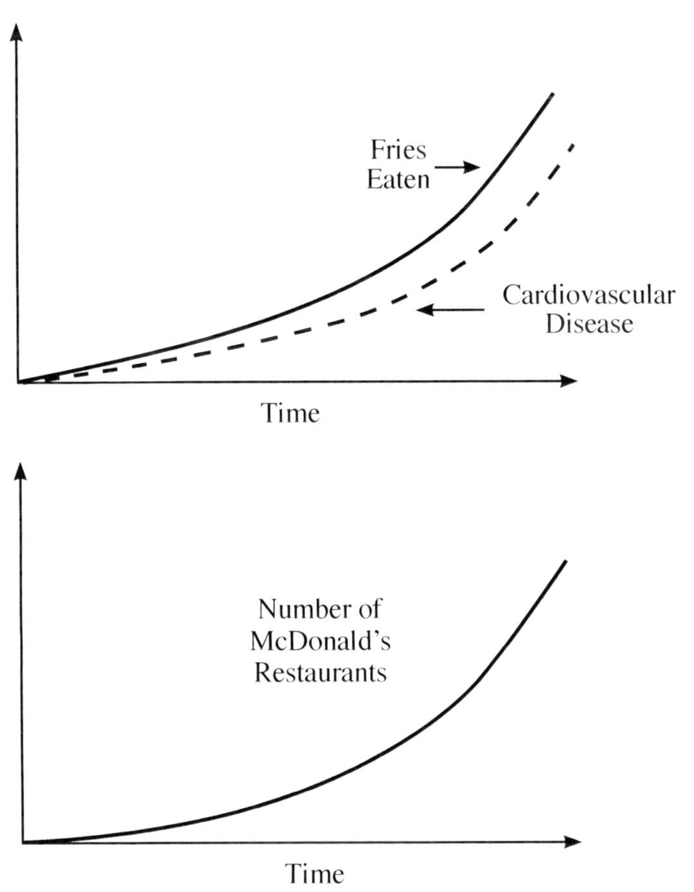

5. Give each student a copy of the Connection Circle template (page 133) and briefly explain the next step in the following Connection Circle Rules. (For a larger copy of the rules to post in your classroom as a reference see page 134).

Connection Circle Rules

1. What's the problem: *What* is changing? *How* is it changing?
2. Choose elements of the story that satisfy *all* of these criteria:
   - They contribute to the problem.
   - They are nouns or noun phrases.
   - They increase or decrease over time.
3. Write your elements around the circle. Include no more than 5 to 10.
4. Find elements that cause another element to increase or decrease.
   - Draw an arrow *from* the cause *to* the effect.
   - The causal connection must be direct.
5. Look for feedback loops. Tell their story.

6. Look for elements in the story that relate to the problem and its possible causes. They must be variables that increase or decrease over time, expressed as nouns or noun phrases.

Keep a focus on the problem and its causes. For example, the author describes the McDonald's recipe for French fries and the properties of various frying oils. While these details are interesting, they are not things that increase or decrease over time, and, except for the effect of saturated fat on cholesterol levels, they do not directly contribute to the problem of increasing cardiovascular disease.

Precise Language is Important in Naming Elements.

Throughout the lesson, guide the discussion to be sure that students are specific in their language. "French fries" figure prominently in the story, but that label is too vague. A more useful label to show the change in quantity might be "French fries sold" or "French fries eaten." Similarly, "McDonald's" is a major topic of the article, but what quantity about McDonald's might change? Phrases such as "number of McDonald's restaurants" and "McDonald's profits" more accurately describe factors in the story that cause change to occur. Finally, do not use words like "more" or "less" in the titles.

Remind students that elements may be tangible, like "number of restaurants," or intangible, like "concerns about health risks" or "desire to change the law." Often intangible elements are keys to the changes in the story.

7. As a class, brainstorm two or three elements, and ask students to write them around the outside of their connection circles. Draw a connection circle on the board or overhead to use as a class example. Below is the beginning of one connection circle for "Eyes on the Fries." Student suggestions will vary.

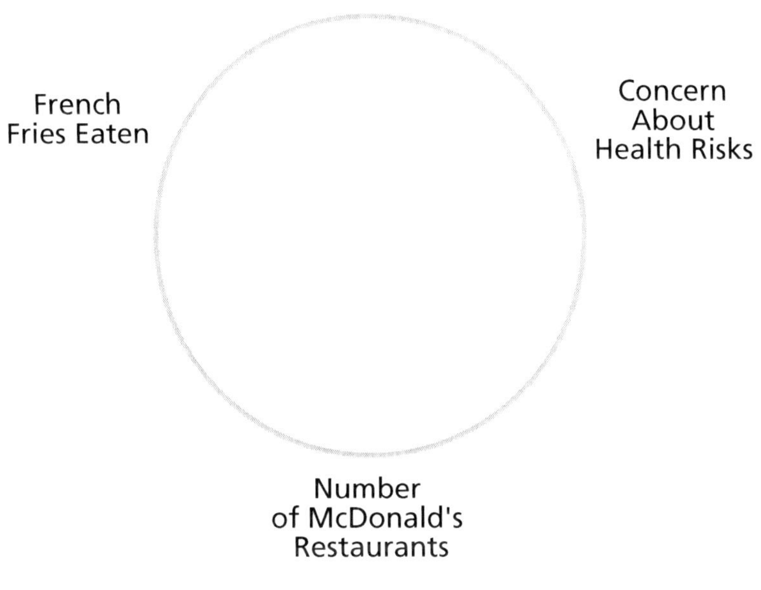

Precise language and clear thinking go hand in hand in using connection circles.

As students refine their mental models, they are always free to change, add or erase elements around their circles. The thinking process is important—not just the product.

8. Allow students time to continue adding elements to their circles as they talk in teams. Encourage dialogue among student teams, but ask each student to draw an individual connection circle. Connection circles may vary within a team. The words around each circle do not have to be the same or in the same order, but they should all be things that work together to contribute to the problem.

9. Start a class discussion by asking volunteers from each team to suggest elements for the sample class circle. Students may add or delete elements from their circles as they hear the ideas of others. Although the class may suggest and discuss many different elements, the final circles should have *no more than five to ten elements.* That way, students begin to clarify their language and their thinking about what is happening and why. The circle below shows an example of one way to represent elements from "Eyes on the Fries."

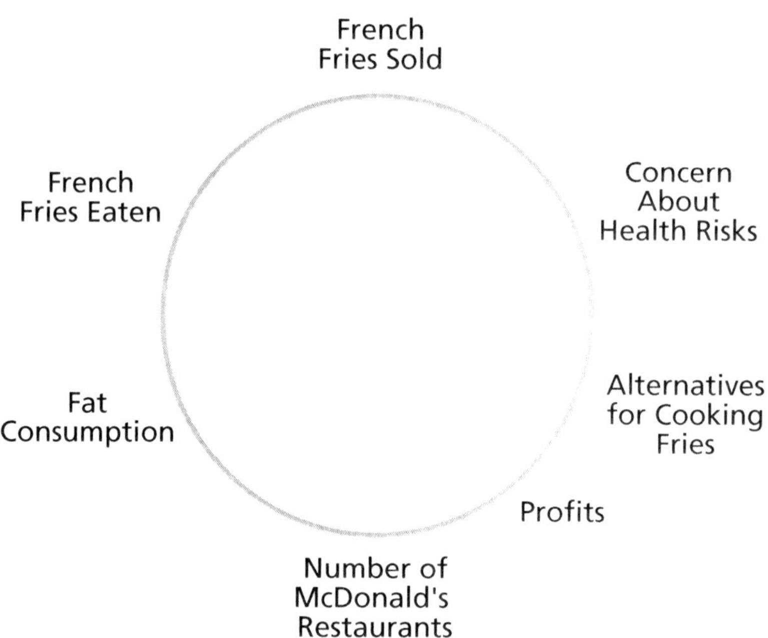

10. Ask a volunteer to describe a causal connection between two of the elements around the connection circle.

- Does an increase or decrease in one of the elements *cause* an increase or decrease in another element? For example, as the number of French fries eaten increases, it *causes* fat consumption to also increase.
- To represent this statement, draw an arrow *from* "French Fries Eaten" *to* "Fat Consumption." Be sure the arrowhead points to "Fat consumption" as shown—*from* the cause *to* the effect.

Students like using connection circles to figure things out. It may appear complicated at first, but after one class demonstration, students are usually ready and able to use the tool to tackle problems in a wide range of applications.

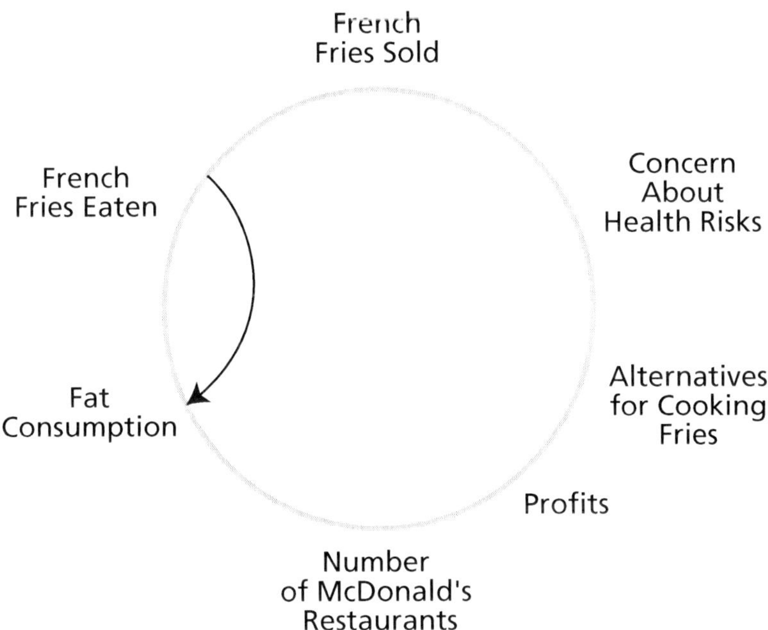

Here are two other possible connections shown in the next circle, on the following page.

- An *increase* in "Fat Consumption" can cause an *increase* in "Concern about Health Risks."
- An *increase* in the "Number of McDonald's Restaurants" will likely cause an *increase* in "French Fries Sold."

Remember these are examples only—student work will vary in the elements chosen and their placement around the circle. Let students generate their own circles to explore and refine their own mental models.

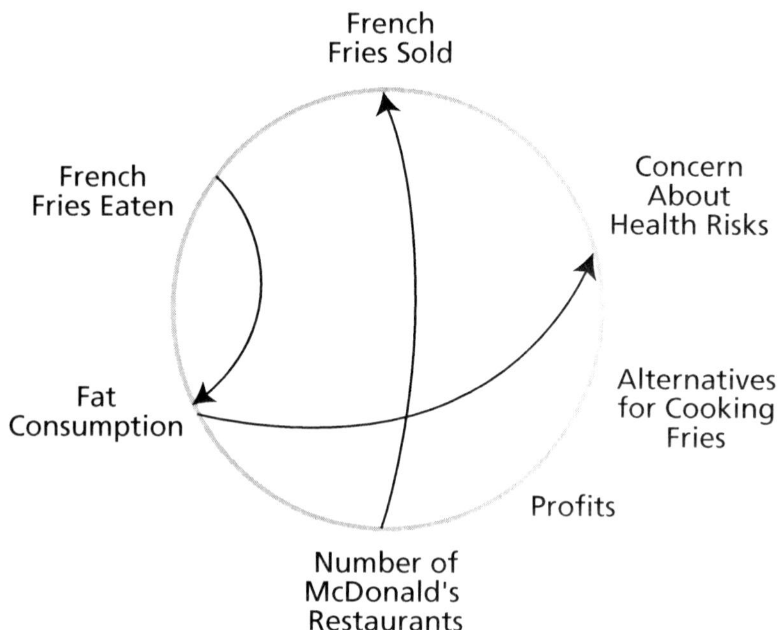

The Connection Circle as a Thinking Tool

The goal of using this tool isn't to find one specific connection circle that will correctly describe a given topic or article. Rather, the circle is designed to generate ideas and connections, and to clarify our thinking about the underlying causes of complex issues. Connection circles help us brainstorm about what is changing and trace webs of causal relationships within systems to understand those changes. The connection circle examples in this chapter demonstrate one way to interpret "Eyes on the Fries," but they are not the only way.

11. Let students work in teams to connect the elements in their connection circles.

- Emphasize that elements are not limited to one connection, and that some elements may not have any connections.
- Students should be prepared to state explicitly how and why the arrow connections work. For example, in our sample connection circle, an arrow leads from "Fat consumption" to "Concerns about health risks." Here's the reasoning: an *increase* in fat in a person's diet causes an *increase* in sus-

ceptibility to higher cholesterol levels, obesity, and other conditions detrimental to well being.

Here is a sample of a complete connection circle with causality arrows drawn. Notice that arrows frequently cross, making the diagram somewhat confusing to follow. Connection circles begin as brainstorming tools and can get messy. However, *do not stop here.* Keep going to help students make sense out of their confusing "spaghetti plates" of connections.

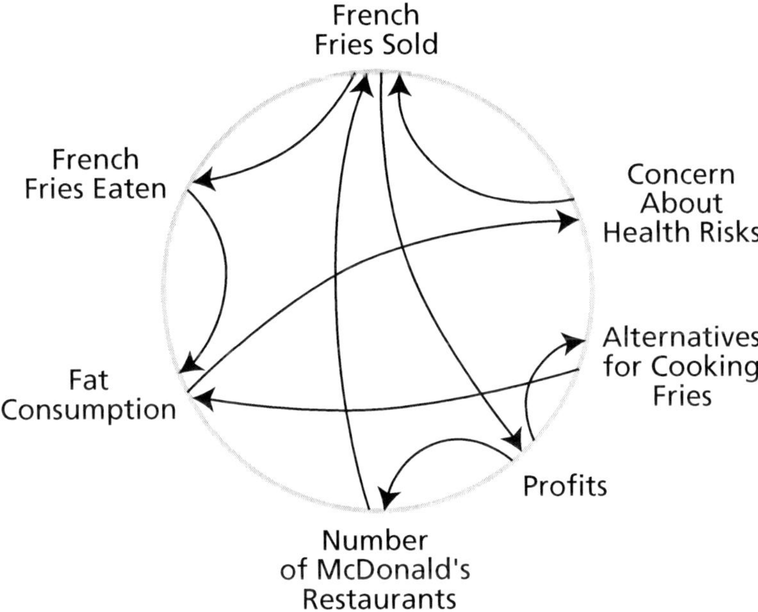

12. After students have had a few minutes to draw their arrows, ask them to search their circles for paths that make a closed loop. In other words, can they begin at one element of the circle, follow connecting arrows to other elements, and end up back at their starting point, as shown on the next page? Focusing first on the elements with the most connections, students trace each loop in a different color.

Do not skip these steps. Uncovering the causal loops extracts meaning from the confusing diagrams. The loops explain the causes of the problem.

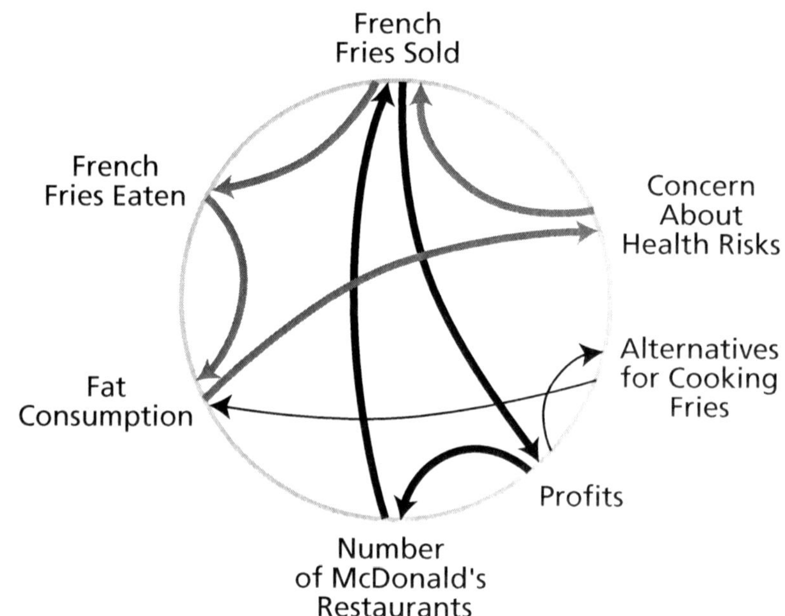

Ask students to draw each closed loop separately and tell the story of that loop. Here is an example from our sample connection circle.

- An *increase* in the number of French fries sold causes an *increase* in profits which can be used to open *more* restaurants. An increase in restaurants causes an *increase* in French fries sold, and the loop begins again, reinforcing itself each time around.

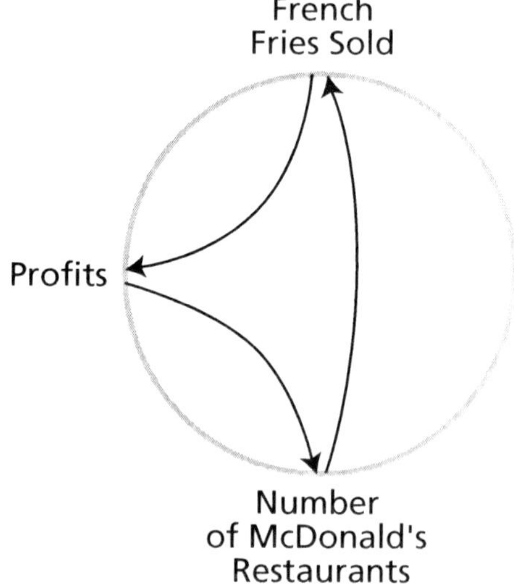

13. Distribute a blank overhead transparency sheet to each team Assign one student in each group to draw a feedback loop on the sheet and prepare to share it with the class. Resume the class discussion with a representative of each team describing the feedback loops and sharing the group's thinking.

Closed pathways are called ***feedback loops***. Tracing the causal links around the loop, a change in one element comes back to effect that element again, and around again.

Another feedback loop from our sample connection circle is drawn below.

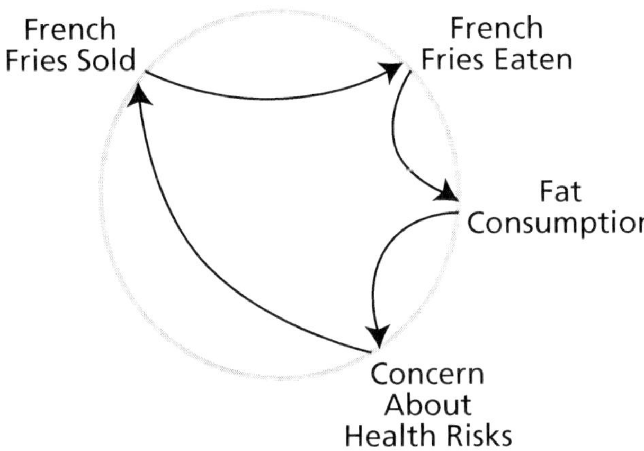

In this loop, an *increase* in fries sold causes an *increase* in fries eaten. That causes an *increase* in fat consumption which in turn *increases* the level of concern about health. When concerns grow sufficiently, it may cause sales of fries to *decrease* as customers try to eat more healthy foods. Continuing around the loop again, fewer fries sold causes fewer eaten and consequently less fat consumed. A drop in fat consumption *decreases* people's health concerns. With fewer health concerns, French fry sales *increase* again, sending the loop around again with changes reversing.

Students may use circle templates to draw their closed loops at first, but soon they will be quickly drawing the loops freehand without the underlying circles, as shown at the end of the lesson.

This feedback loop is *self-balancing*. Tracing around the loop, an initial increase in one element comes back around to cause a decrease in that element, balancing back and forth each time around the loop.

14. When the work of each team is displayed, challenge students to discover loops that share a common element. In our sample connection circle, "French fries sold" appears in at least two feedback loops. As students talk their way around the loops, they will be describing the changing behaviors of the elements in the story. The diagram below shows two intersecting feedback loops drawn together.

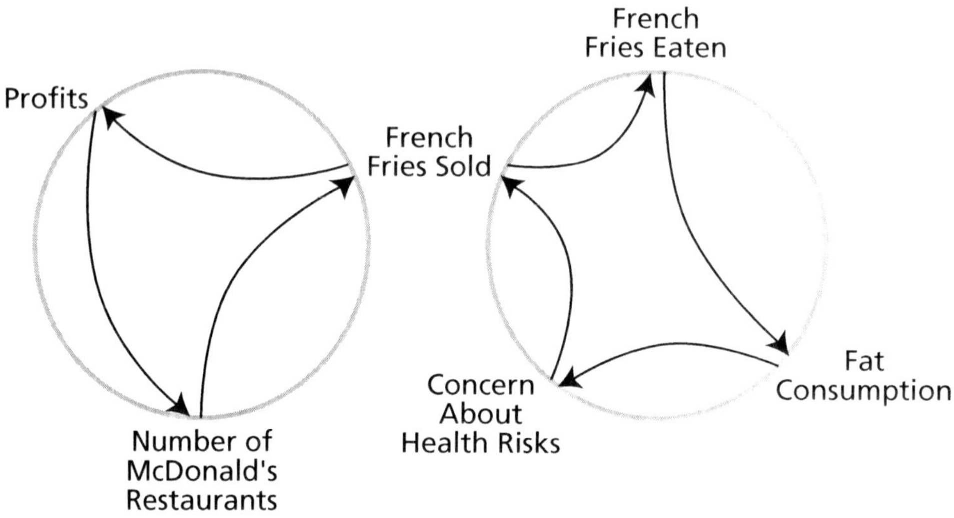

As students uncover feedback loops in their connection circles, they are surprised to find that many changes are interdependent and simultaneous. They are beginning to make sense of complexity.

Mental Models

Everybody needs a way to make sense of the world. You could say that we build "mental models" of the way things work. Reading comprehension strategies are often tools to help build mental models of the author's message and the ideas presented. A connection circle works in this way by constructing pathways of causality. We reason out how and why things changed—this increased, causing a second thing to increase, which caused the first thing to decrease, and so on. Lots of elements can be changing at one time or in some sequence that isn't linear, and the connection circle can represent that.

Bringing the Lesson Home

? How has your perception of the problem changed?

Ask students to reflect on how they originally viewed the problem and how their thinking has changed. In the process of developing their connection circles, students are often surprised to discover that a problem does not have simply one cause. Instead, problems and their solutions arise out of interdependent webs of causes and effects. With connection circles and feedback loop diagrams, students can begin to probe and appreciate this complexity in the systems around them.

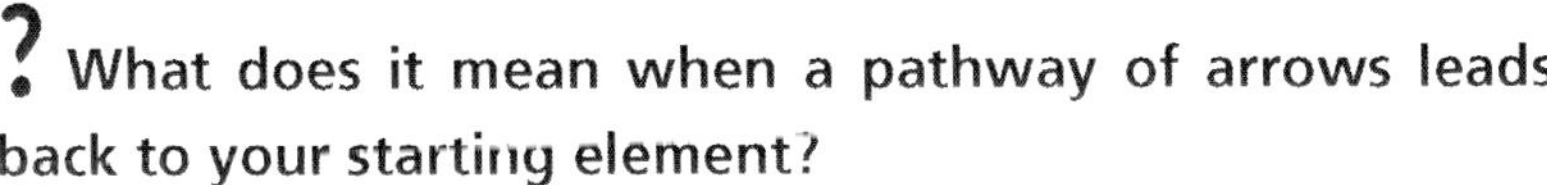

? What does it mean when a pathway of arrows leads back to your starting element?

When an arrow pathway loops back to the original element, there is feedback in the story. Each closed loop is a feedback loop. When one element in the loop changes, the effect ripples through the whole loop, affecting the original element as well.

For example, as the number of restaurants goes up, the amount of French fries sold also goes up. That causes profits to increase which will tend to increase the number of restaurants being opened, starting the process again. This is a ***reinforcing loop,*** *commonly known as a vicious or virtuous cycle.*

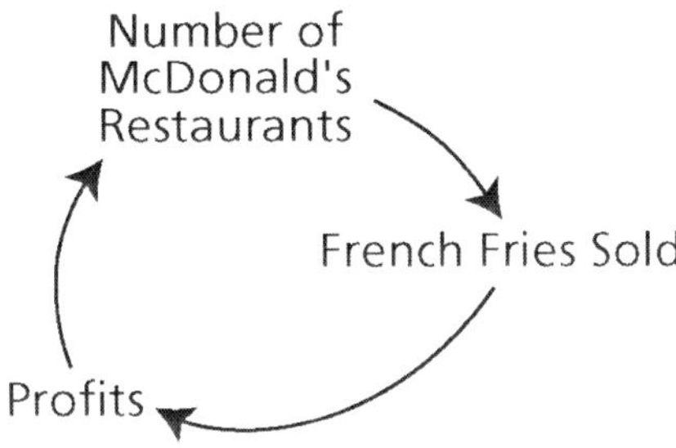

The purpose of a connection circle is to uncover the causal loops that explain *why* the problem occurs.

There are two kinds of feedback loops: reinforcing loops and balancing loops.

Another kind of feedback loop is a ***balancing loop****. In contrast to a vicious cycle, a balancing loop does not spiral in the same direction, but rather see-saws back and forth. For example, "French fries sold" increases "French fries eaten." That leads to more fat consumption and on to greater health concerns. If health concerns grow strong enough, French fry sales will be driven down. Trace the loop around a second time and notice what happens to the change among the elements.*

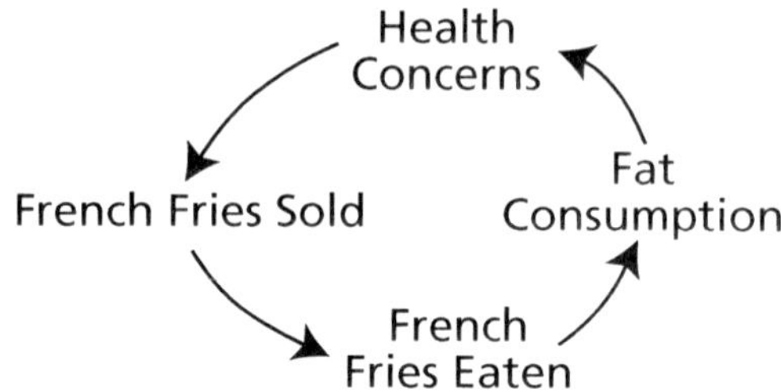

When concern grows strong enough, the number of French fries sold decreases. The number of French fries eaten goes down, fat consumption is reduced, and eventually concerns lessen. With less concern about health, people will buy more French fries again.

? What happens when elements from the connection circle are in more than one feedback loop?

The loops will interact in ways that make the behavior interesting, and often quite complex. As demonstrated in the previous paragraph, the sale of French fries creates profits but also creates health concerns. Profits increase the number of restaurants, and more restaurants mean more French fries are sold. But, meanwhile, health concerns tend to reduce the number of French fries sold. The loops push in different directions, causing tension and complexity in the story.

Although it is not always possible to do, identifying multiple feedback loops usually brings the reward of deeper insights. There are seldom simple answers to real world problems. Connection circles can help us understand change more clearly.

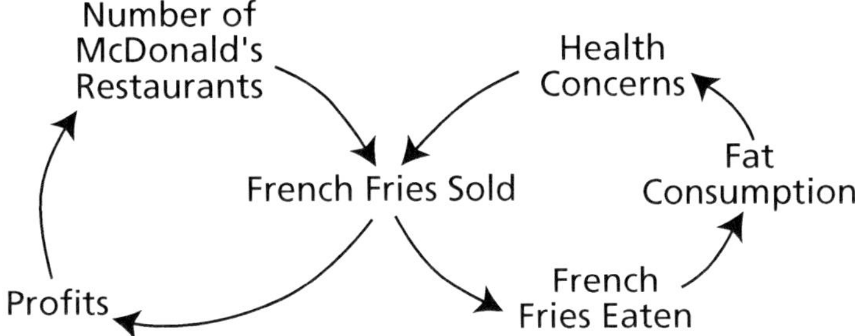

? Can students add other loops to their diagrams?

Yes. As they tell the story of their causal loop diagrams, ask student to think about which loops might be the most important driving forces and also which other loops might be missing. For example, in exploring solutions to the problem, students may want to consider the effects of alternative fats on cardiovascular illness and related health concerns. Use the diagram as a springboard for discussion.

? Can students draw causal loop diagrams like these without using connection circles?

Yes. The purpose of a connection circle is to help students uncover the feedback loops that are causing the problem. With practice, students can learn to focus on the problem, identify contributing factors, trace feedback loops in their connection circles, draw them separately freehand, and use the loops to explain why the problem occurs. Eventually we hope that they can find the feedback loops in a story without using connection circles at all.

NOTES

1 We have revised our earlier explanation of connection circles in this third edition of *The Shape of Change* to make the purpose more clear. Readers can find more about this lesson and its next steps in our second book, *The Shape of Change: Stocks and Flows* (2007), also available from the Creative Learning Exchange.

2 The connection circle was conceived by Julia Hendrix, a fifth grade teacher in Carlisle, Massachusetts when she used the circle in the *Connections Game* (Lesson 9) as a template for examining causal connections in a story. Alan Ticotsky and Rob Quaden have since adapted and refined the method and application of the tool to help students probe causality and feedback in a range of complex systems.

3 "Eyes on the Fries," by Rene Ebersole, appeared in the student magazine *Current Science*, March 1, 2002. It is reproduced by permission beginning on page 135.

Lesson 11

Keystone Species in an Ecosystem

Using a Connection Circle to Tell the Story

Ecosystems are built upon complex interrelationships among organisms and their habitats. Often, a change in the population of one species causes unexpected changes in other species. Understanding and representing a web of changes is challenging for the scientists who study them, let alone for readers who try to comprehend these complex situations. In this lesson, students read a chapter from a skillfully written science book and use connection circles to unravel a mystery of nature.[1]

As in previous lessons, students will frame their inquiry with these questions: *What* is changing? *How* is it changing? *Why* is it changing?

MATERIALS

- Overhead projector or display board
- Several different colored markers for each student
- *Connection Circle* template for each student (page 133)
- Posted copy of "Connection Circle Rules" (page 134)
- Copies of "The Case of the Twin Islands" (page 137)

How It Works

In her informative and entertaining book, *The Case of the Mummified Pigs and Other Mysteries in Nature,*[2] Susan E. Quinlan has written fourteen true stories that describe the research of ecologists who puzzle out how and why ecosystems behave as they do. Readers discover the interesting and often surprising connections among organisms through the work of detectives who find clues to nature's riddles.

A connection circle is a thinking tool, a way to surface and examine mental models—not a mold for one "right" answer.

The chapter, "The Case of the Twin Islands," examines why the ecosystems in the waters off two neighboring Aleutian islands are so different. As students use connection circles to trace causal relationships in the story, they discover the role of a keystone species, a species vital to the stability of the whole ecosystem. Students learn how feedback loops maintain a delicate balance in an ecosystem and what happens when that balance is disturbed.

Connection Circles

The purpose of a connection circle is to help students focus on the problem presented by the author and to uncover its causes. Here is a quick overview:

- First, students briefly define the problem: What is the author concerned about? What is the main problem? *What* is changing over time?
- Next, *how* is it changing? In a few words, or with a quick behavior over time graph, students describe how the problem is increasing or decreasing over time.
- Finally, students look for elements in the story that contribute to the problem. They use a connection circle to organize their thoughts, find cause and effect relationships, and trace the feedback loops that tie them together to explain *why* the problem occurs.

Procedure

1. Read "The Case of the Twin Islands," reprinted with permission in the Appendix (page 133). Students may read independently, share reading, or listen to it read aloud.

2. Create connection circles summarizing the situation described in the story. If students are drawing connection circles for the first time, follow the procedure outlined in Lesson 10, "Do You Want Fries with That?" (page 103).

If students are already familiar with connection circles, give each student a Connection Circle Template (page 133), review the rules, and ask pairs of students to begin choosing elements for their circles. See the Appendix (page 134) for a larger copy of the rules to post in your classroom for easy reference.

Connection Circle Rules

1. What's the problem: *What* is changing? *How* is it changing?
2. Choose elements of the story that satisfy ***all*** of these criteria:
   - They contribute to the problem.
   - They are nouns or noun phrases.
   - They increase or decrease over time.
3. Write your elements around the circle. Narrow it down to 5 to 10.
4. Find elements that cause another element to increase or decrease.
   - Draw an arrow *from* the cause *to* the effect.
   - The causal connection must be direct.
5. Look for feedback loops. Tell their story.

It may help you to also read Lesson 10 for another connection circle example.

3. What's the problem? *What* is changing? Ask students to quickly identify the problem that the author is presenting. They may say, "The sea otters have disappeared from the waters around Shemya while the sea urchin population has grown there."

A behavior over time graph is a line graph sketch that shows how something changed over time. What was the general pattern of the behavior?

Ask students to define the problem more precisely by describing *how* the populations changed over time in a graph or briefly in words. These are examples. They are just quick rough sketches of the general patterns of behavior. (Students may prefer to sketch separate graphs for each population.)

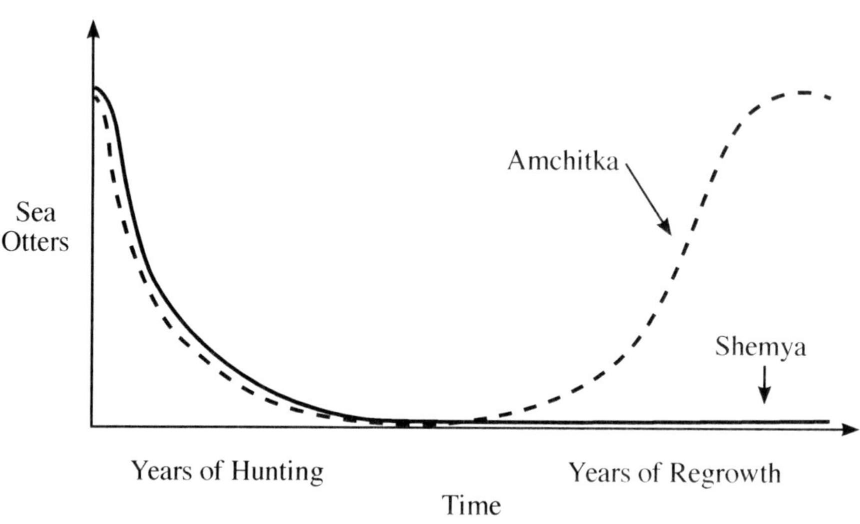

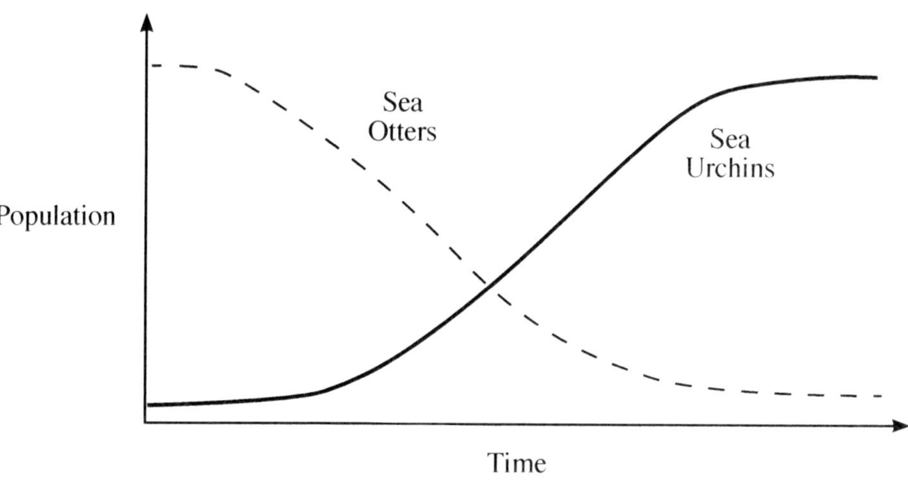

4. Remind students to choose elements that describe the problem and its possible causes. Here, our main concern is the sea otter population that has decreased over time. The population of sea urchins is also important. Other variables in the story contribute to the increase and decrease of these species.

Elements can be tangible or intangible. Do not use words like "more" or "less" in the labels.

5. Once students have drawn their connection circles with causal arrows, share them as the focus of a class conversation.

- Draw a large circle on the board or overhead projector.
- Have each team suggest an element to put on the circle.
- As a class, refine the list to include *no more than five to ten* elements.
- Ask each team to describe a causal arrow and explain their reasoning for direct causality. Encourage other teams to ask clarifying questions. Students should refer to the text when explaining their reasoning.

Here is one example of a connection circle for "The Case of the Twin Islands." Expect student examples to vary.

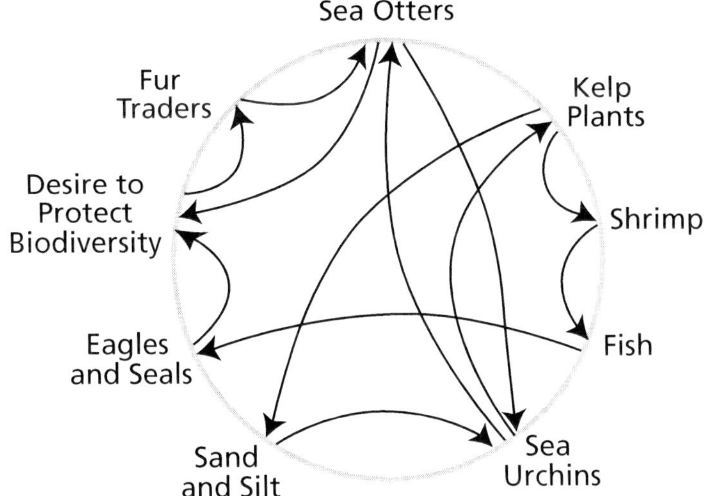

A connection circle is a thinking tool, a way to surface and examine mental models—not a mold for one "right" answer.

Remember, these are only sample drawings. Let students present their own ideas and encourage them to weigh the ideas of others. Students are always free to change their drawings as they continue to refine their mental models together.

Ask students to explain their arrows: How did a change in one element cause a change in another?

- An *increase* in the number of fur traders caused a *decrease* in the number of sea otters because traders hunted and killed sea otters. Also, a *decrease* in traders caused an *increase* in sea otters because they could multiply unharmed.
- An *increase* in the shrimp population caused an *increase* in the number of fish because fish eat shrimp. A *decrease* in the number of shrimp caused a *decrease* in the number of fish.
- An increase in kelp plants caused an *increase* in sand and silt because kelp calmed the waters allowing sediment to be deposited. The increased sediment then buried the sea urchins causing them to decrease. Students might draw an arrow suggesting that an increase in kelp caused a decrease in urchins, but this is not a *direct* cause. Remind students to be very careful in their thinking about what caused what.

6. Ask teams of students to trace a closed "loop." Can they start at one element, follow the arrows around the circle and return to where they started? Each of these pathways is a *feedback loop* that tells part of the story. Trace each loop in a different color. (It helps to start with an element that has many connections to and from it.)

After students trace a loop, ask them to draw a simplified drawing that includes only the elements from the traced loop, as shown in the following examples. Again, student drawings will vary.

The circle below shows one large feedback loop. Tracing it reveals a story.

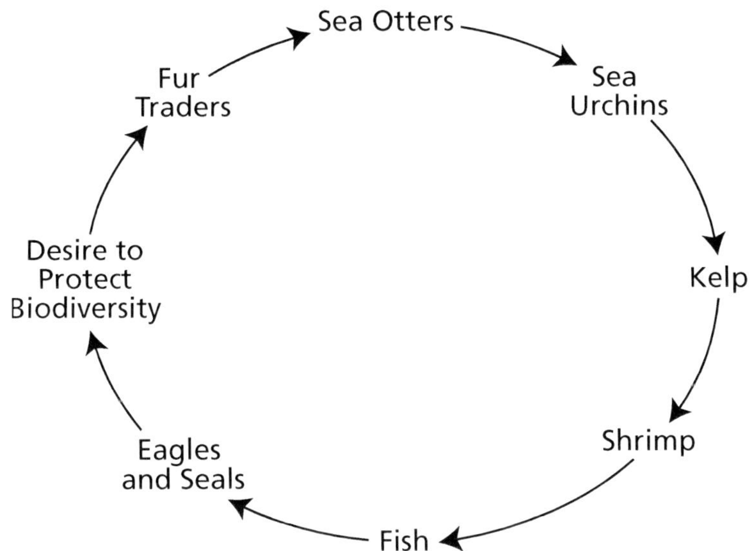

The purpose of a connection circle is to uncover the feedback loops that explain *why* the problem occurred. Don't skip this step.

Starting at the top, an *increase* in sea otters caused a *decrease* in sea urchins because sea otters eat urchins. Fewer urchins allowed the kelp plants to *increase.* An *increase* in kelp caused an *increase* in shrimp, which then caused an *increase* in fish, which then caused an *increase* in eagles and seals. With abundant wildlife, people were less worried about biodiversity. A *decrease* in the desire to protect biodiversity allowed the number of traders to *increase,* so the number of sea otters began to *decrease.*

This is a ***balancing feedback loop***. We started with an increase in sea otters, but going around the loop, the chain of events caused sea otters to decrease. If we traced the loop again, the decrease in sea otters would then become an increase, balancing back and forth each time around the loop.

Do not present these examples to students! Allow them to discover the feedback in the story for themselves. Let representatives from each team present feedback loops and share their stories with the class.

The story gets complicated, but don't worry. It is easier when students construct and talk about their own circles. This is the reason for doing connection circles in the first place: Students can understand and communicate ideas that are difficult to express using more conventional tools.

7. Look for other feedback loops. Here are some examples:

Otters and Fur Traders

Here is a possible loop linking otters and fur traders.

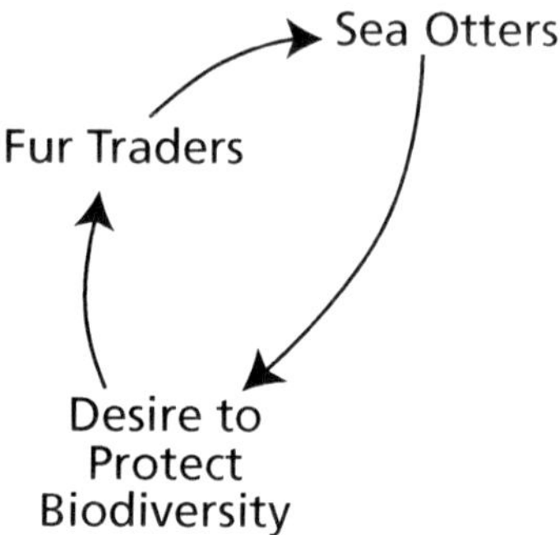

Tracing the loop, an *increase* in fur traders in the 19th Century caused a *decrease* in sea otters to dangerously low levels. An awareness of the decline caused an *increase* in the desire to protect biodiversity. This led to a *decrease* in hunting. This is also a ***balancing loop***—any change works to restore itself around the loop again.

Students trace the different loops on their original connection circles in different colors before drawing separate feedback loops. They can draw these loops freehand without using connection circles as templates.

Sea Urchins and Kelp

Here is another feedback loop. Sea urchins eat kelp plants. The kelp plants calm the water movement and trap sand and silt on the ocean bottom. Sand and silt smother sea urchins.

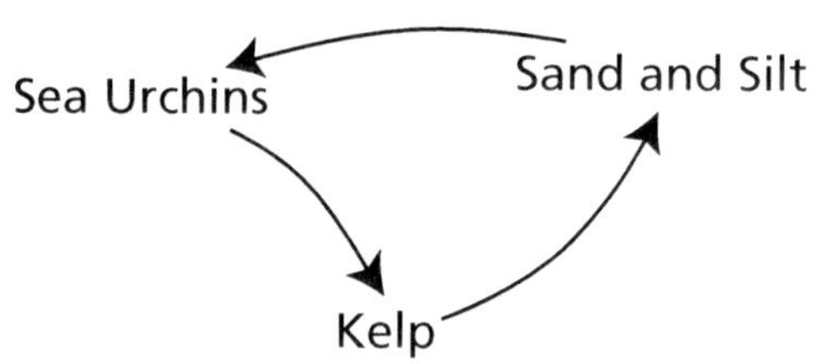

Tracing the loop for the circumstances around Shemya Island, an *increase* in sea urchins caused a *decrease* in kelp plants. Fewer kelp plants meant less sand was deposited. A *decrease* in sand provided a more suitable habitat for a *further increase* in sea urchins and *another decrease* in kelp plants. In this spiral, the sea urchins continued to multiply and the kelp disappeared.

However, around Amchitka Island, the opposite occurred. An initial *decrease* in sea urchins caused an *increase* in kelp plants. More kelp caused more sand. More sand meant *even fewer* sea urchins and *more and more* kelp. This time the spiral drove the sea urchin population *down* and the kelp thrived to harbor greater biodiversity.

This is a good example of a ***reinforcing loop***—sometimes also called a virtuous or vicious cycle. Any change gets amplified over and over again, spiraling either up or down.

Reinforcing loops drive accelerating growth or decline in systems. Balancing loops work to keep reinforcing loops in check. When something disrupts the balance of an ecosystem, a reinforcing loop can spur a rapid growth or decline of a species—a clue to the mystery in our story.

Sea Otters and Sea Urchins: Predators and Prey

Because sea otters prey upon sea urchins, an *increase* in sea otters causes a *decrease* in sea urchins. A *decrease* in urchins then causes a *decrease* in otters as their food supply dwindles. Tracing around the loop again, a *decrease* in otters allows the urchins to reestablish themselves. This is another ***balancing loop***—any change restores itself, balancing back and forth each time around the loop.

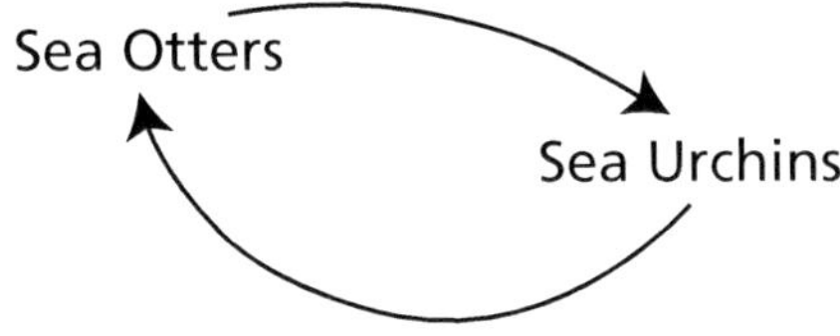

Tracing the story of each loop explains why the behavior changed over time.

The sea otter/sea urchin loop on previous page is typical of predator/prey feedback loops in nature. The populations balance each other. Too many predators will reduce the prey population to levels that will cause the predators to run short of food. When the prey population expands too much, more predators will hunt them and bring down their numbers.

8. While sharing feedback loops with the whole class, look for elements that appear in more than one loop. Most stories contain overlapping loops. This diagram connects all the previous loops.

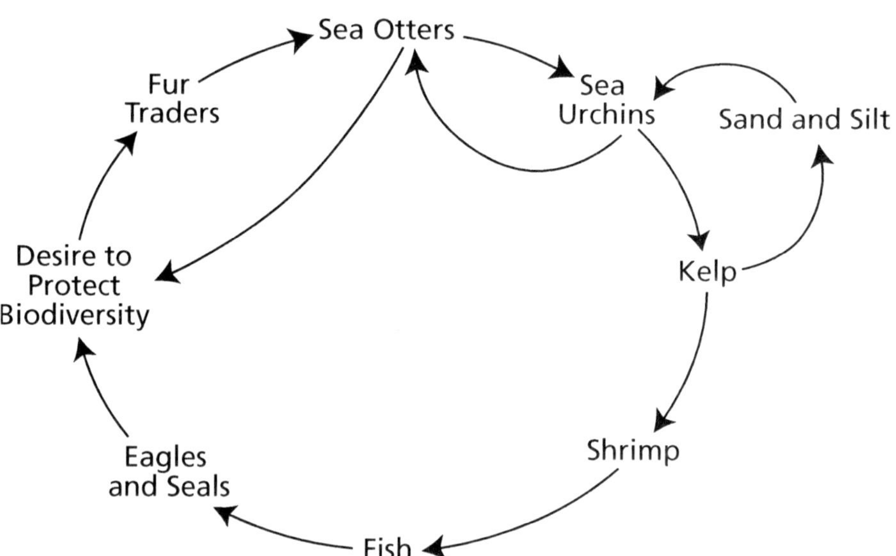

An ecosystem is a delicate balance of many feedback loops. As students uncover these interdependencies, they begin to appreciate the complexity of natural systems.

Tracing the intertwined loops, notice how kelp plants provide food for shrimp, triggering a biodiversity increase, while also causing sand and silt to build up. The sand and silt loop drives the sea urchin population down, further enabling the kelp to grow. In this diagram, sea urchins and sea otters both have two arrows leading from them, signifying multiple outcomes caused by changes in their populations.

9. Ask students to revisit their original behavior over time graphs defining the problem, or have each team choose an element from the circle and sketch how it changed from the time when hunters arrived in the late 1800s to the time when "The Case of the Two Islands" was written. Emphasize that the general shape of the graph is important—it cannot be precise because we have no specific data. Share the graphs and ask students to explain how they relate to the feedback loops they have uncovered.

Bringing the Lesson Home

Give students a chance to bring the lesson full circle. What did they learn? Posing stimulating questions like these will help students ask better questions themselves.

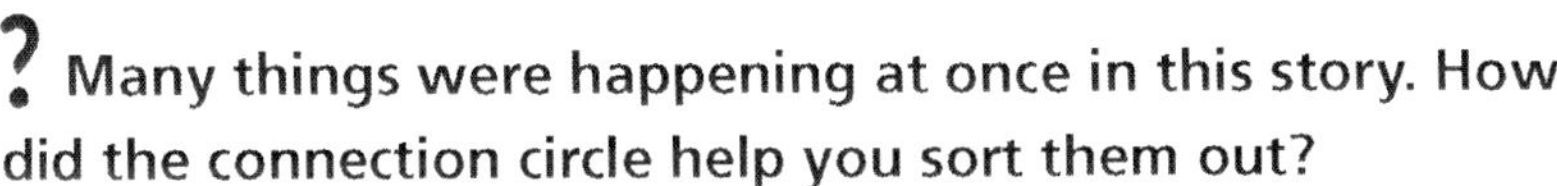

? Many things were happening at once in this story. How did the connection circle help you sort them out?

The mystery of the twin islands often seems baffling at first. Encourage students to reflect on their thinking and on the process of understanding complexity by looking for the interwoven causal loops underlying the problem.

? Did you solve the mystery of the twin islands? What effect did sea otters have on the sea urchin population and the balance of the two ecosystems?

Around Amchitka Island, the sea otter population increased. This caused a decrease in the number of sea urchins. That allowed the kelp forests to grow thickly because they were not being destroyed by sea urchins. The kelp provided habitat for shrimp, which fed many fish. The fish became food for seals and eagles. The increased kelp also sheltered the deposits of sand and silt on the ocean floor, which smothered the bottom dwellers who might try to live there.

In using connection circles, the thinking process is important—not just the product.

In contrast, sea otters had not returned to Shemya Island and a large population of sea urchins lived in the waters there. The sea urchins prevented the growth of kelp, so few shrimp and fish could survive in the inhospitable environment. Bottom dwellers thrived since the sand and silt did not build up over the ocean floor, but these creatures were not desirable food for most fish species. With few fish to attract them, seals and eagles did not colonize Shemya Island and its surrounding waters.

? How did hunters affect the islands' ecosystems?

Fur traders hunted sea otters to the brink of extinction. The decline of the sea otter population allowed sea urchins to proliferate, and the urchins devastated the kelp forests. When kelp forests decrease, many marine animal species are deprived of habitat and their numbers decline as well. Without hunters, sea otters could thrive around Amchitka Island.

? Author Susan Quinlan calls the sea otter a "keystone species." What does she mean?

When the sea otter was removed from the Aleutian Islands, the ecosystem collapsed and became barren of many species. Similarly, if the keystone in an arch is removed, all the other stones will fall. Any species that is disproportionately important (i.e., compared to its population) in the maintenance and balance of an ecosystem, and whose removal disrupts or destroys the food web, is thought to be a keystone species. Some scientists believe that only predators can be keystone species but others disagree.

? What are the keystone species in ecosystems where we live?

Among animals generally considered to be keystone species are prairie dogs, beavers, freshwater bass, gray wolves, and salmon.

Feedback Loops Tell the Story

Feedback loops explain ***why*** the ecosystems were so different. An ecosystem is a delicate balance of feedback loops. Positive loops drive rapid population growth or decline, but nature provides balancing loops to keep positive loops from spiraling out of control. When hunters disturbed the balance by removing the sea otters from the ecosystem, the sea urchin population boomed causing many other changes to the ecosystem.

Additional Background Information

Students often generate many good questions that go beyond the original story. Here is some more background information that might be helpful.

Students have used connection circles to find the causes of change over time. Eventually, they will come to recognize the feedback loops in the systems around them without the need of this tool.

? Why had sea otters come back to Amchitka but not Shemya?

The story only tells us that a few otters had escaped hunters but "they had not returned yet to Shemya Island." Researchers have proposed several theories to explain the abundance of sea otters on some islands and their scarcity on others. Among the causes hypothesized are coastal currents, algae production, complex factors affecting otter prey, predation on otter pups, and environmental contamination. Interested students can pursue this story further.

? In the absence of sea urchins, do sea otters eat so much of another species that it becomes depleted?

Sea otters can deplete their food sources rapidly. As is the case with other species, feedback loops in the environment operate to reduce otter populations when food is scarce and allow it to increase when prey is abundant.

? What is currently happening to the sea otter population in the Aleutian Islands?

James Estes and other scientists have continued to study the sea otter population and discovered more threats since 1990. It was estimated that between 150,000 to 300,000 otters lived in the Pacific Coast region before the hunters arrived in the 19th Century. A treaty in 1911 stopped hunting but only about 1,000 otters were left.

In the 1970s, the otter population near Alaska was estimated to have recovered to over 100,000. But in the years leading to the beginning of the 21st Century, they declined again. The culprit this time may be a different species of hunter—killer whales. Killer whales usually prefer to eat sea lions and seals, but those populations have declined due to reduced fish stocks. Killer whales have turned to sea otters and have reduced their numbers to dangerously low levels again. Kelp forests have been noted to be in serious decline by year 2000. Students will recognize familiar feedback relationships in these stories too.

NOTES

1 We have revised this lesson from the version in the earlier edition of *The Shape of Change* (2004) to make our explanation of connection circles more clear. For more information on this lesson and its next steps, also see Lesson 11 in *The Shape of Change: Stocks and Flows* (2007) by Quaden, Ticotsky and Lyneis, also available from The Creative Learning Exchange at *www.clexchange.org.*

2 "The Case of the Twin Islands" is a chapter from *The Case of the Mummified Pigs and Other Mysteries of Nature*, by Susan E. Quinlan, illustrated by Jennifer Owens Dewey, published by Caroline House, Boyds Mills Press, Inc., 1995. For your convenience, the chapter is reprinted with permission on page 133. We urge you to get the book and use connection circles to explore it's many other intriguing stories.

Name____

Connection Circle Template

1. What's the problem: *What* is changing? *How* is it changing?
2. Choose elements of the story that satisfy *all* of these criteria:
   - They contribute to the problem.
   - They are nouns or noun phrases.
   - They increase or decrease over time.
3. Write your elements around the circle. Narrow it down to 5 to 10.
4. Find elements that cause another element to increase or decrease.
   - Draw an arrow *from* the cause *to* the effect.
   - The causal connection must be direct.
5. Look for feedback loops. Tell their story.

Connection Circle Rules

1. **What's the problem: *What* is changing? *How* is it changing?**
2. **Choose elements of the story that satisfy *all* of these criteria:**
   - They contribute to the problem.
   - They are nouns or noun phrases.
   - They increase or **decrease over time.**
3. **Write your elements around the circle. No more than 5 to 10.**
4. **Find elements that cause another element to increase or decrease.**
   - Draw an arrow *from* the cause *to* the effect.
   - The causal connection must be direct.
5. **Look for feedback loops. Tell their story.**

Eyes On The Fries

Americans love french fries. On average, each person in the United States eats 30 pounds of french fries every year. That adds up to a countrywide annual total of more than 8.5 billion pounds of french fries—a weight equal to about 18,889 Statues of Liberty!

That humongous appetite for french fries is widening waistlines and contributing to the epidemic of cardiovascular diseases (CVD), say nutrition experts. Cardiovascular diseases, such as heart attack and stroke, are ones that affect the heart and the blood vessels. Roughly 58 million Americans—almost one-fourth of the nation's population—have some form of cardiovascular disease, according to the National Center for Chronic Disease Prevention and Health Promotion.

Despite that alarming number, Americans aren't curbing their appetite for french fries. Maybe it's time for a more healthful fry.

PERFECTING THE FRY

The french fry became a national staple back in the 1950s after a milk shake-machine salesman named Ray Kroc visited a small burger stand in San Bernadino, Calif. Kroc had heard that the stand used at least eight of his machines to mix more than 40 shakes at once. He had to see that. What impressed Kroc even more were the stand's french fries—salty and golden crisp on the outside, soft and rich on the inside.

Kroc envisioned a string of restaurants selling those fries all over the country. He bought the stand's franchise rights from brothers Mack and Dick McDonald and became the proud father of the McDonald's fast-food chain.

STANDARDIZED FRIES

Before McDonald's, the quality of fast-food french fries varied from restaurant to restaurant. Kroc turned the preparation and cooking of fries into a science. He made his fries from only top-quality Idaho russet potatoes that had a specific water-to-starch ratio. Starch is a white, granular type of carbohydrate. Carbohydrates are nutrients made of carbon, hydrogen, and oxygen that are the main source of fuel for the body's cells.

Potatoes with too much water and not enough starch make soggy fries. To keep McDonald's fries from being soggy, Kroc sent technicians to the potato fields to monitor the potatoes' water content with scientific instruments called hydrometers.

"Eyes on the Fries" by Rene Ebersole appeared in the student magazine *Current Science*, March 1, 2002. It is reproduced with permission.

Kroc didn't want McDonald's fries to be too crunchy, either. When potatoes are harvested, they're rich in sugars, another type of carbohydrate. Sugars are simpler in chemical structure than starches are and have a sweet taste. If you slice and fry a fresh potato, the sugars in it will caramelize (liquefy) and the fries' outsides will brown before their insides are fully cooked. To make fries crispy on the outside and fluffy on the inside, Kroc cured, or stored, his Idaho russets at a warm temperature for a few weeks until most of the sugar had converted to starch.

IT'S ALL ABOUT OIL

The taste of a french fry also depends on the cooking oil in which it's deep-fried. From its first days, McDonald's used cooking oil containing beef tallow, a white fat rendered from cattle. Fats are nutrients that the body uses as a source of energy as well as to make hormones, cell membranes, and blood vessels. Fats enrich the taste of food, and beef tallow gave McDonald's fries a subtle beefy flavor.

Cooking oils made from animal fats contain saturated fats, which are fats with molecules that carry as many hydrogen atoms as possible. The problem with saturated fats in the diet is that they increase one type of cholesterol in the body called low-density lipoprotein (LDL) cholesterol, say health experts. Cholesterol is a soft, waxy substance the body uses to build new cells and repair old ones. Studies have shown that too much LDL cholesterol in the body clogs the arteries and is associated with increased risk for cardiovascular disease.

In the 1990s, McDonald's and other fast-food chains responded to a public health outcry by switching to vegetable oils containing polyunsaturated fats, which lower LDL cholesterol. That switch might not have fixed the problem, however. Restaurants reuse the oil in which they make fries. In order to make vegetable oils suitable for repeated deep-frying, the oils must be altered through a chemical process called hydrogenation. Hydrogenation creates another type of fat: trans unsaturated fat. "Trans fats are similar in structure and function to saturated fats," said Alice Lichtenstein, a nutrition professor at Tufts University and the vice chair of the American Heart Association's nutrition committee. "And they also increase LDL cholesterol."

HEALTHFUL CHOICES

If fast-food chains want to make fries that are better for human hearts, said Lichtenstein, they should switch to oils that contain unsaturated fats, such as olive or canola oil. Unfortunately, those oils can't withstand repeated deep-frying. Any restaurant that uses those oils would have to change them more frequently. And that would likely drive up the cost of french fries.

Until fast-food chains switch to cooking oils that are more nutritious, what can fry lovers do? Well, says Lichtenstein, one place to start might be thinking twice the next time someone asks, "Would you like me to super-size those fries?"

THE CASE OF THE TWIN ISLANDS

AMCHITKA AND SHEMYA ISLANDS lie close together in the Aleutian Island chain in the Gulf of Alaska. Both islands are made of the same kinds of rocks, and the same kind of rocky ocean floor occurs around each island. They are both surrounded by clear, unpolluted waters of the same temperature and saltiness. The marine environments of the two islands are nearly identical. However, the two islands are home to very different groups of marine plants and animals. Marine scientists James Estes, Norman Smith, and John Palmisano wondered how the islands could be so alike, and yet so different.

From *The Case of the Mummified Pigs and Other Mysteries of Nature*, written by Susan E. Quinlan, illustrated by Jennifer Owens Dewey, published by Caroline House, Boyds Mill Press, Inc. Reprinted by permission.

These scientists could explain just one difference in the life around the two islands. Amchitka Island is home to several thousand sea otters, while none live around Shemya. This difference is due to history. Sea otters are large fur-bearing marine mammals. Their fur is one of the softest and warmest furs in the world, so sea otters were once hunted by people. In the late 1800s, fur traders from Russia, Asia, and North America searched for otters in every bay and inlet of western North America. They killed all the otters they found in order to get their furs. They nearly killed off all the sea otters on Earth.

Fortunately, however, a few sea otters escaped the hunters. These otters survived in hidden coves in Alaska and in Monterey Bay, California. After decades of protection from fur traders, sea otters had slowly returned to their former abundance in a few areas, including the waters around Amchitka Island. But they had not returned yet to Shemya Island.

Estes, Smith, and Palmisano suspected that sea otters might be the cause of all the other differences in marine life around Amchitka and Shemya Islands. To find out if their hunch was right, these scientists visited both islands and dived around them several times. They counted the numbers, sizes, and kinds of marine plants and animals around each island.

Amchitka Island, home to thousands of sea otters, was

also home to hundreds of seals. There, bald eagles swooped low over the sea to catch fish in their talons. Underwater the scientists found a forest of giant kelp, a kind of marine plant. Huge brown fronds of the kelp rose up from the ocean bottom toward the sunlit surface. Many shrimplike animals and lots of fish lived amidst the waving kelp fronds. But few animals lived on the ocean bottom.

In contrast, Shemya Island, which had no sea otters, also had few seals and no bald eagles. Underwater the biologists found almost no kelp, few shrimplike animals, and few fish. But here, the ocean bottom was swarming with sea urchins, chitons, limpets, blue mussels, and barnacles.

The scientists couldn't figure out what was going on without knowing more about the connections among the ocean creatures. So they read many reports by other scientists. Information about the food of sea otters gave the ecologists their first clue.

Sea otters dive underwater to catch their food, which includes many kinds of marine animals. Sea urchins are one of their favorite foods. Because they are large animals, sea otters need a lot of food. A single adult sea otter must eat nine to thirteen pounds of marine animals every day. Estes's team quickly realized that a population of thousands of sea otters would soon eat all the large marine animals within their reach. That explained why few sea urchins were found near Amchitka Island. Any urchins

A kelp forest and many sea otters surround Amchitka Island.

within easy reach of the diving sea otters had been eaten there. But around Shemya Island there were no sea otters to eat them, so the sea urchins thrived.

What difference did it make that sea otters had eaten most of the sea urchins around Amchitka? Since sea urchins graze on kelp and algae, Estes's team suspected that sea urchins might affect the kelp. Studies by other scientists proved that their suspicions were correct.

Sea urchins not only eat kelp, they also gnaw through the bases of kelp fronds. This breaks the kelp's anchor hold on the ocean bottom, and the urchin-gnawed kelp soon washes ashore to die. When lots of sea urchins are around, they eat through all the bases of the giant kelp. So kelp cannot grow on a site patrolled by hordes of sea urchins. That explained the absence of kelp on Shemya, where the ocean bottom was carpeted with giant sea urchins. It also explained why kelp had formed an underwater forest on Amchitka, where sea otters had eaten all the large urchins.

The scientists soon tied other differences in the animal life of the two islands to the presence and absence of the kelp forest. Shrimplike amphipods and isopods live in calm waters and feast on dead kelp. The kelp forest of Amchitka provided a perfect habitat for these animals. In contrast, bottom-dwelling animals were smothered by the sand and silt that settled in waters calmed by Amchitka's kelp forest.

Many kinds of fish prey on shrimplike animals, but few

Sea urchins thrive around Shemya Island.

fish can eat bottom-dwelling animals like sea urchins, chitons, barnacles, or mussels. Consequently fish were more numerous in the kelp forest of Amchitka than in the waters around Shemya. Harbor seals and bald eagles eat fish. So they were more numerous around Amchitka, too.

Estes's team concluded that when the sea otters around Amchitka Island had eaten all the big sea urchins, the kelp forest was allowed to grow. The kelp forest in turn provided habitat and food for shrimplike animals, which then became food for fish. Fish, in turn, provided food for seals and eagles. So all the amazing differences in the marine life around Amchitka and Shemya Islands could be traced to the presence or absence of a single animal species—the sea otter.

When stone layers build an archway, they place a single, wedge-shaped stone at the top of the arch. This single stone keeps the other rocks in place and holds the arch together. If the keystone is removed, the archway falls apart. Ecologists had long suspected that certain species were keystones of living communities. The investigations of Estes's team showed that sea otters are a keystone in the North Pacific. Through a tangle of connections, sea otters affect many other parts of the world. Populations of kelp, invertebrate animals, fish, seals, and eagles are tied indirectly, but indivisibly, to the welfare of sea otters.

The fur traders of the 1800s had no idea that their relentless harvest of sea otters would cause dramatic changes in the marine environment. And in the 1960s, no one expected striking changes in the marine environment as sea otters returned to their former homes. But the removal, and addition, of this single animal species caused many dramatic changes.

Today ecologists recognize that all living things are tied together by invisible connections. And some species, like the sea otter, are keystones. As thousands of species of plants and animals become endangered or extinct due to the activities of humans, ecologists worry. Which of the rapidly disappearing species are keystones? And what unexpected changes will occur when the keystones are removed from nature's living arches?

About Us

About the Authors

Rob Quaden and Alan Ticotsky are teachers in the Carlisle Public Schools in Carlisle, Massachusetts. Quaden is an eighth grade algebra teacher. Ticotsky is a classroom teacher who has taught in elementary and middle school and published science curriculum books. They have served as district math and science curriculum coordinators. For many years, Quaden and Ticotsky were systems mentors supported by the Waters Foundation, working with their colleagues to develop and implement system dynamics lessons throughout Carlisle's K–8 curriculum. They have conducted system dynamics training programs for teachers in Carlisle and beyond. Debra Lyneis works at the CLE helping teachers publish their system dynamics curriculum materials for other teachers to use. She served on the Carlisle school board.

The Creative Learning Exchange

The Creative Learning Exchange is a non-profit organization in Acton, Massachusetts dedicated to promoting learner-centered learning and system dynamics in K–12 education. Under the direction of Lees Stuntz, the CLE publishes and disseminates classroom curriculum materials developed by teachers, distributes a quarterly newsletter, hosts a biennial conference for teachers, sponsors an annual student exposition, maintains a listserv, and provides system dynamics training materials and programs for teachers. Information is available at www.clexchange.org.

The Waters Foundation

Through the vision and generosity of Jim and Faith Waters, The Waters Foundation K–12 Educational Partnership supported systems thinking and system dynamics in a dozen school districts across the country for many years. The Waters Foundation supported Quaden and Ticotsky during the years they were developing the lessons in ***The Shape of Change***. The foundation develops and disseminates curriculum materials, conducts action research, and provides training opportunities to teachers through their website, www.watersfoundation.org.

System Dynamics

System dynamics is a field of study and a perspective for understanding change. Using computer simulation and other tools, system dynamics looks at how the feedback structure of complex systems causes the change we observe all around us. System dynamics was developed by Professor Jay W. Forrester at MIT and is applied in many areas including ecology, business management, economics, and psychology. Now, system dynamics is helping teachers make K–12 education more learner-centered, engaging, challenging and relevant in our rapidly changing world. ***The Shape of Change*** introduces young students and their teachers to some of the basic concepts of system dynamics as a way to observe and think about change.

THE Shape OF Change
Stocks and Flows

Rob Quaden, Alan Ticotsky
and Debra Lyneis

Illustrated by Nathan Walker

Creative Learning Exchange
Acton, Massachusetts
2007

To Jay W. Forrester,
Celebrating fifty years of system dynamics

Graphic Design/Layout: Amanda Wait, *www.MiceSentiments.com*
Illustrations: Nathan Walker, *www.NathanWalker.net*

ISBN: 978-0-9753169-4-8

The lessons in this book build on the original lessons in ***The Shape of Change***, 2004, by the same authors.

Both books are available from:
The Creative Learning Exchange
www.clexchange.org
milleras@clexchange.org
978-635-9797
Acton, Massachusetts

Printed in USA by Instant Publisher.com

Table of Contents
The Shape of Change: Stocks and Flows

Acknowledgements

Once again, we would like to thank all those who helped us with our first book, ***The Shape of Change.*** They gave us the springboard for this next step, ***The Shape of Change: Stocks and Flows.***

The Shape of Change
Stocks and Flows

What is changing?

How is it changing?

Why is it changing?

This book builds on the lessons we developed in our first book, ***The Shape of Change.***[1] We invite you to help students deepen their understanding of the constant change that surrounds them.

In ***The Shape of Change***, students engaged in games and other classroom activities to focus on *what* was changing. Then, they used behavior over time graphs to express and examine *how* those patterns of change took shape.

- In the In and Out Game, students enacted and plotted linear growth.
- In Making Friends, they saw the line on their graph curve upward in a pattern of exponential growth as new friends doubled each round.
- In the Mammoth Game, they watched their herds of mammoths decline to extinction in a downward curve of exponential decay. Then, they saw the same pattern when their boiling water cooled to room temperature in It's Cool.
- In playing and graphing The Infection Game, they watched a disease spread through their class in an S-shaped pattern until everyone was infected.
- In The Tree Game and The Tree Game Puzzle, students observed and graphed the sustainability of their forests under varying planting and harvesting policies.
- The Rainforest Game let students experience and graph the effect of delays on their policy outcomes.

- The last three lessons helped students uncover feedback loops in stories of change over time, changes that they could make explicit with graphs.

Now, ***The Shape of Change: Stocks and Flows*** will take the next step—to help students understand *why* these things changed. Students will learn that all change over time can be viewed as a process of accumulation:

- In "The In and Out Game, the number of friends on the team is an accumulation that grew as new friends joined each round.
- In "The Mammoth Game, the number of mammoths in the herd is an accumulation that increased when mammoths were born and decreased when they died.

The level of water in a bathtub is an accumulation that increases by the flow of water in through the faucet and decreases by the flow of water out the drain over time. We'll use this analogy throughout the book.

We call these accumulations "Stocks." The amounts entering and leaving the stocks over time are called "Flows." Envisioning change over time in this framework helps students understand the similar structures that underlie all change.

Frequently Asked Questions

? Why would students need to learn about stocks and flows?

Learning about stocks and flows gives students a way to visually represent and examine the causes of change over time in a common language that applies across disciplines.

? Does this approach engage kids?

Yes. Using the language of stocks and flows to explore the causes of change raises the level of dialog, reflection, and critical thinking in the classroom because students must make their assumptions very explicit. Students use the diagrams to share and refine their thinking together.

? So what? Does an understanding of stocks and flows apply beyond the classroom?

As students proceed through the lessons, they will begin to recognize similar stock/flow structures in the systems that surround them. Students will learn that stocks are changed only by their flows, so any policy to change a stock—in the game or in real-life—must focus on altering its flows. Students can build practical problem-solving skills based on this basic understanding of how the system works.

? Where does this idea of stocks and flows come from?

Stocks and flows are basic building blocks in the field of system dynamics.[2] *System dynamics looks at how feedback processes within a system cause the changes we observe. Stocks and flows, together with feedback loops, cause change over time in the systems that surround us. Don't worry. We'll explain feedback loops one step at a time too.*

? Do we need any special materials, equipment or training to do these lessons?

You and your students will need to be familiar with the lessons in ***The Shape of Change****. It is important that students construct understanding from their own experience of the hands-on classroom activities and the graphs they drew. Beyond that, all you need are pencils and paper, a chalkboard and chalk. The lessons in this book build on one another in sequence.*

? At what ages can students do these lessons?

The original lessons in ***The Shape of Change*** *were written for students in Grades 3-8, although they have been widely adapted for younger and older students, including adults. With our own students, we would follow each of the original lessons with a discussion of stocks and flows, building this abstract understanding on the students' concrete experience. Younger students who play the In and Out Game or Making Friends can briefly learn the vocabulary of stocks and flows. By middle school, students who play the Infection Game are ready to use the concepts in more complex ways, while still referring back to the earlier lessons. With practice, students learn to recognize basic feedback loops and stock/flow structures in systems around them.*

A Problem-Solving Process

Our stock/flow maps present one mental model of a problem, but students may come up with other maps. In the later lessons, they may define a problem differently or include other details. Use this opportunity to discuss differences and similarities. A stock/flow map can help students surface their assumptions and examine the causes of change in an objective way. It can also help them be explicit and internally consistent in their reasoning. A stock/flow map is not an "answer;" it represents a thinking and problem-solving process.

? How is this book different from *The Shape of Change, Stocks and Flows: A Beginning*?

*In **A Beginning**, we presented stock/flow maps for the first few lessons of The Shape of Change. For this book, we have learned more, revised those first lessons and completed the rest.*

Looking back at ***The Shape of Change***, we'd like to repeat our earlier invitation: Teachers and students will be happy that thinking, not memorizing, is the key to learning from these activities. Try these lessons and watch your students start paying attention to the shape of change.[3]

NOTES

1 ***The Shape of Change***, by Rob Quaden, Alan Ticotsky and Debra Lyneis, 2004, is available from The Creative Learning Exchange at *www.clexchange.org*.

2 The field of system dynamics was founded by MIT Professor Jay W. Forrester fifty years ago, based on his earlier work in feedback control systems. System dynamics uses computer simulation to understand how feedback processes and stocks/flows cause change in fields as diverse as business management, psychology, public policy, economics, biology, environmental science, and more, with the goal of understanding and improving the behavior of systems. You do not need computer modeling to benefit from the lessons in this stock/flow book. However, if you are interested in learning more, simple computer modeling lessons for many of the lessons in ***The Shape of Change*** are referenced at the end of each lesson in the original book and are available at *www.clexchange.org*.

3 We welcome your feedback and any classroom suggestions: *lyneisd@clexchange.org*. Thank you.

The In and Out Game

In Lesson 1 of ***The Shape of Change***, students played a game to understand how things change over time. Players physically moved into and out of a "stock." They observed how the total number of students in the stock changed as students entered and left, and they used behavior over time graphs to record and interpret the changes. See Pages 7–16 of ***The Shape of Change*** for the complete lesson.

Overview

The In and Out Game illustrates two fundamental concepts in a concrete way.

- **Stocks** are accumulations, or quantities that can increase or decrease over time.

- Stocks are controlled by **flows**, which represent the movement into or out of the stocks.

For example, the amount of water in a bathtub can be represented by a stock. Water flowing in through the faucet and water flowing out through the drain can be represented by flows. The amount of water in the bathtub at any point is determined by how much water has flowed in and out over time.

Seeing the Structure

1. Introduce the students to the symbols of a stock/flow map. Stocks are accumulations and are drawn as rectangles. In the In and Out Game, the number of students who are in the circle at the start of each round is represented by a stock. Have students suggest a name for the stock. The name of a stock should be a noun or noun phrase.

Players in the Stock

2. A stock can be changed only by a flow. Ask students how the stock of "Players in the Stock" changed over time. Students who have played the game will know intuitively that people entering or people leaving caused changes to the stock. These are the flows. (It is sometimes helpful to identify the flows using "–ing" words to denote actions, such as entering, leaving, going in, going out, etc.)

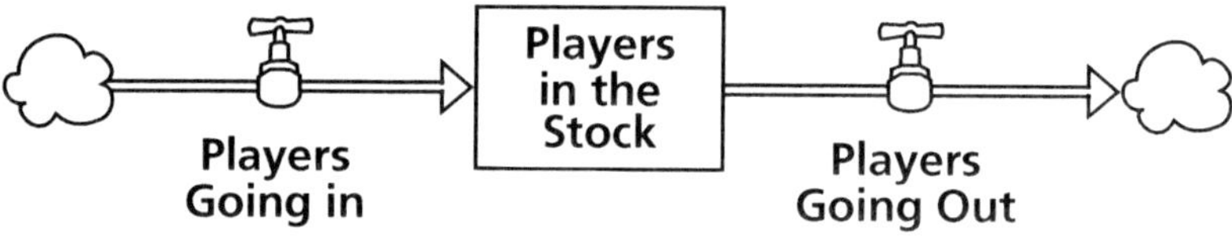

3. In this map, the pipes represent the flows. The valves in the center of each pipe indicate that the flows can be controlled. For example, in the game, the rule for the number of students entering and leaving was changed several times.

The **clouds** represent the boundaries of the map: in this game, it is not important where the incoming people come from, or where the leaving people go. We are only concerned with the flow of people into and out of the stock.

Time is implicit in every stock/flow map. Stocks increase or decrease as quantities flow in and out over time.

4. Time is implicit in a stock/flow map. The stock accumulates and drains as quantities flow in or out *over time*. In the In and Out Game, players entered and left *each round*. In a bathtub, water flows in or out in gallons of water *per minute*.

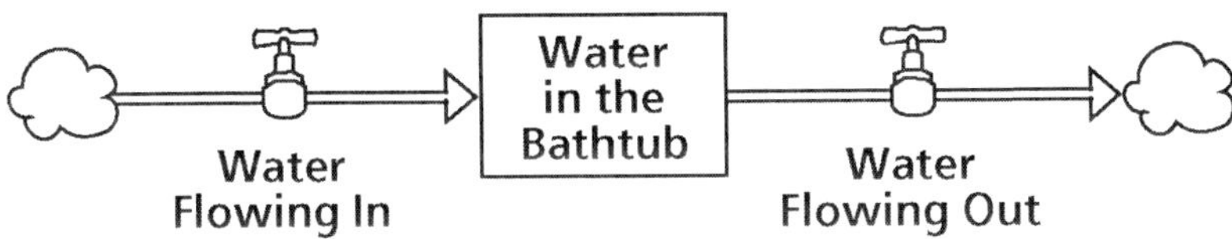

? Can you think of real-life examples of stocks and flows?
Encourage students to draw their examples in the form of stock/flow maps. Ask the students to sort their maps into categories and explain their reasoning. It is very powerful for students to see that a wide variety of examples can be classified using this generic structure. These are some examples:

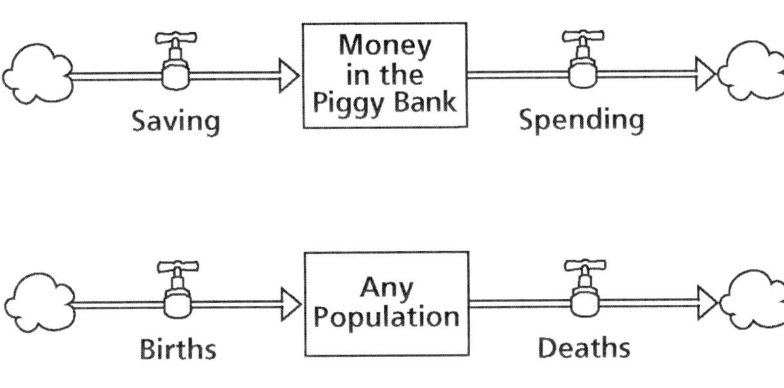

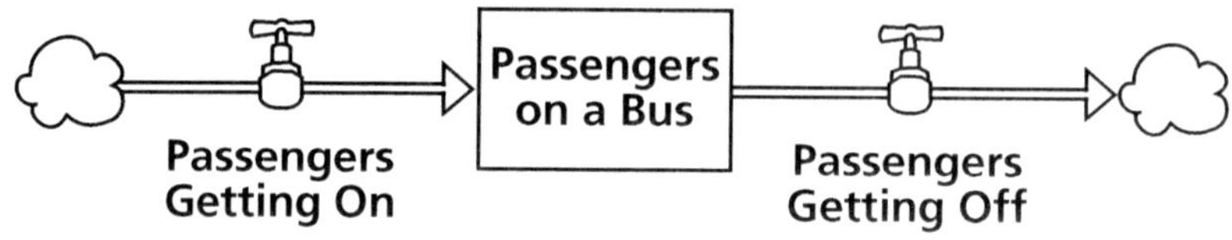

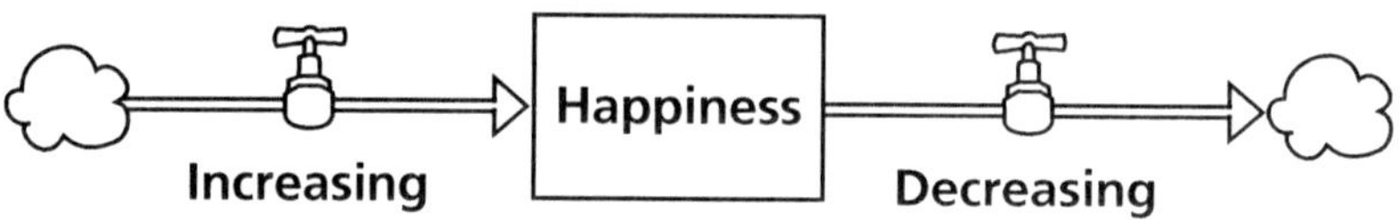

A stock can also have just one flow.

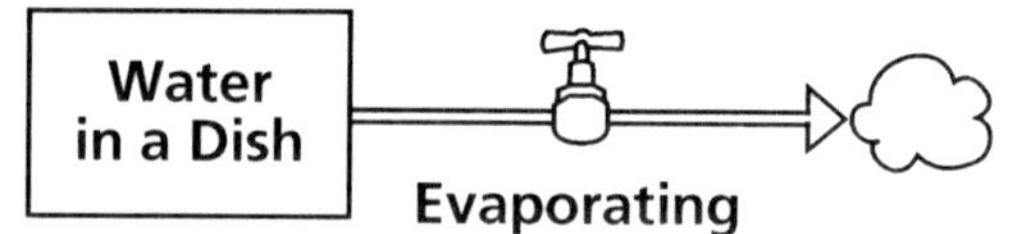

? Thinking back to the In and Out Game, how could you explain the graphs in terms of stocks and flows?

The stocks increased over time because the inflows were greater than the outflows. For example, in Game 1, the inflow was two students entering each round, and the outflow was one student leaving each round, so the stock of students grew by one student each round. In Game 2, with five students entering and only two students leaving, the stock grew even faster each round.

The game is a discrete activity. We connect the dots to help students see the patterns more clearly.

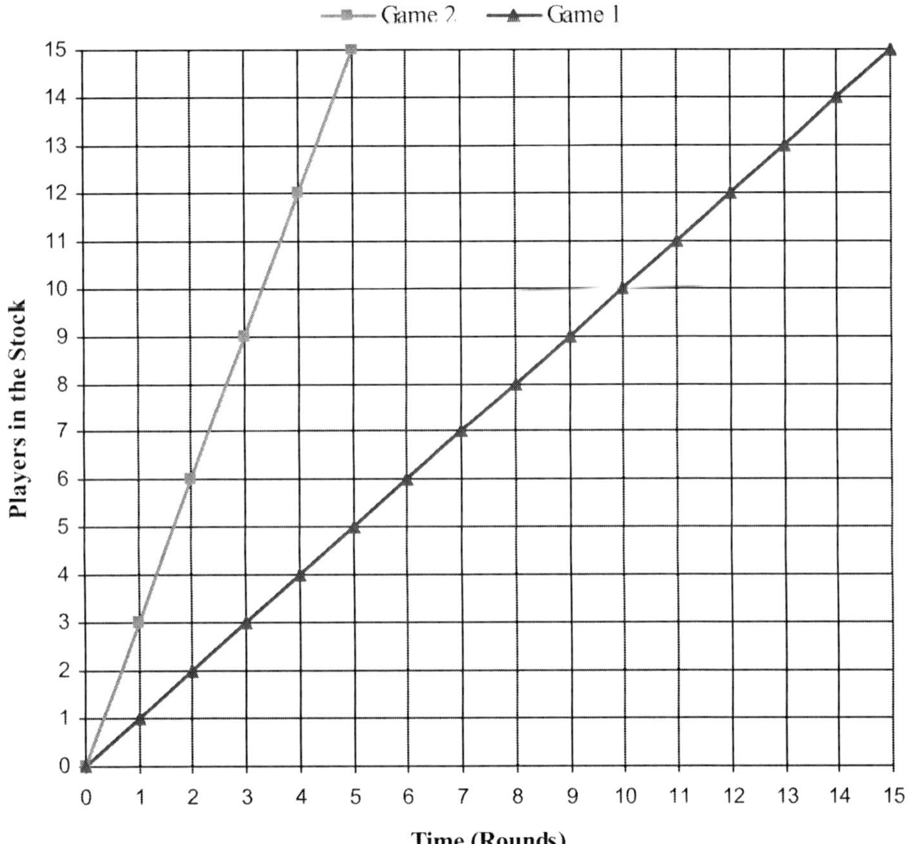

The total number of players in the stock depended on how many students flowed in and out each round.

? Take another look at your examples of stocks and flows. How can a stock change?

If you have a bathtub, you can change the level of water in it by pouring water in through the faucet or letting water out through the drain. Although you can alter the rates of flow by adjusting the faucet or slowing the drain, the flows in and out are the only ways to change the water level in the tub.

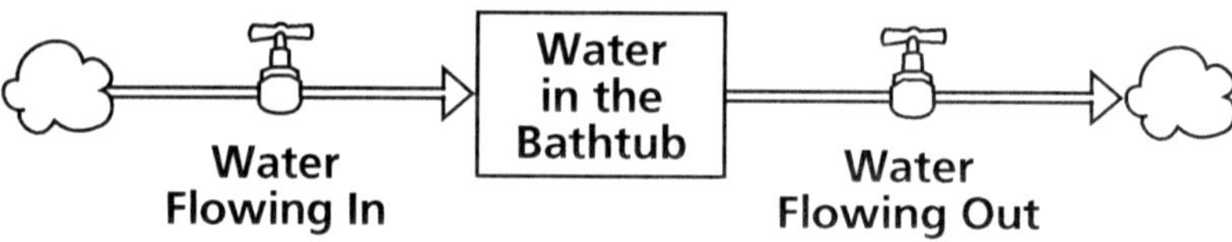

If you have money in a piggy bank, you can accumulate more money if you save more and/or spend less. Any amount of money you deposit will increase the balance, but larger deposits will cause it to grow more quickly and smaller deposits will cause it to grow more slowly. The same thing works for withdrawals. Any withdrawal will drain the balance, but bigger expenditures will drain it more quickly. To build a bigger nest egg, you need to increase the inflow or decrease the outflow of money, or both.

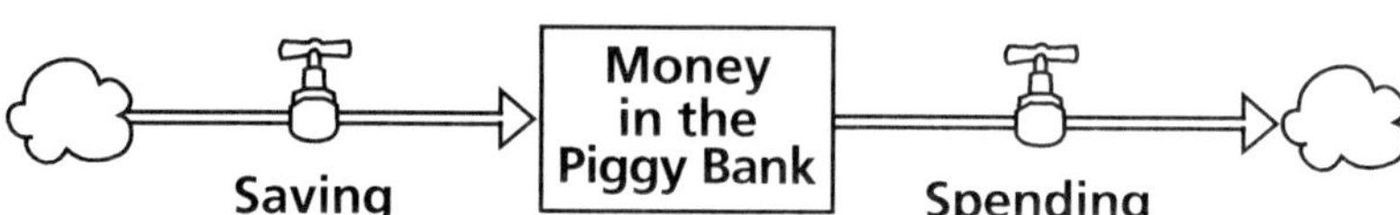

Tell the story of other examples to see how stocks and flows can help you think about change in the real world. Stocks can be changed *only* by their flows.

If you have a landfill where trash is buried, the landfill will continue to fill up because there are no outflows. You can slow the rate of filling by encouraging recycling, but trash will still pile up. You cannot decrease the stock of trash without adding an outflow: digging trash up hauling it somewhere else—where the same problem will arise again.

How to Identify Stocks and Flows

If you could stop time and take a snapshot of a system, you would see the stocks—the quantities that have accumulated over time. You would see an amount of water in the tub, an amount of money in the bank, a pile of trash. The stocks define the state of the system at any point in time.

A snapshot of water in the tub at any moment would not tell you how fast the water is filling or draining over time, however. The inflows and outflows define how the stock changes over time. Water flows in or out of the tub in a number of gallons per minute; money is saved or spent in dollars per week; trash piles up in truckloads of trash per day.

Any change over time can be viewed this way.

Making Friends

In Lesson 2 of ***The Shape of Change***, students played a game to observe and compare how the number of friends grew as new friends were added each round, first by a constant number and then by doubling. See Pages 17–25 in ***The Shape of Change*** for the complete lesson.

Overview

Of the two games played in Making Friends, Game 1 is based on the same stock/flow structure as the inflow of the In and Out Game. During each round of the game, the number of new friends is constant. This causes the total number of friends to increase at a steady rate.

However, the structure of Game 2 is completely different. In that game, the number of existing friends *caused* an increase in the number of new friends, because *each* existing friend chose a new friend each round. As a result, the number of friends increased at an increasing rate. This represents the fundamental concept of **feedback**.

Seeing the Structure

1. Ask students to draw a stock/flow map of Game 1. Point out that the map looks similar to the In and Out Game.

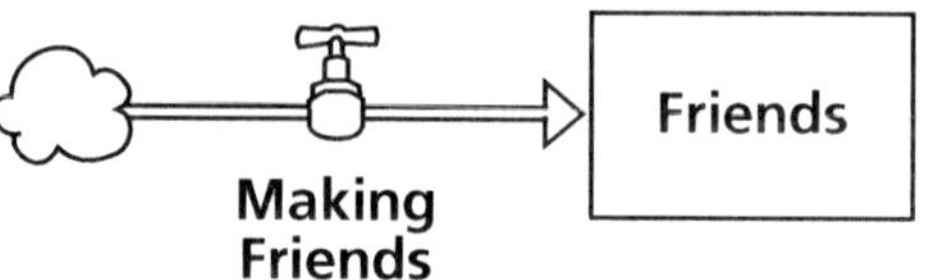

2. Ask why this map would not explain Game 2. Students should realize that the flow "Making Friends" changed throughout the game. It was not constant.

3. Ask students to explain why the number of friends in Game 2 increased so much faster. The number of friends in the stock determined the number of new friends flowing in because each friend recruited a new friend each round. In other words, the stock influenced the flow. To show this on the map, draw a connector arrow from the stock to the flow.

The curved arrow is not a flow—no friends are moving from the stock. Rather, the arrow indicates that information about the size of the stock affects the size of the flow.

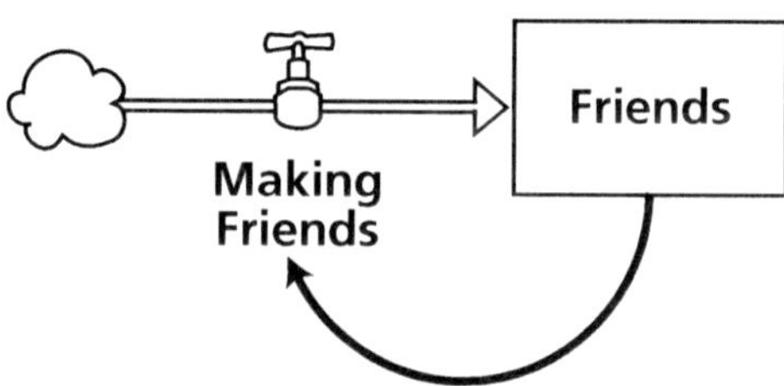

This is an example of **positive feedback**, also called **reinforcing feedback**. The stock increases the flow, which increases the stock, which in turn increases the flow, etc. This process goes on and on, increasing the value of the stock faster and faster.

Refer back to the game. At first, one friend chose one friend, making two friends in the stock. In the next round, the two friends each chose a new friend, making four friends in the stock. Then those four friends each added a friend to make a total of eight friends in the stock, and so on, doubling each round.

A Causal Loop

This drawing is another way to show feedback. The causal arrows mean that an increase in friends on the team causes an increase in making new friends, which in turn causes an increase in the friends on the team, and so on. A causal loop diagram is a quick sketch of the feedback loop, while a stock/flow diagram shows us more precisely how the changes work. We use them together to think about change over time.

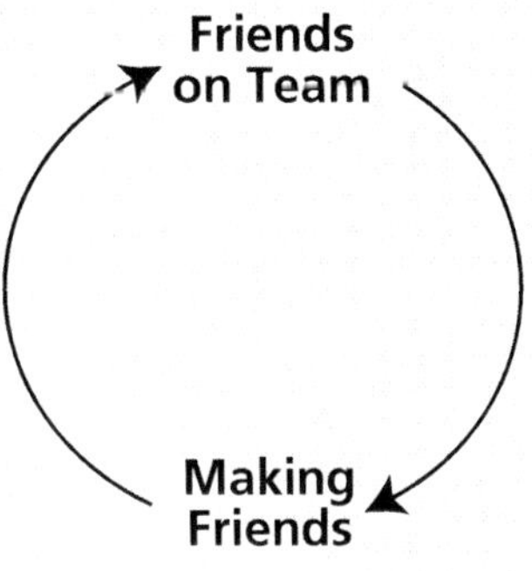

4. Ask students to think about real-life examples of positive feedback.

Positive feedback is another name for a vicious (or virtuous) cycle. Growth that is gathering speed can also be called snowballing, escalation or compounding growth. It is a feedback loop that reinforces itself.

Example 1:

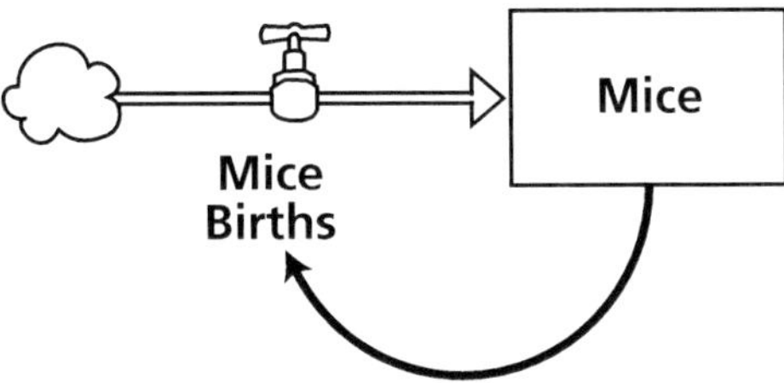

If you start with just a few mice, they give birth to baby mice, which grow into adult mice, which give birth to more baby mice, etc. Given that most people consider mice pests, this is an example of a vicious cycle.

Note that the map of mice is incomplete and does not show the complete dynamics of mice populations. For example, the map does not show mice deaths and it does not specify a birth rate. (More on these later.)

There are countless examples of positive feedback in the world around us.

Example 2:

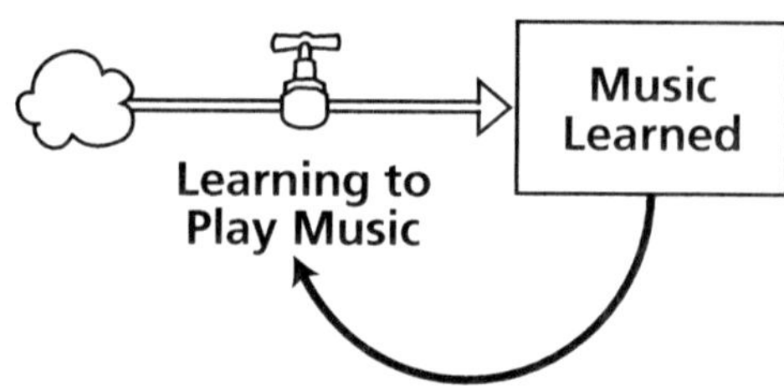

Once you learn to play a simple piece of music, you are able learn a more complicated piece, and so on. Here the reinforcing loop would be a virtuous cycle.

Example 3:

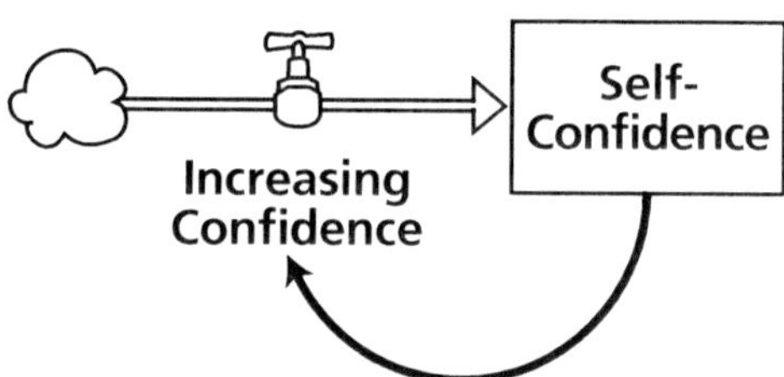

The more self-confidence you have, the more willing you are to take on new situations, which then increases your self-confidence.

Example 4:

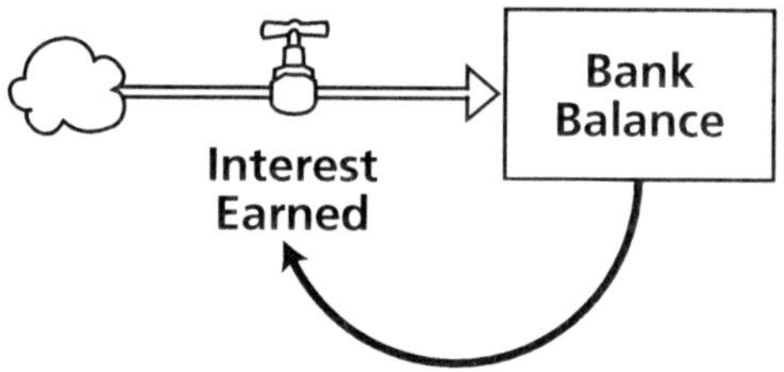

The more money you have in a bank account, the more interest you earn, giving you even more money in the account, and so on.

5. After drawing each map, trace the feedback loop by following the direction of the flow and the connector. To understand how the stocks and flows change, it is helpful to draw up or down arrows to show increases or decreases around the loop.

Using the mice example, show an initial **increase** in the number of mice by placing an up arrow near the stock:

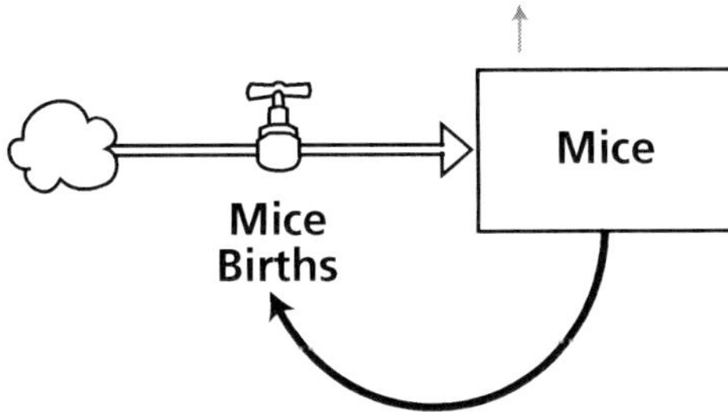

Tracing the connector, the increase in the number of mice will **increase** the number of mice births because more mice will have more babies. Show this by drawing an up arrow near the flow:

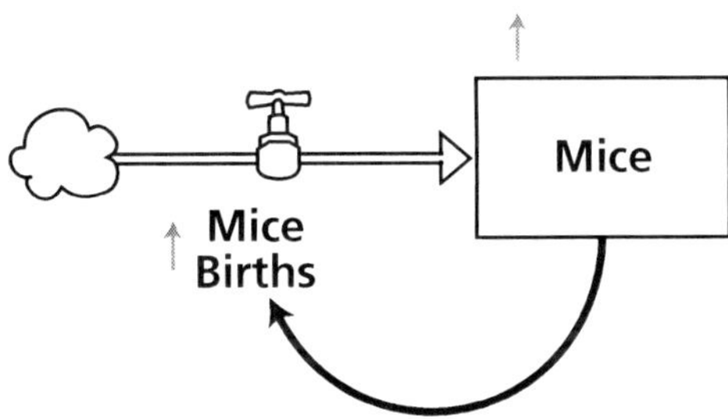

Following the flow "pipe," this increase in mice births further **increases** the number of mice above what it would have been otherwise. Add another up arrow near the stock:

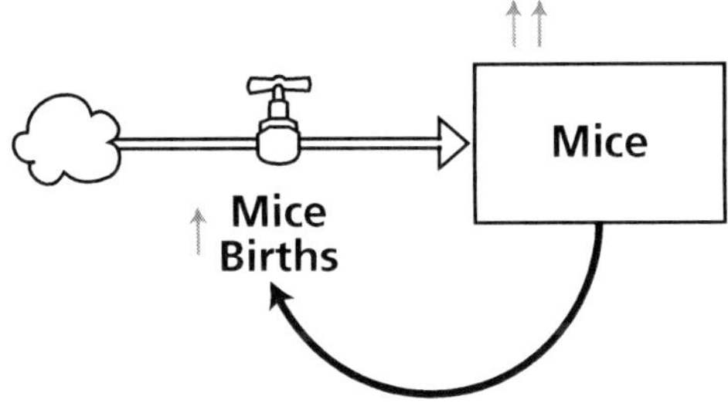

Time is implicit in a stock/flow diagram. A certain number of mice are born *per year*, adding to the total number of mice in the stock over time.

An increase in mice further **increases** the mice births:

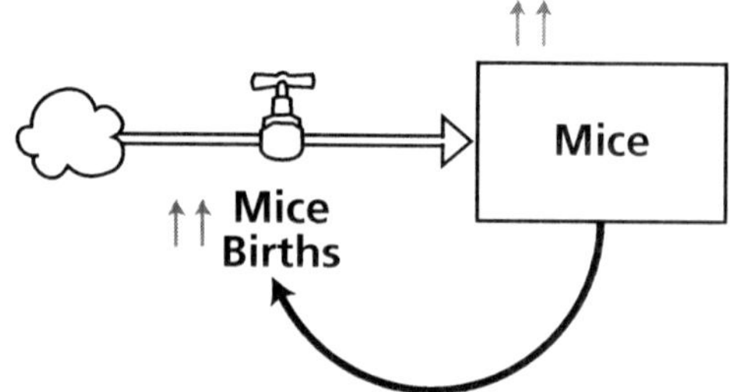

Mice births always increase the population, but increasing the births produces even more mice than there would have been otherwise.

No matter how long we follow this process, more and more arrows will line up, all pointing in the same direction. This indicates that the number of mice will increase at a faster and faster rate.

6. Note that we started this process by **increasing** the number of mice. We could also have **decreased** the number of mice at the start, in which case the initial arrow would point down:

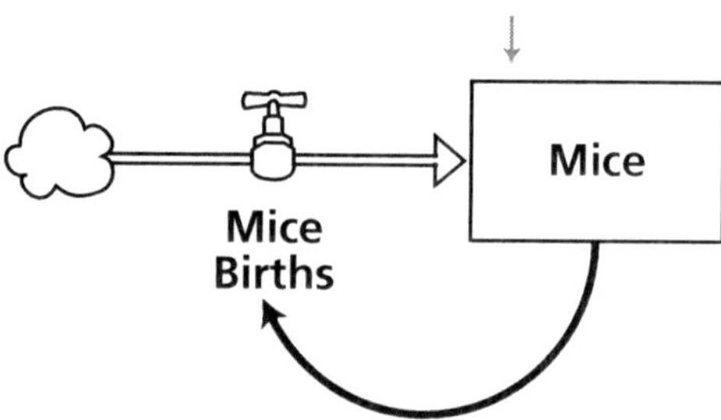

The result of this decrease would be that, all other things being equal, the number of mice births would also **decrease**. Show this by placing a downward arrow near the flow:

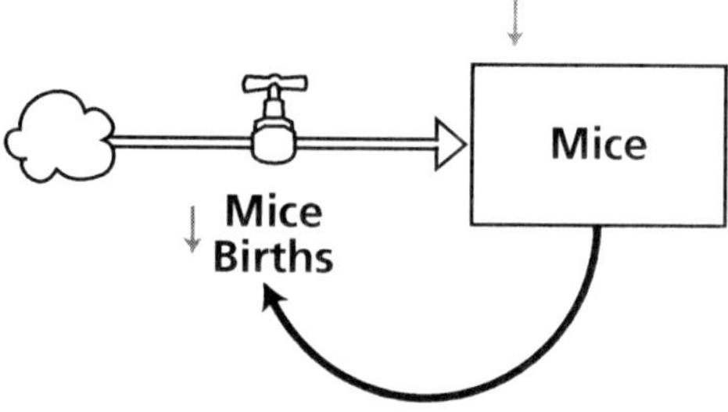

If the number of births decreases, the number of mice **decreases** relative to what it would have been if there had been no decrease in the number of births. (With any new births, the number of mice is still growing, but because fewer mice produce fewer births, the stock is growing at a slower rate.) Show this by adding another downward arrow near the stock:

In a reinforcing loop, any change is amplified each time around the loop.

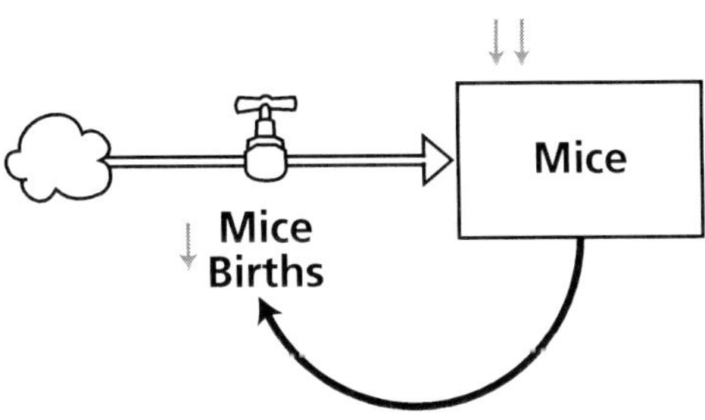

The situation with the downward arrows is analogous to the one with the upward arrows. No matter how long we continue the process, more and more arrows will line up, all pointing in the same direction.

7. There are two distinct, but related concepts that need clarification.

- First, note that, all else being equal, an **increase** in the stock leads to an **increase** in the flow and that a **decrease** in the stock leads to a **decrease** in the flow. In other words, the change from the stock to the flow is in the ***same*** direction. This is shown by either adding the letter S (for "same") or the "+" sign near the arrowhead. Doing so eliminates the need for the up/down arrows, although they are helpful at first.

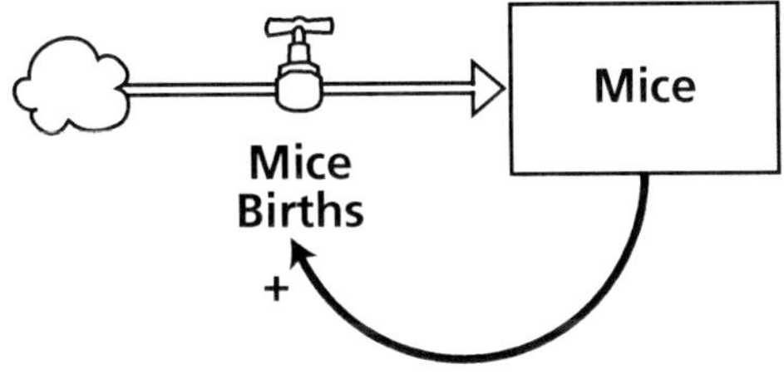

- The second concept is that positive feedback produces a **reinforcing loop**. Each time around the loop, an initial increase (or decrease) is reinforced again and again. To show that the number of mice will increase faster and faster (with more arrows always pointing in the same direction) write an "R" in the loop for "Reinforcing."

In this book, we will use a "+" sign to show change in the same direction.

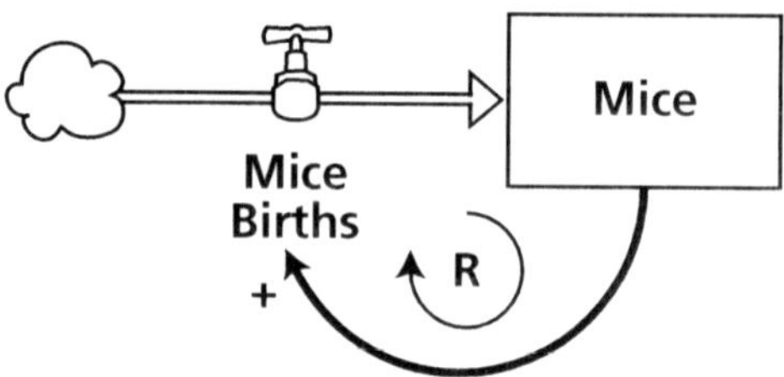

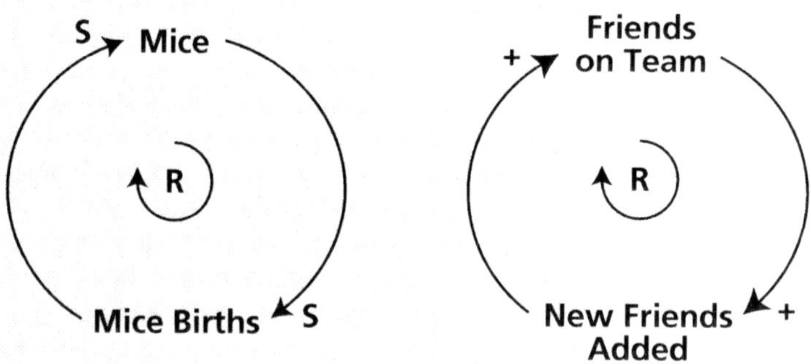

Causal Loop Drawings

An increase in mice causes an increase in baby mice which causes an increase in the number of mice above what would have been otherwise, and so on around the loop. Likewise, a decrease in mice triggers a decrease in births, producing fewer mice than there would have been otherwise, and so on. The "R" label tells us that this is a reinforcing feedback loop.

Now we can also complete our Making Friends causal loop diagram. The "+" sign also shows a change in the same direction. An increase (decrease) in one variable causes an increase (decrease) in the next variable, beyond what it would have been.

? How do these stock/flow maps relate to the graphs we drew of the friends game in *The Shape of Change*?

In the first game, the number of new friends was constant each round, so the line on the graph showed linear growth, a straight line. In the second game, however, the number of new friends depended on the number of friends already on the team because ***each*** *friend chose a new member for the team each round. More friends led to even more friends. This escalating growth appeared as a curved line on the graph.*

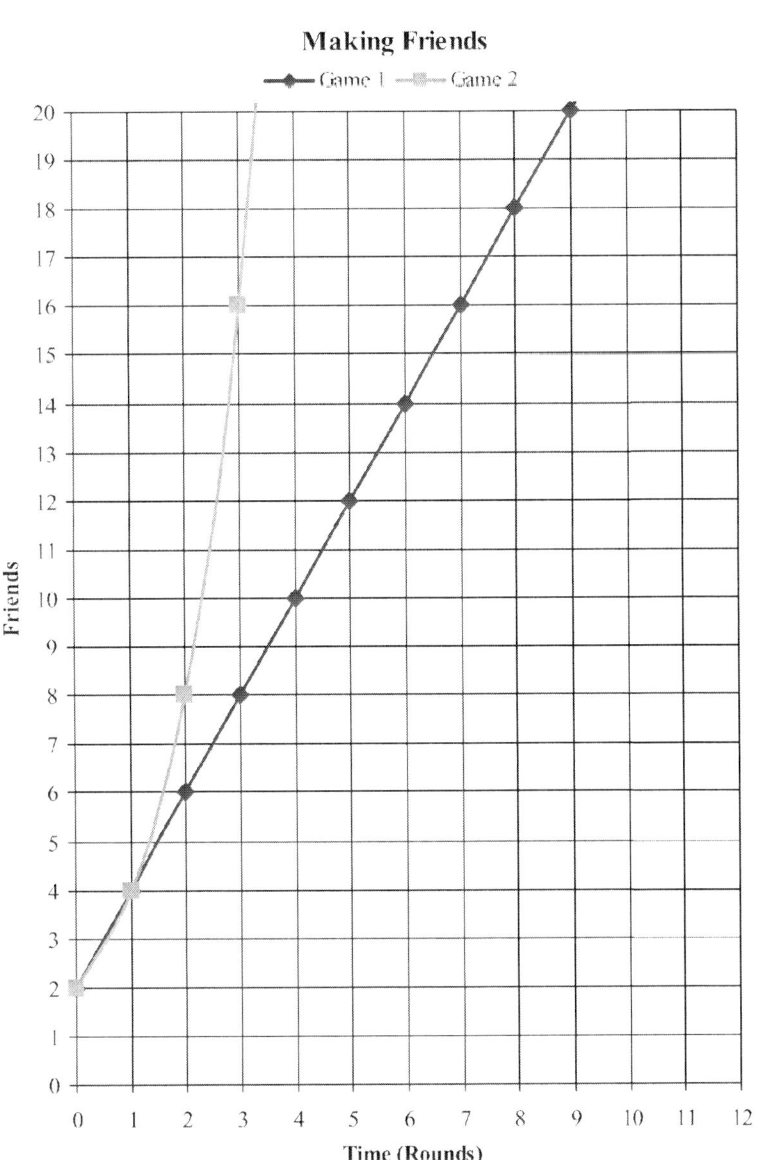

The game is a discrete activity. We connect the dots to help students see the patterns more clearly.

? In Game 2, we could play only three rounds before running out of players. What would the graph look like if we had enough students to play ten rounds?

Growth would escalate rapidly. Starting with one student on the friends team and doubling the number of members each round, there would be more than a thousand members after ten rounds!

*A reinforcing feedback loop produces this pattern called **exponential growth**.*

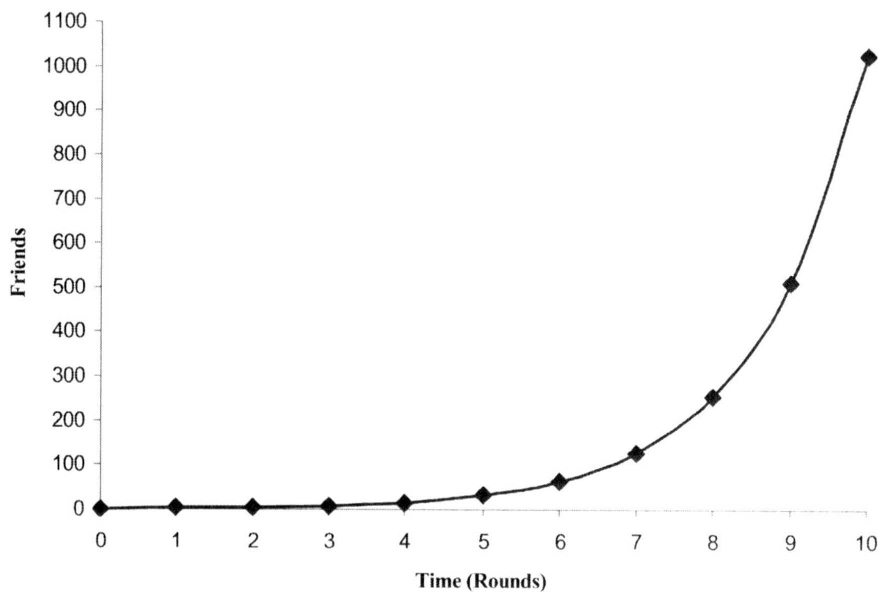

? Think about our mice. Does our stock/flow map produce this same behavior for them? What about money in the bank and the other examples we discussed?

Yes, they are all examples of reinforcing feedback loops that can cause the stocks to grow exponentially until something limits their growth.

? Think again about the Making Friends game and graph. Tell the story of this completed stock/flow diagram.

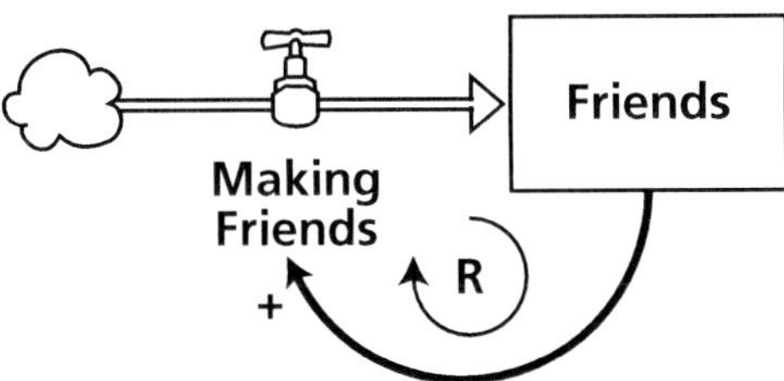

The total number of friends on the team, the stock of Friends, is increased by the inflow of new friends each round. As players make new friends, the team grows.

This map describes the second game when the number of friends on the team affected the flow of new friends because each friend chose a new friend each round. The more friends there were on the team, the more new friends were added (a change in the same direction labeled "+"). The number of friends kept growing at an increasing rate, producing a steepening curve on the graph. We call this pattern exponential growth, a hallmark of a reinforcing feedback loop (labeled "R").

If, partway through the game, we decreased the stock by taking some players out of the game, that would cause a decrease in the number of new friends below what it would have been otherwise (a change in the same direction). With fewer new friends, the team would grow more slowly than it would have otherwise. Like the mice population, the team would still grow but at a slower rate.

The stock/flow maps lay out the structure for us. The causal loop diagrams and the behavior over time graphs give us another view of the same thing. Used together, they help us understand how and why things change over time.

The Mammoth Game

In Lesson 3 of ***The Shape of Change***, students explored theories of extinction as they played a dice game and graphed the population growth and decline of their herds of mammoths. See Pages 27–38 in ***The Shape of Change*** for the complete lesson.

Overview

Building a stock/flow map of the Mammoth Game adds new elements beyond the map of the Making Friends game. Making Friends is based on reinforcing feedback which results in exponential growth. In addition to producing reinforcing feedback, the Mammoth Game also produces balancing feedback which results in exponential decay.

Seeing the structure

1. After playing the Mammoth Game, develop a stock/flow map with the students. Ask students to name the stock, the quantity that can increase and decrease over time. Students should have no difficulty suggesting mammoths.

Think of a bathtub again. The accumulation of water in the tub changes as water flows in through the faucet and out through the drain. The size of the mammoth population is controlled by the flows of births and deaths over time.

Mammoths

2. Ask students to describe what happened to the mammoths in the game and how that can be shown on the map. With each roll of the dice, new mammoths were born and old mammoths died. Again, students should have no difficulty explaining that the stock of mammoths was increased by births and decreased by deaths each year.

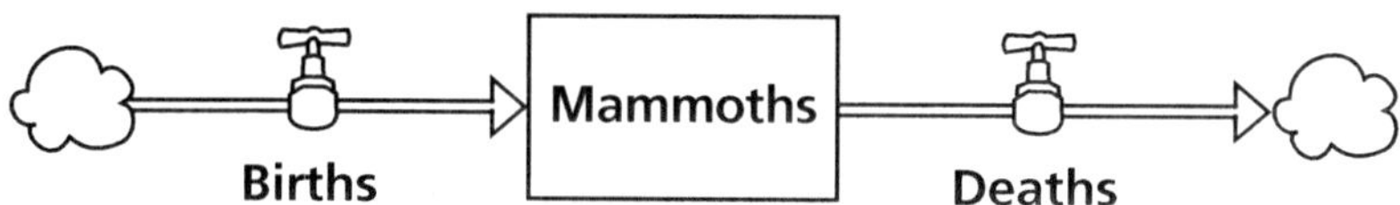

3. While this map is a good start, note that it implies a **constant** flow of births and a **constant** flow of deaths. However, this is not what happened in the game; the flow of births was determined, in part, by the number of mammoths. It might be helpful to give an example from the game: when you have 20 dice, there will be more rolls of "one," on average, than when you have only 10 dice. Or, thinking about mammoths, there will be a greater number of baby mammoths born each year in a large herd than in a small herd. Ask students how to represent this on the stock flow map.

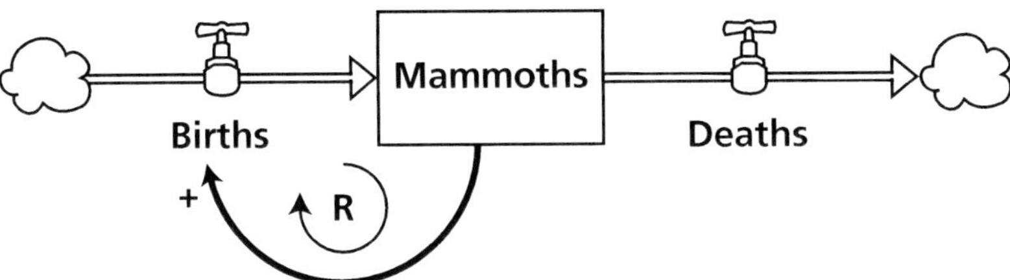

(Notice that this is like the structure of Making Friends when the number of friends already on the team influenced the number of new friends added each round.)

Similar reasoning can be applied to the flow of deaths. The number of deaths each year also depended on the number of mammoths.

The "clouds" signify the boundaries of the system. We are interested in how the population changed with births and deaths. We are not concerned with the mammoths before they were born or after they died.

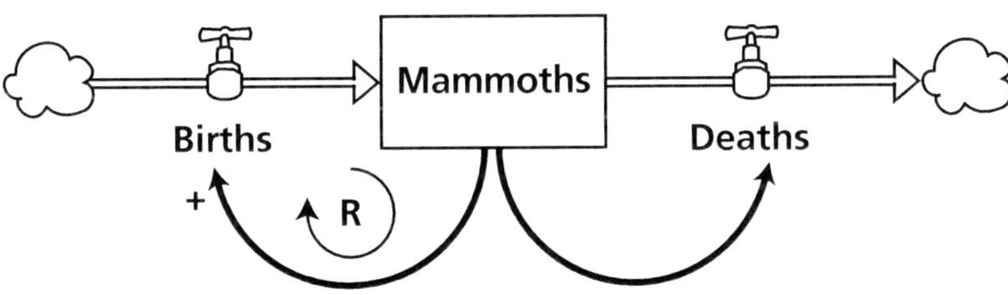

4. The stock of mammoths influencing the inflow of births is an example of a reinforcing loop leading to exponential growth as we saw in Making Friends. But the stock of mammoths did not increase in this game. In fact, it declined to extinction. Why? Because mammoths were also dying.

Examine the outflow of deaths more closely with students.

The feedback between the stock of mammoths and the outflow is an example of a ***balancing loop***. With all else equal, an **increase** in the number of mammoths will lead to an **increase** in the number of deaths. However, this **increase** in the number of deaths will lead to a **decrease** in the number of mammoths. Use the arrow technique to make this more explicit.

Start by increasing the number of mammoths and show this by drawing an arrow pointing upward near the stock:

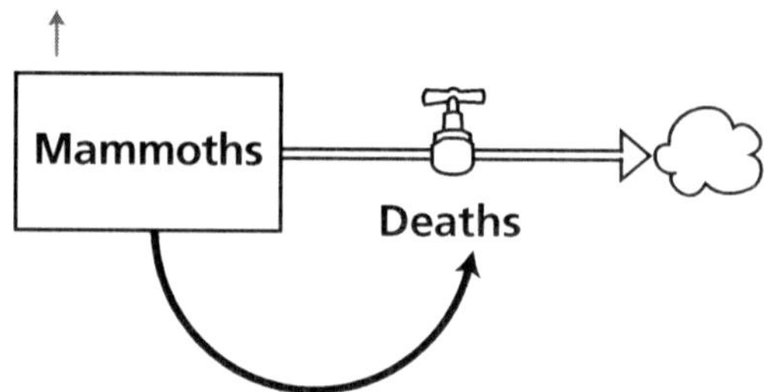

Ask students how this affects the number of deaths. An **increase** in the number of mammoths causes an **increase** in the number of deaths above what it would have been otherwise, a change in the same direction.

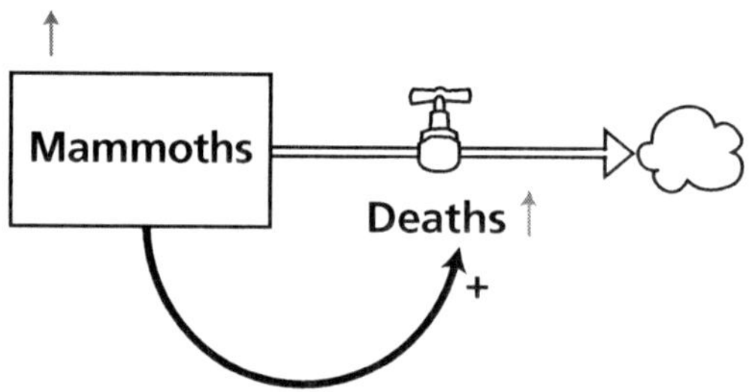

What happens to the stock next? The **increase** in deaths leads to a **decrease** in the number of mammoths below what it would have been. Add an arrow pointing downward:

In a balancing loop, any change reverses direction each time around the loop.

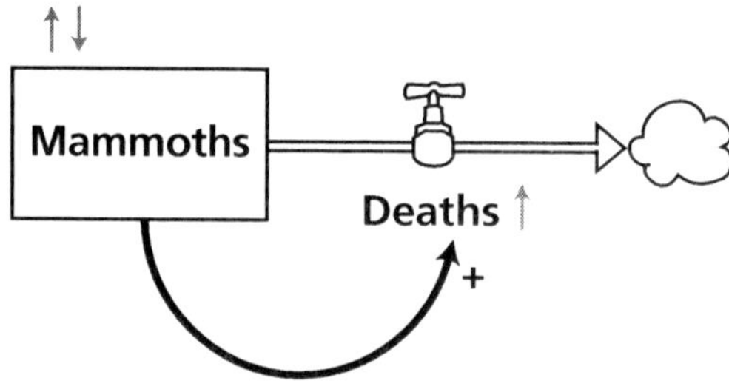

Ask students to add the next arrow. A **decrease** in the number of mammoths leads to a **decrease** in the number of deaths:

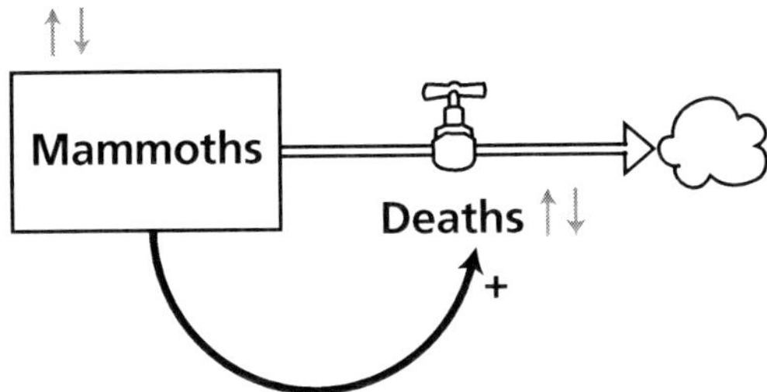

This **decrease** in deaths in turn leads to a relative **increase** in the number of mammoths: the number of mammoths is higher than it would have been if the number of deaths had not changed because mammoths are dying at a slower rate.

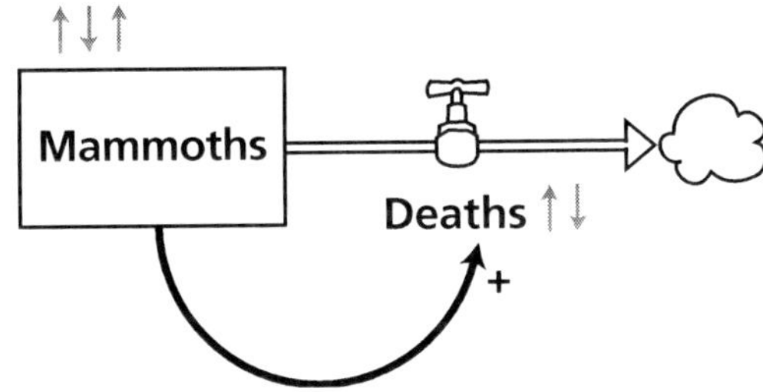

Notice that the arrows reverse during each "cycle." No matter how long we repeat the process, the arrows will keep turning up and down, "balancing" back and forth.

5. Like the situation in Making Friends, the flow of births and the stock form a ***reinforcing loop***. An **increase** in the stock of mammoths leads to an **increase** of the inflow and a **decrease** in the stock leads to a **decrease** of the inflow. The change from the stock to the inflow is in the same direction.

However, in the Mammoth Game, the flow of deaths and the stock form a ***balancing loop***. All else equal, an **increase** in the outflow of deaths causes a **decrease** in the stock of mammoths, while a **decrease** in the outflow causes a relative **increase** in the stock. As we saw using the arrows, any change reverses direction each time around the loop.

The balancing deaths loop caused the population to decline approaching zero. Balancing loops can also cause stocks to grow toward a goal. More on that later.

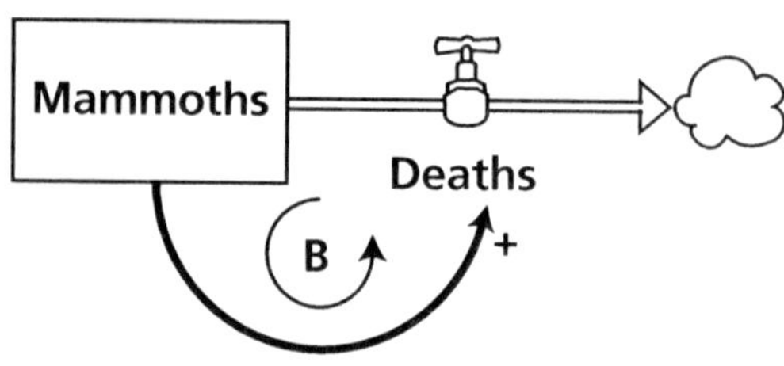

Our balancing feedback loop produces a graph that declines at a decreasing rate, a behavior called ***exponential decay.*** The number of mammoths approached zero. They became extinct.

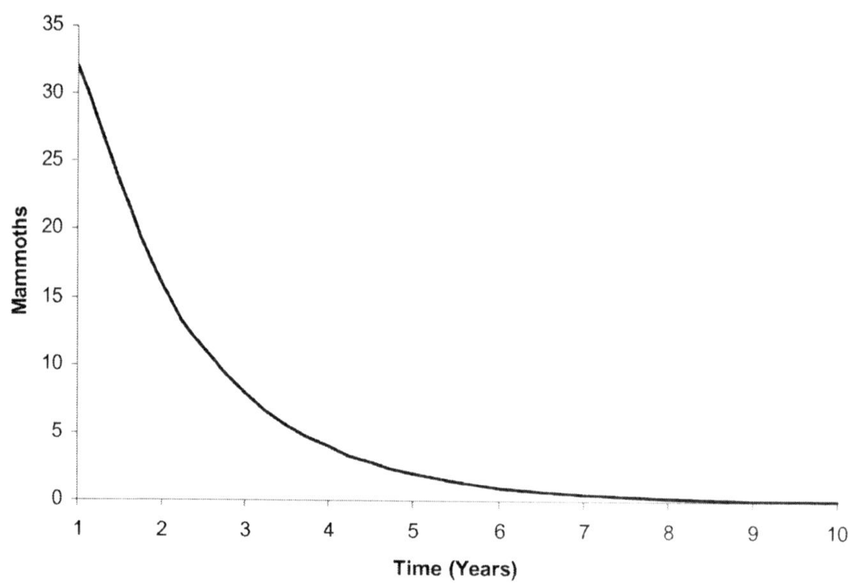

6. Refer back to the stock/flow map and ask students to explain the difference between the two mammoth games in terms of the stock/flow map. All the elements of the first map are needed in a map for the second game. However, in the second game there were more ways for the mammoths to die. Put another way, the fraction of mammoths that died was higher. This can be reflected in the map by adding the Death Fraction.

The death fraction shows in a more precise way that the number of deaths is influenced by more than the stock of mammoths. It depends on the number of mammoths and on the fraction of mammoths that dies every year.

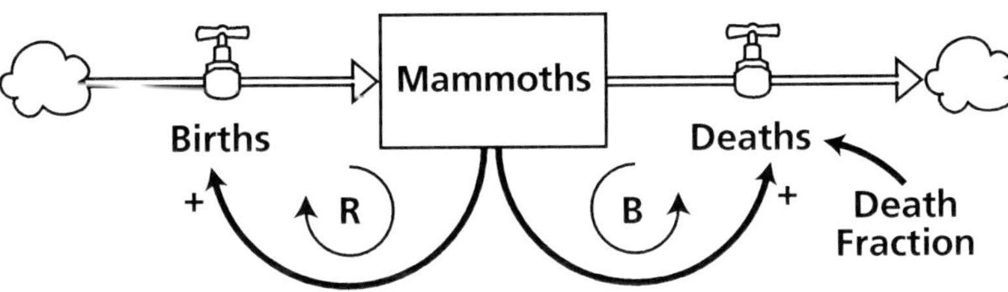

? How does this explain the similarity as well as the difference between the two mammoth games.

In the first game, 2 out of 6 mammoths died each year on average; in the second game with the addition of human hunters, 3 out of 6 mammoths died each year. Both games exhibit exponential decline because there were more deaths than births each year, but in the second game, the fraction of deaths was larger, resulting in a quicker decline of the population.

7. Students should see that the symmetry between births and deaths can also be extended to the birth and death fractions. The flow of births is influenced by the stock of mammoths as well as a birth fraction. In the case of the game, that fraction was 1/6. The birth fraction represents factors other than total population that influence the birth rate, like the percentage of the population that is female, the percentage of females of child-bearing age, etc. The higher the birth fraction, the more births.

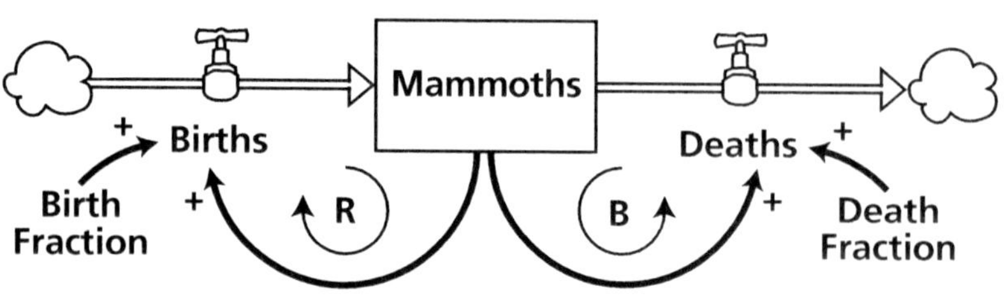

We will use a minus sign "-" to show a change in the opposite direction.

8. This map is a complete mental model of the Mammoth Game. The stock of mammoths is changed over time by flows of births and deaths each year. The flows in turn are influenced by the stock. This sets up two feedback loops: one reinforcing loop and one balancing loop. It is the relative strength of the two loops that determines the fate of the population over time.

A Causal Loop Drawing

The causal loop on the right tells us that an increase in mammoth births causes a relative increase in the mammoth population, which further increases the number of births—changes in the same direction labeled "+." This is a **reinforcing** feedback loop much like Making Friends; alone, it would cause exponential growth.

Meanwhile, an increase in the population causes an increase in the number of deaths. This increase then leads to a relative decrease in the population—a change in the opposite direction labeled "-" (or "O" for opposite"). This is a **balancing** feedback loop causing exponential decay. Both loops influence the population simultaneously.

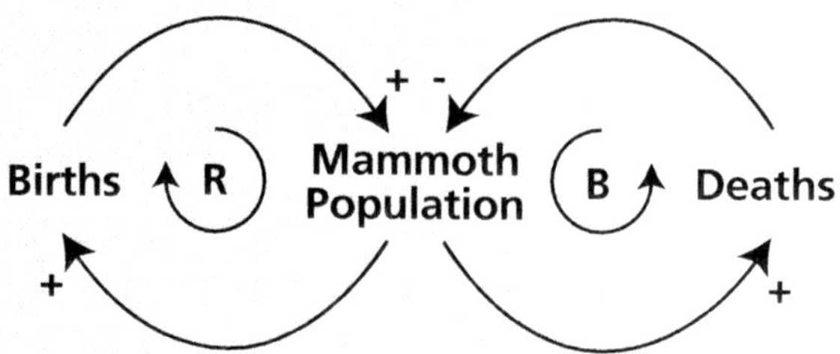

? What causes the mammoth population to increase?

If the birth fraction is higher than the death fraction, then there will be more births than deaths each year. The reinforcing feedback loop will dominate and the population will grow exponentially.

? What causes the mammoth population to decrease?

If the death fraction is higher than the birth fraction, then there will be more deaths than births each year. The balancing feedback loop will dominate and the population will decay exponentially approaching zero.

? Can the population stay the same size?

Yes, a population can remain stable at a constant level if the birth fraction equals the death fraction at any value. The total population does not change because an equal number of mammoths are born and die each year.

? Does this map apply only to mammoth populations?

These principles apply to all populations.

? How does the stock/flow map give us a better understanding of how a population changes.

The stock/flow map shows us that any population is an accumulation over time that is increased by births and decreased by deaths. Since a stock can be changed only by its flows, understanding how a population changes means taking a closer look at the birth and death flows(and migration flows in some populations). In the Mammoth Game we saw that increasing the outflow of deaths caused the population to decline more rapidly. Other things being equal, decreasing the inflow of births would also cause the population to decline.

Different birth and death rates would play out simultaneously to cause a population to grow, decline or stabilize over time.[1] Seeing the structure helps us to understand the behavior we observe.

NOTE

1 These relationships can be quantified and simulated in a system dynamics computer model. Students can experiment with different birth and death rates to observe how the mammoth population would change over time under varying conditions. For a simple system dynamics computer model of the Mammoth Game with complete instructions for using it with students, see "The Mammoth Extinction Game" by Stamell, Ticotsky, Quaden and Lyneis (1999), available for free from the Creative Learning Exchange at *www.clexchange.org*.

It's Cool

In Lesson 4 of ***The Shape of Change***, students conducted a scientific experiment to measure, record and graph the changing temperature of a cooling cup of boiling water. See Pages 39–50 in ***The Shape of Change*** for the complete lesson.

Overview

In the cooling activity, the stock is the heat in the water and the flow represents the loss of that heat into the air. However, unlike the birth and death fractions in the Mammoth Game, the rate of cooling is not constant. As students observed in their experiment and graph, the water temperature dropped quickly at first, but as the difference between the water temperature and the room temperature narrowed, the rate of cooling decreased until the water eventually reached room temperature.

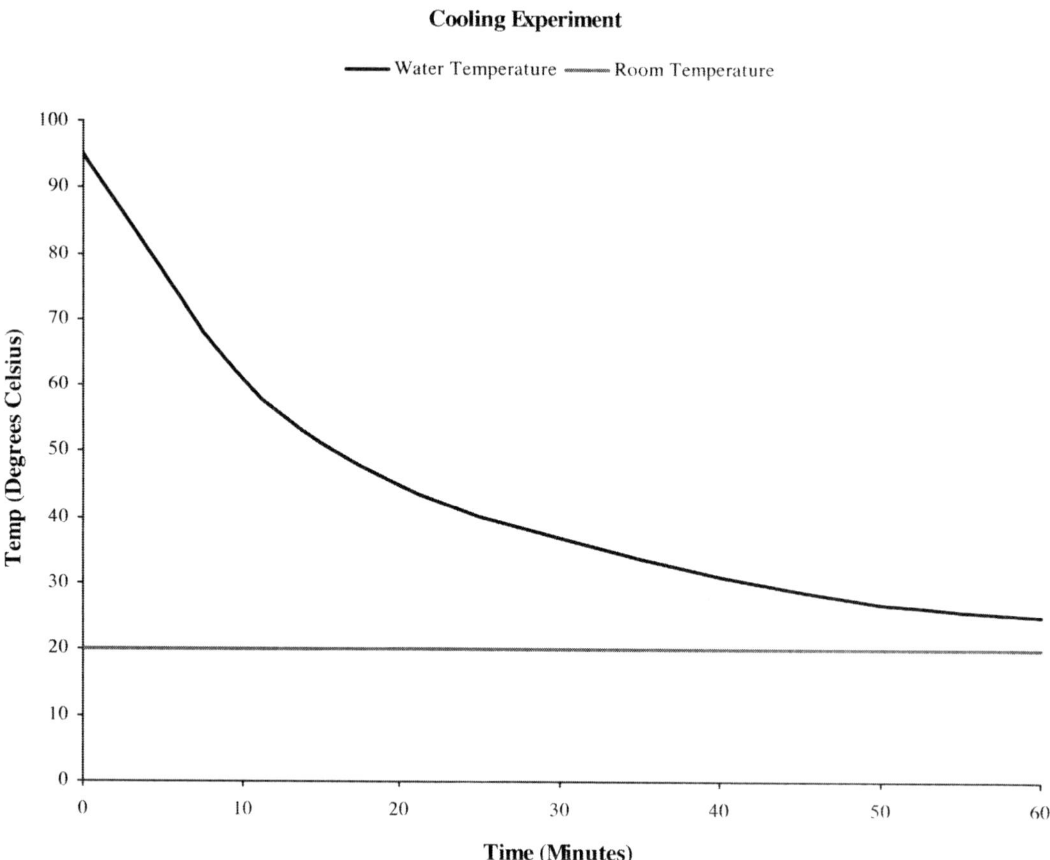

Building a stock/flow map of the cooling process will help explain why the temperature graph did not produce a straight line and why this exponential decay approached room temperature.

Seeing the Structure

1. Ask students to identify the stock and flow in the cooling experiment.

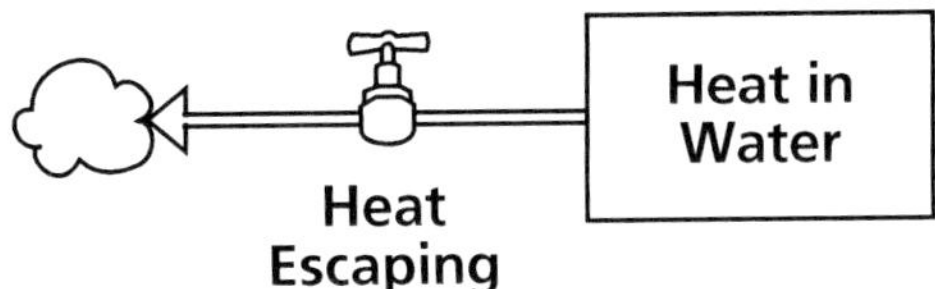

Notice that the outflow is draining toward the left this time. Flows can go in any direction. The arrow tells the direction of the flow.

2. Be sure students understand the difference between heat and temperature. (See "How It Works" on Page 39–40 of ***The Shape of Change.***) Heat energy accumulates and dissipates; it is measured in degrees of temperature. Connect the stock to water temperature to show that we would need to convert the heat energy to degrees Celsius.

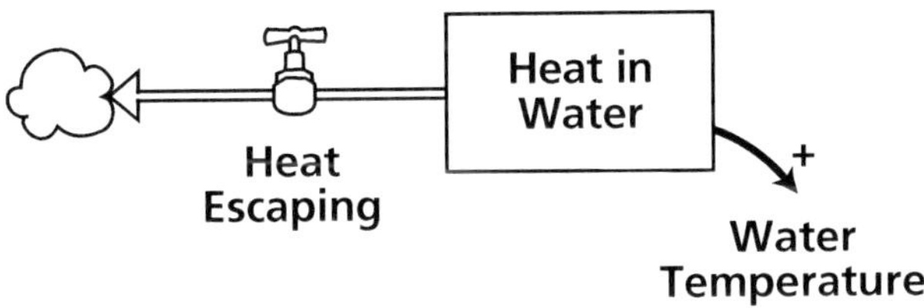

3. Ask students to name factors that affect the rate at which heat escaped from the water. Factors typically mentioned include the insulating properties of the container, the surface area of the water exposed to air, the shape and size of the container, and so on. For simplicity, bundle these factors together into one variable labeled "Effect of Cooling Factors" to represent the effect of all these factors on how quickly the heat escapes the water. The higher the rate, the faster heat escapes.

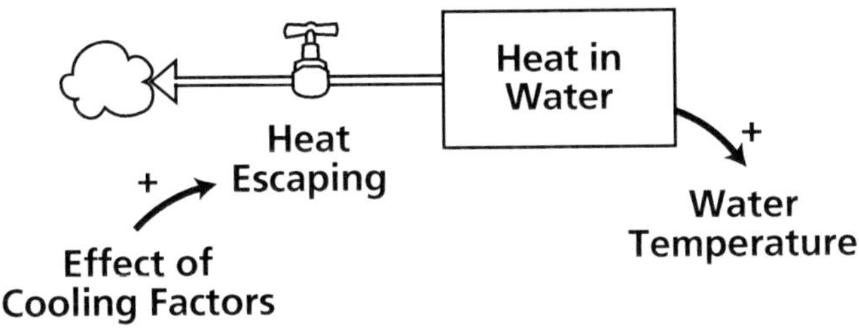

4. Remind students to think about the shape of the temperature graph. The cooling was steepest at the beginning when the difference between the water temperature and room temperature was greatest. Later, when the difference was smaller, the rate of change slowed down and leveled off.

Add "Room Temperature" to the diagram.

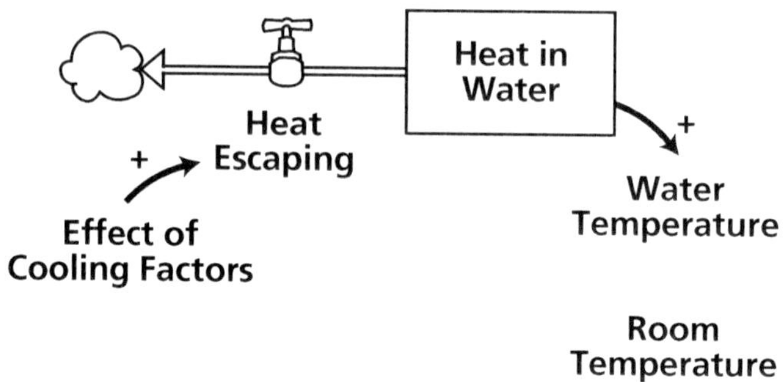

5. Remember that the difference between the room temperature and the water temperature determined how quickly the heat escaped. Add a variable named "Difference" to represent the gap between the two measurements. The higher the water temperature, the greater the difference.

Heat always flows from an area of higher temperature to an area of lower temperature, flowing more quickly when the temperature difference is greater.

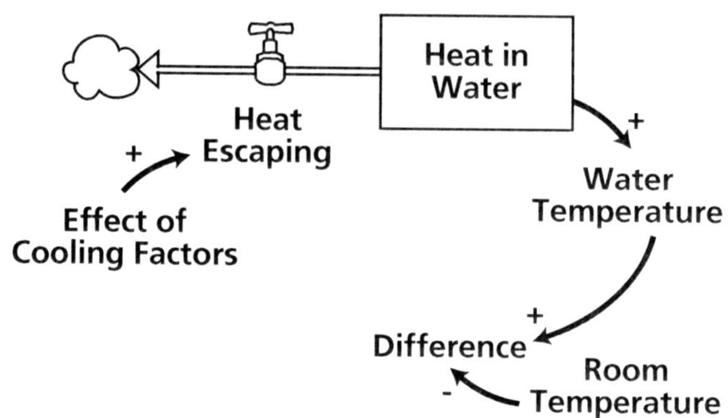

6. Finally, the size of the difference between the water tem-perature and the room temperature affected the rate of heat escaping. When the gap was large, heat escaped quickly, as it did in the early stages of the experiment. As time passed, the room temperature stayed constant while the water temperature dropped, reducing the difference between the two measurements.

When "Heat Escaping" increases, "Heat in the Water" decreases.

Connect "Difference" to the "Heat Escaping" flow to show that the temperature difference caused the rate of heat escaping to change—the greater the difference, the higher the rate.

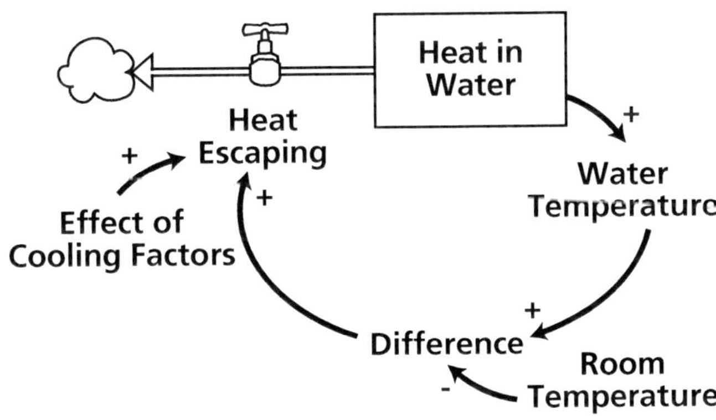

The stock/flow map now explains how the unique cooling factors of the container and the difference between the water temperature and room temperature affected the rate of cooling. It explains how the accumulation of heat energy dissipated over time.

The cooling experiment is an example of a balancing feedback loop at work. The water temperature approaches room temperature at a decreasing rate.

7. Trace the feedback loop in the stock/flow map using up and down arrows if necessary. When the stock of "Heat" **increases,** "Water Temperature" **increases.** Since "Room Temperature" is constant, the "Difference" **increases.** A larger "Difference" causes "Heat Escaping" to **increase,** which makes "Heat" **decrease** this time. When elements reverse in a feedback loop, the loop is ***balancing.***

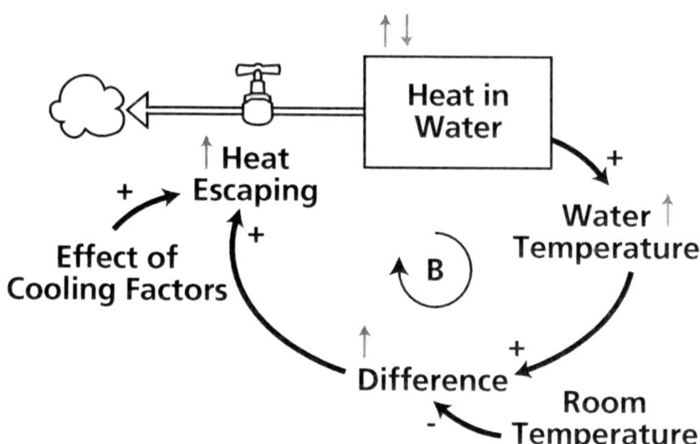

8. Look at the cooling graph again and relate it to the stock/flow map. The balancing loop produces an **exponential decay** graph of temperature. The graph curves with a high rate of decline at first and flattens, eventually approaching room temperature.

This graph is like the exponential decay caused by the balancing loop in the Mammoth Game. When the herd was large, many mammoths died. As these deaths reduced the size of the population, there were fewer and fewer deaths each year, and the population slowly approached zero—extinction.

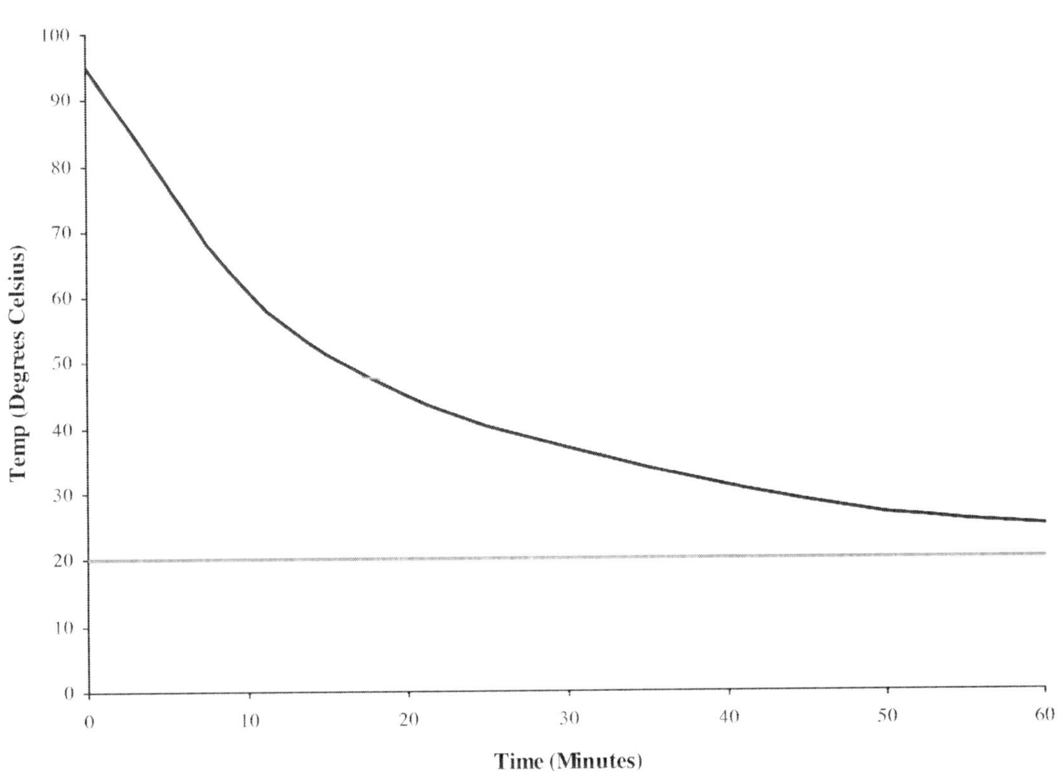

? In this lesson we measured the temperature of a cooling cup of boiling hot water. Why did the water approach room temperature?

The water approached room temperature because the heat was flowing out of the water and into the cooler air. It flowed most rapidly at the beginning of the experiment when the gap between the water temperature and the room temperature was the greatest. As the gap closed, heat escaped more slowly. When the water finally reached room temperature, it stayed at room temperature.

An Extension

For a further challenge, some students may be able to apply what they have learned in a broader way.

What would happen if we started with ice cold water instead of boiling hot water?

The heat would flow from the warmer air into the cooler water, again flowing most rapidly when the temperature difference was greatest at the beginning. Eventually, the water would warm up to room temperature and stay there.

Does our stock/flow map apply to ice water too?

Yes, it does. To make it clearer, we would change "Heat Escaping" to "Heat Transferring" which means that the heat always moves from the warmer area to the cooler area whether you start with boiling water or ice water. The arrowheads on both ends of the flow show that the flow can go either way.

For boiling water, the heat flows ***out*** *until the water reaches room temperature. For ice water, the heat flows* ***in*** *until the water reaches room temperature. The stock of heat increases.*

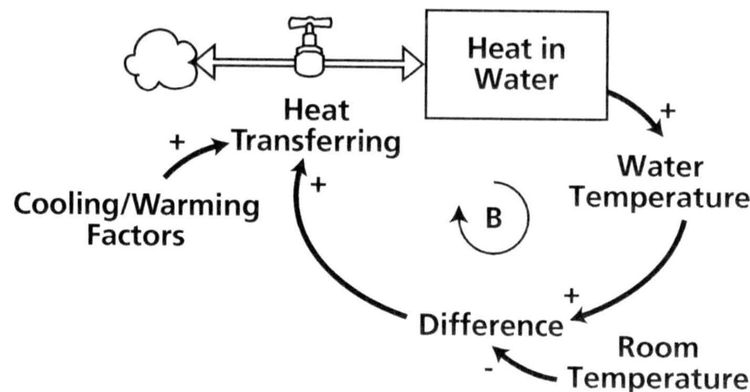

An arrowhead at both ends of the flow indicates that heat energy can flow into or out of the stock, depending on whether you start with very hot or very cold water.

? What would the graph of a warming cup of water look like?

It would be similar to the cooling experiment, except this time the water is approaching the goal of room temperature from below as it warms up.

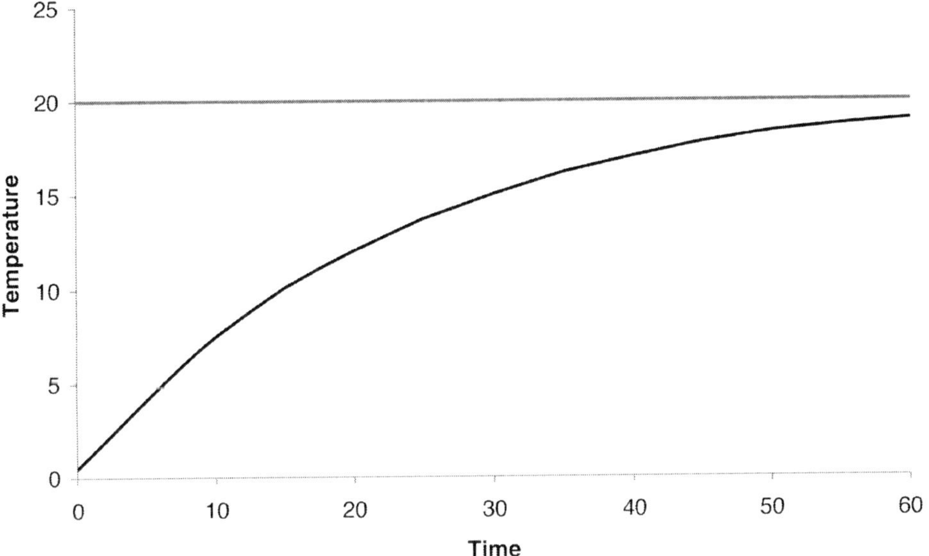

For ice water, the balancing loop causes the water temperature to rise approaching room temperature.

A Causal Loop Drawing

This diagram gives us a picture of the balancing feedback loop—the water temperature adjusts to approach room temperature. Our stock/flow diagram gives us a more precise "operational" view of how the heat accumulates or dissipates over time. We use both diagrams to understand the behavior we observed and graphed.

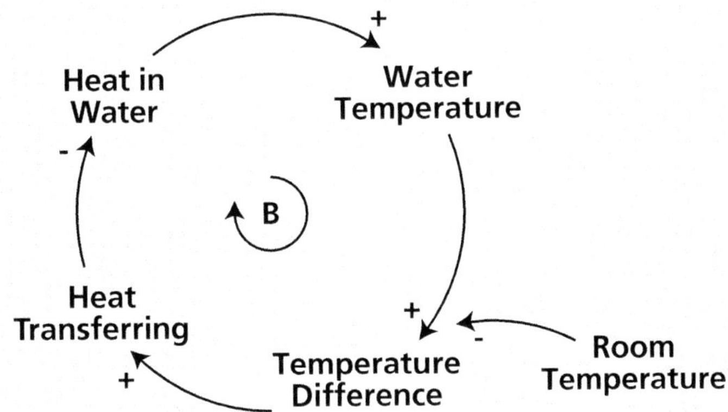

Another View

An even simpler generic depiction of the balancing loop could show the temperature adjustment without the intervening temperature/heat conversions. The rate of change declines as the gap closes, until the water temperature reaches the goal of room temperature. In this lesson, however, we included the conversions because the concept of heat energy as a stock was a focus of the science lesson.

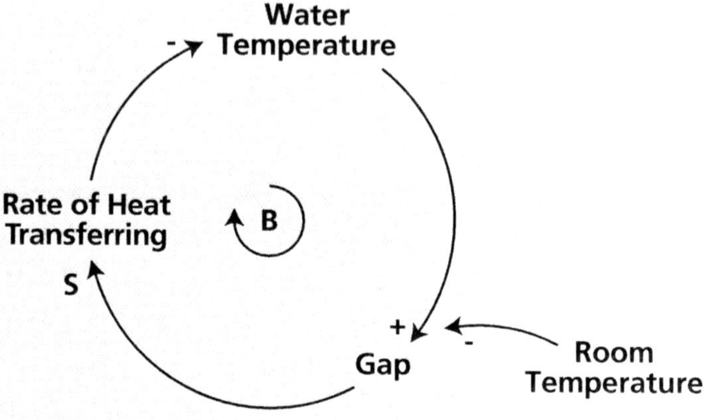

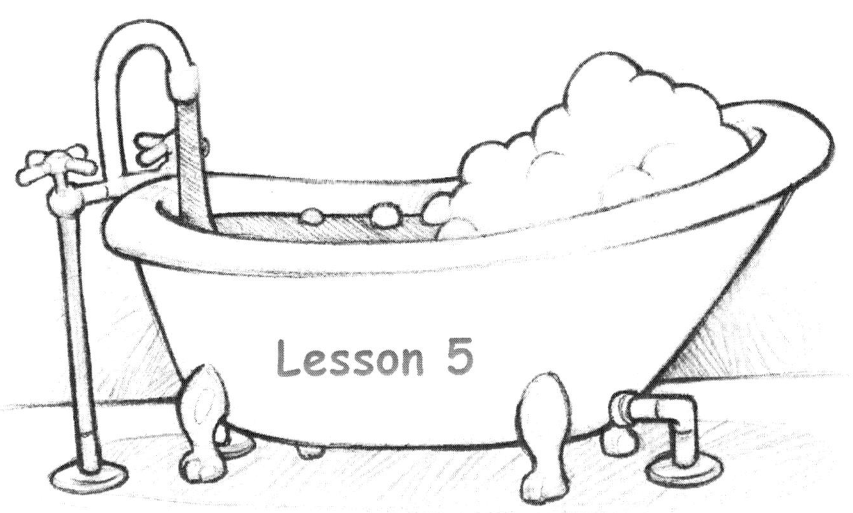

The Infection Game

In Lesson 4 of ***The Shape of Change***, students played a game to simulate the spread of an infection. As they multiplied their secret numbers together, the infection (the number zero) spread through the class in a pattern of S-shaped growth. See Pages 51–64 in ***The Shape of Change*** for the complete lesson.

Overview

The Infection Game stock/flow map combines all the elements that were used in the previous lessons. Students apply all that they have learned about behavior over time graphs, stocks and flows, and reinforcing and balancing feedback loops to understand how and why the infection spread among them. There are two stocks and two feedback loops in this simulation.

Seeing the Structure

1. Review the Infection Game graph of the total number of players with zero. Briefly discuss what happened in the game to produce this behavior.

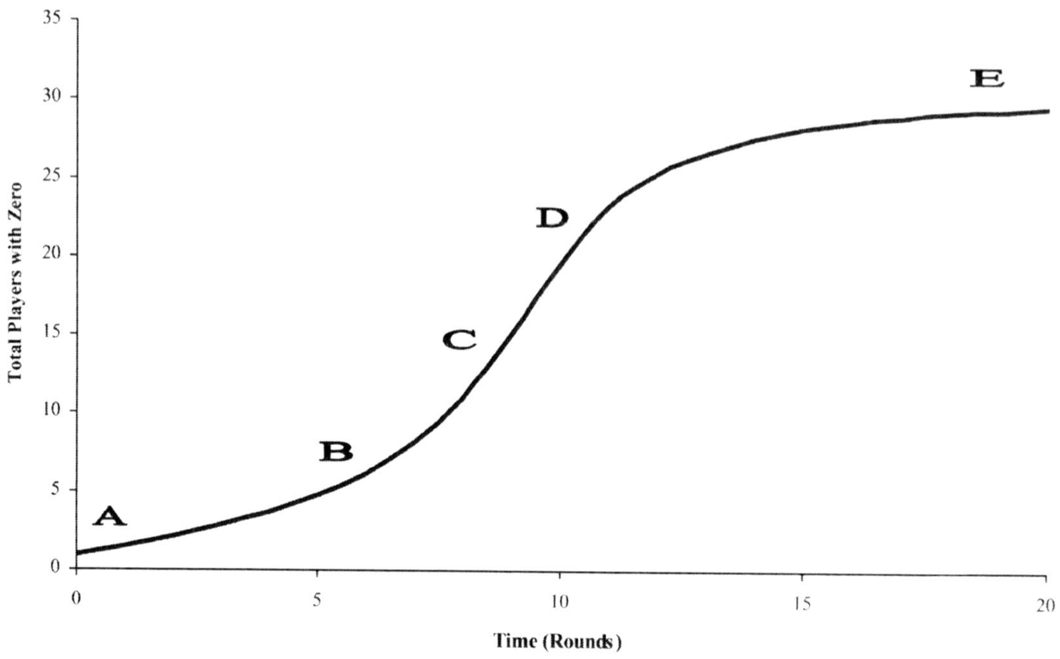

At first (point A) few people were infected with zero, but as more people became infected and they infected others, the rate of infection increased (point B). Eventually, the rate of infection slowed (point D) because many people were already infected. Eventually everyone was infected (point E).

Look closely at the graph for hints about what structure could be causing the behavior you observed.

2. Notice that the first section of the graph (at points A and B) is like the upward curving exponential growth graphs we saw for Making Friends and the Mammoth Game births. As each friend chose a new friend, more new friends led to more friends on the team, which led to even more new friends, and so on. Mammoth births led to even more births. These were examples of positive feedback loops.

Think about what happened in the Infection Game. At first only one person was infected, but as more people had zero, the infection spread more and more quickly. More infections led to even more infections. A **reinforcing feedback loop** must be at work here too, causing the **exponential growth** we see in the graph at the beginning of the game. Maybe a loop like this one was causing the growth:

Causal loop drawings are only very rough sketches. A stock/flow map will show more precisely how the system works.

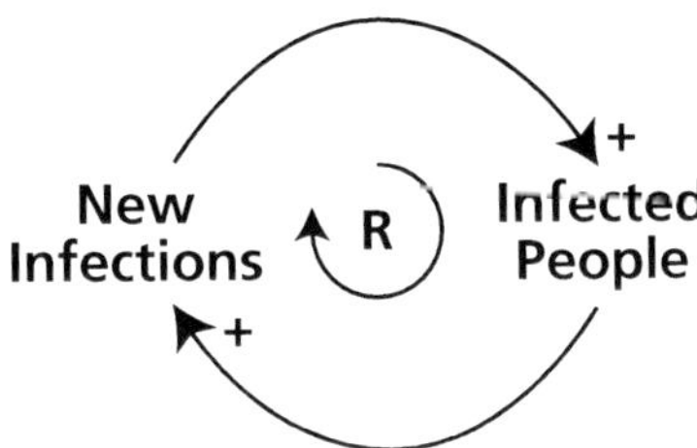

3. Now take a look at the next segment of the graph (starting at point C). Notice that the growth is slowing as the number of infected people approaches the total number of players in the game. As more people became infected, there were fewer and fewer healthy people left to infect, until finally everyone in the class was infected (at point E).

The growth in the number of infections in this graph segment appears to be *approaching a goal*, similar to the pattern of ice water warming up to room temperature caused by a balancing feedback loop in Lesson 4. We also saw balancing loops cause decay toward a goal when boiling water cooled to room temperature in Lesson 4 and when mammoths approached extinction in Lesson 3. These balancing loop examples have different stock/flow structures, but they all grow (or decay) quickly at first and level off as they approach a goal. Goal-seeking is the distinguishing feature of all balancing loops.

All balancing feedback loops are goal-seeking.

A **balancing loop** must be causing the **leveling off** of the infected population in the Infection Game. Maybe a loop like this one was also at work:

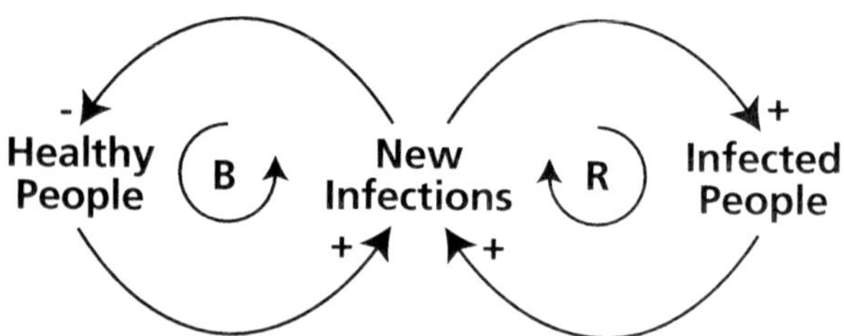

An increase in New Infections caused a decrease in the number of Healthy People. Fewer Healthy People led to fewer New Infections because an infected person was less likely to encounter a healthy person to infect. Healthy People still decreased, but at a slower and slower rate.

Thinking About Feedback Loops

We have studied our graph looking for clues as to what feedback loops could be causing the S-shaped growth we observed in the game. Based on what we have learned in previous lessons about basic feedback loops and stocks and flows, we have hypothesized that a reinforcing loop could be causing the initial growth in infections until a balancing loop takes over to slow the growth, and we have drawn very rough sketches of those feedback loops. Next, we will construct a stock/flow map to think much more carefully about how this system actually works, why it produces the behavior we observe, and how we could use that understanding to effect change.[1]

That's the general idea. Of course, students will have difficulty recognizing the signs of reinforcing and balancing loops or drawing initial causal loop diagrams until they have practiced with basic structures and their patterns of behavior in a variety of systems.

If your students are not ready to draw these feedback loops yet, then just discuss the graph segments in terms of what feedback processes *might* be involved (without drawing causal loop diagrams) and build the stock/flow map to uncover them. The goal is to help students build an intuition about how feedback systems work. With practice, they will deepen their understanding of how the structure of a system creates its behavior.

4. Ask students to identify one or more stocks in the game. Students generally will come up with "Infected People" and "Healthy People."

5. Ask what happened in the game and how to show that on the map. Again, students will have no difficulty seeing that there was a flow of people from Healthy to Infected. They may describe the flow as "people getting sick" or "catching the disease." Draw a flow from one stock **to** the other.

Conserved Flows

We know that stocks can be changed only by flows. In some one-stock models such as the In and Out Game and the Mammoth Game, inflows originate from "cloud" symbols. The source of the flow lies outside the boundary of the stock/flow map. Similarly, outflows often drain into "clouds." When players leave the In and Out Game, or after mammoths die, we no longer track their behavior.

The Infection Game has two stocks, and players move from one to the other during the simulation. The total number of players always remains the same. People in the game are either healthy or infected, but they do not leave the game. The flow that links the stocks conserves the number of players at a constant level.

6. Refer back to our graph of players infected with zero. Let's think first about what could be causing the accelerating growth at the beginning of the game. As more people became infected the rate of getting sick increased. Ask students to think about similarities to the Friendship Game and mammoth births and suggest a structure for the growth in infections.

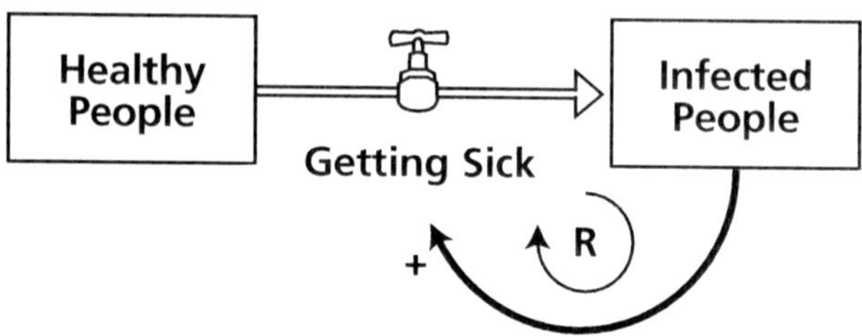

This is a **reinforcing feedback loop**. As more people got sick, there were more infected people, leading to even more people getting sick.

7. However, in the game, this exponential growth did not keep going forever. Refer again to the graph and ask students to relate what happened. As more people got sick, there were fewer and fewer encounters with healthy people to infect. In the end, it was hard for an infected person to find a healthy person at all —nearly everyone was already infected. The rate of Getting Sick depended on an infected person meeting a healthy person.

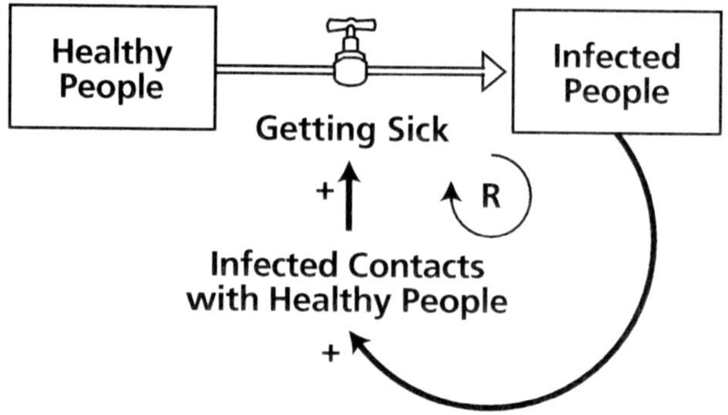

8. Infected people encountered fewer and fewer healthy people as the game went on. Ask students to think about how and why Infected Contacts with Healthy People changed.

Think of the game. How likely was it for an infected person to meet a healthy person when nearly everyone was still healthy at first, or when only a few people were still healthy at the end of the game? Using numbers and assuming there were 50 players in the game, how likely was it when 40 out of 50 were healthy, when 25 out of 50 were healthy, or when only 5 out of 50 were still healthy? The number of Infected Contacts with Healthy People depended on the proportion, or fraction, of the class that was still healthy. When a larger fraction of the class was healthy, the chance of an infected person meeting a healthy person was higher.

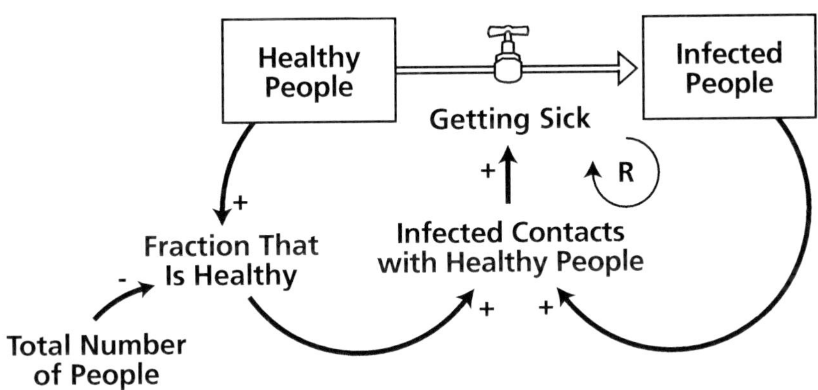

The Fraction That Is Healthy is the fraction of the whole class that is still healthy. It is the likelihood that an infected person will meet a healthy person.

9. Ask students to trace this loop and tell its story in terms of the game, using up and down arrows if that helps. As the fraction of the population that is healthy grows smaller, there are fewer infected contacts with healthy people, causing fewer new people to get sick. The rate of Getting Sick slows down. As long

as any people are still getting sick, the number of healthy people is decreasing, but at a slower and slower rate until there are no healthy people left.

This stock/flow map captures the dynamics of the Infection Game. Its two feedback loops are both necessary and sufficient to explain the S-shaped growth we observed.

This is a **balancing feedback loop** causing the number of healthy people to approach zero (and, consequently, the number of infected people to approach the total number of people.)

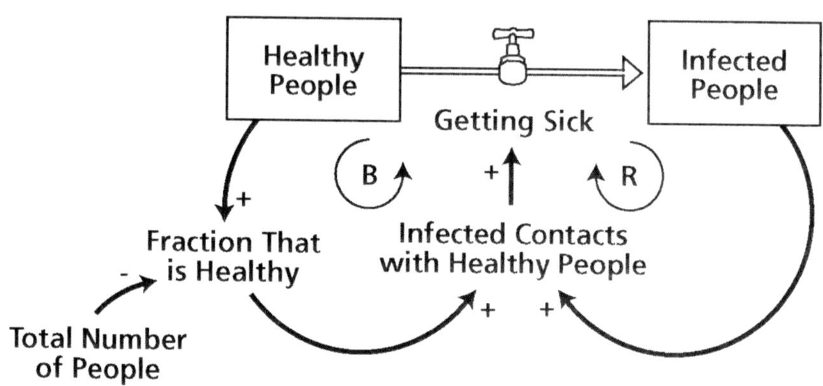

? Two feedback loops caused the infection to spread through the class in a pattern of S-shaped growth. Were both loops active all the time?

Yes. The reinforcing loop caused healthy people to become infected. This loop was dominant at first because there were plenty of healthy people to infect; the infected population could grow more and more rapidly. The balancing loop limited that growth, but its effect did not dominate until there were fewer and fewer healthy people left to infect. People were still becoming infected, but at a slower and slower rate.

The shift in dominance from the reinforcing to the balancing loop occurred at point C on our graph. We also saw this on our graphs of new infections in ***The Shape of Change****.*

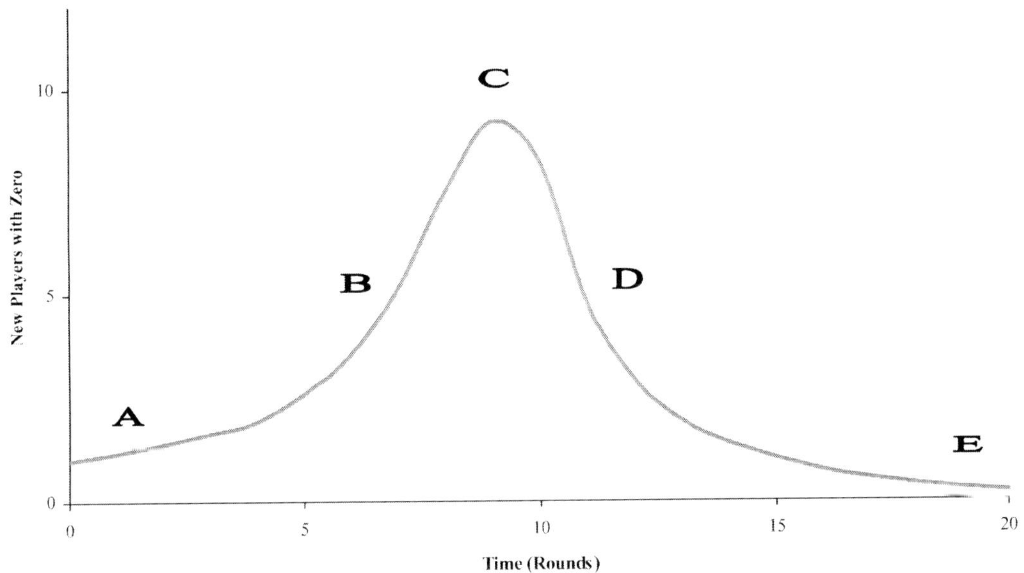

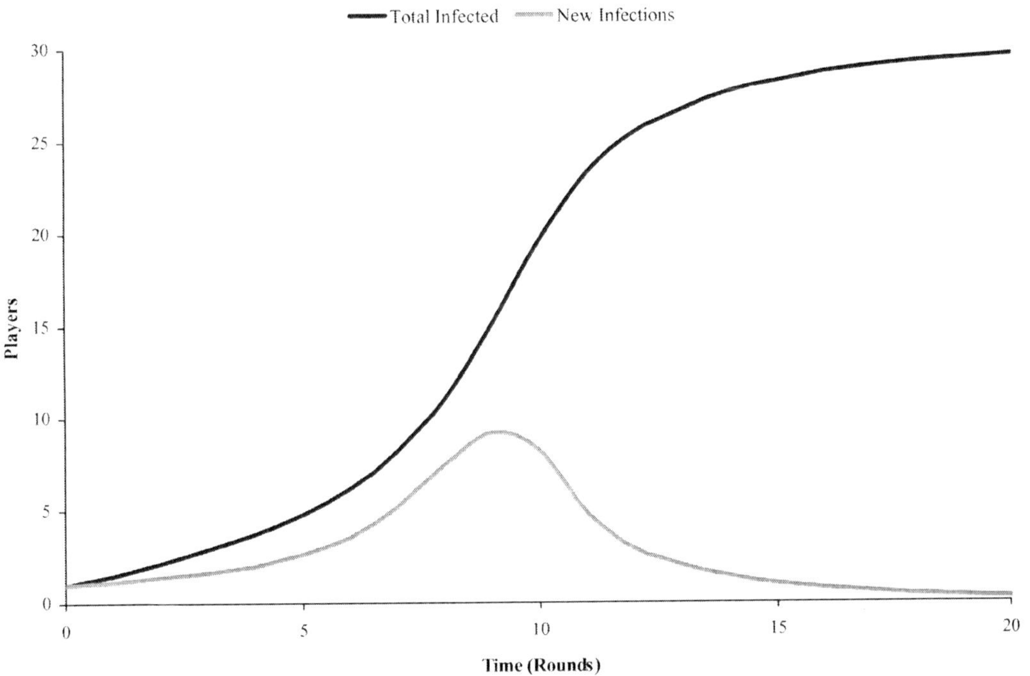

The number of New Infections (or New Players with Zero) is the number of people getting infected each round. In our stock/flow map, we labeled that flow Getting Sick. Total Infected is the stock of Infected People that have accumulated over time as a result of the flow.

? Our stock/flow map explains what happened in our Infection Game, but the game and the map are simplifications of real-life epidemics. What else is missing?

We have made two important simplifying assumptions in the Infection Game.

First, we assumed that every contact of an infected person with a healthy person resulted in transmission of the infection. In the real-world, infectivity is rarely, if ever, 100%. You do not catch a cold every time someone sneezes near you. In reality, only a fraction of exposures result in an infection, with some illnesses being catchier than others. We would show this in our stock flow map by showing that the ***Infectivity*** *of the illness affects the flow of people getting sick.*

Also, in the game, every person contacted one other person during each round. In the real world, infected people may have different numbers of contacts, depending on whether they stay home or go to school when they are sick, for example. We would show this on our map by adding a ***Contact Rate.***

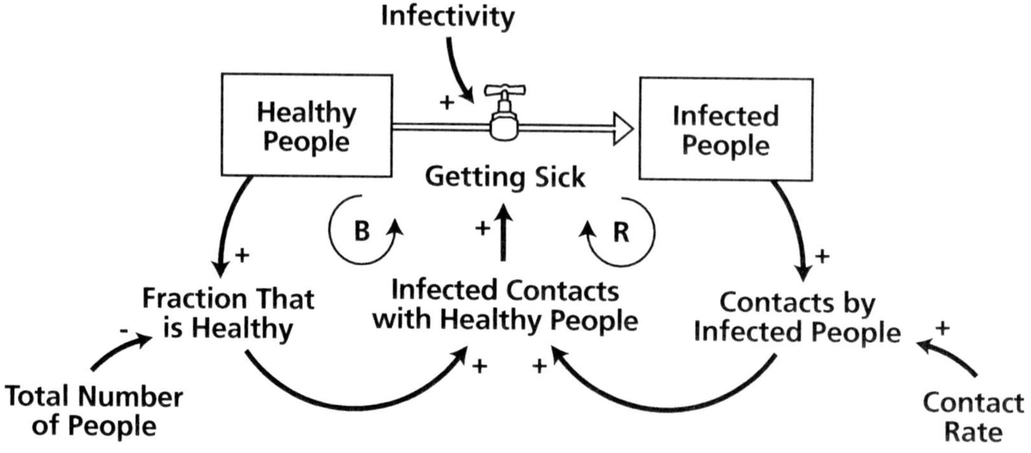

It is interesting to note that neither of these additions would change the underlying behavior of the system. The reinforcing and balancing loops would still work in the same way to produce S-shaped growth, although the changes would happen more or less quickly depending on the different contact and infectivity rates.

The object of the Infection Game is to understand, in its simplest form, how an epidemic spreads. How do the reinforcing and balancing feedback loops control the behavior? Can we use this understanding to change the system?

? What else is missing?

Students may suggest many other differences between the game and reality. For example, in real-life, some people may recover from an illness while other people may die. People can develop immunities to some illnesess but not to others. New people may enter the population through births or immigration, for example. There may be delays in incubation times. There might be vaccines or quarantine policies.

Use our basic stock/flow diagram as a springboard to discuss all these issues. However, we do not need to add these complexities to our stock/flow diagram to explain the basic dynamics of an epidemic.

? Does this remind you of other contagions?

Students may suggest many different examples including the spread of a computer virus, a fad, a social movement, or a rumor. All of these "infections" have the same basic structure and behavior.

NOTE

1 Students can gain valuable insights and inquiry skills approaching a problem in this way. For an even more rigorous analysis, the next step would be to build a system dynamics computer simulation of our stock/flow map one loop at a time to see if it can actually generate the graph's behavior, and use it to experiment with policies to change the behavior. But, that is far beyond the scope of this book—a challenge for another day.

The Tree Game

In Lesson 6 of ***The Shape of Change***, students simulated the planting and harvesting of trees in a forest. They graphed their stock of trees over time to observe the effect of their policies on the sustainability of the forest. See Pages 65–72 in ***The Shape of Change*** for the complete lesson.

Overview

Two ideas underlie this lesson. First, the lesson illustrates another way that stocks and flows can work together: an outflow from one stock is controlled by a second stock.

Second, students get more practice anticipating and observing how a stock changes with different inflow and outflow rates. In the In and Out Game, for example, it was simple to predict how many players accumulated in the stock because the flows were constant and easy to compute. In each of the succeeding lessons, however, the rates of flow have changed over time. Students have had to think more carefully about how the changing inflows and outflows affected the quantities in the stocks. They have done this by relating their classroom game experiences to the graphs they produced and to their stock/flow maps. In the process, they are building their own intuition about how and why quantities increase and decrease over time.

Seeing the Structure

1. Ask students to draw a stock/flow map of the game. Students will have no difficulty coming up with trees, trees planted, and trees cut. Draw the following map and ask students why it is an **incomplete** representation of the tree game.

2. This map shows that both flows are constant. However, in the game, the flow of plantings was **constant** at 4 trees per year while the flow of cutting **changed** each year by doubling.

3. Ask students how to represent the doubling of the outflow. Some students will suggest feedback from the stock to the outflow. Help students understand that this is **incorrect** by drawing the connector and tracing the loop.

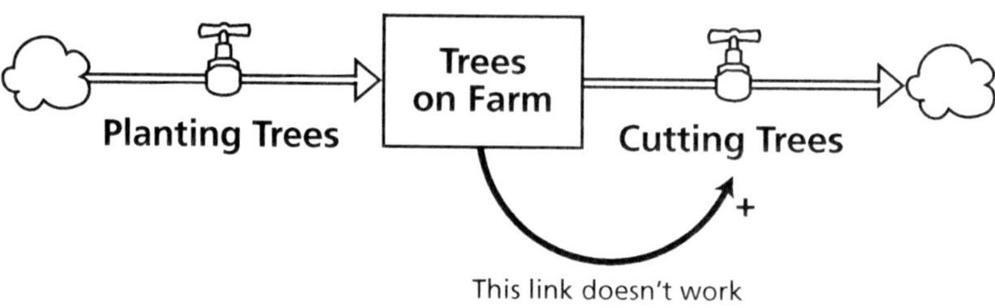

This map says that the number of trees on the farm determines the number of trees that are cut each year. An **increase** in the stock of trees results in an **increase** in the flow of trees cut. This **increase** in the flow will result in a **decrease** in the stock. This in turn will **decrease** the flow. (This is just like the balancing loop for deaths in the Mammoth Game that caused exponential decay.)

However, in the Tree Game, as the stock of trees on the farm **decreased**, the flow of cutting continued to **increase**. This link doesn't work.

Tell the story of each connection as you draw it. Does it make sense?

4. Ask students what determined the increase in cuttings. The cuttings increased because more people wanted the trees. Help students identify this desire for trees as the concept of demand. Demand is represented by a stock that controls the rate of cutting trees. An increase in the demand causes an increase in the number of trees cut.

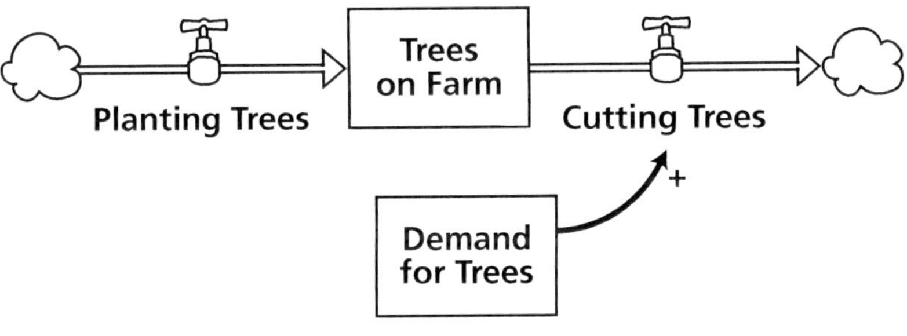

Often a flow is influenced by another stock. In the game, the number of trees cut each year depended on the demand for trees, not on the stock of trees. Perhaps a growing population needed more lumber for housing.

5. In the game, the demand continued to rise. Ask students for suggestions to represent increasing demand. Add an inflow to show how demand was building over time.

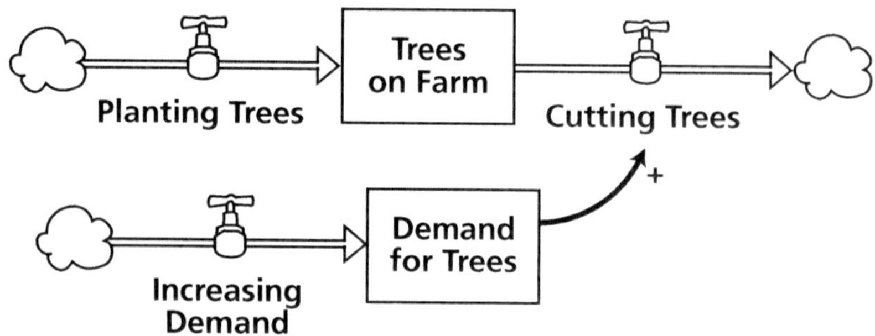

6. Remember that the flow of increasing demand was not constant. Rather, in our game, it doubled every year. A feedback loop is needed, like the doubling process in Making Friends. (This is a very simplified view of demand, defined as doubling in this game. When the need for lumber increased, people who bought our trees came back to buy more.)

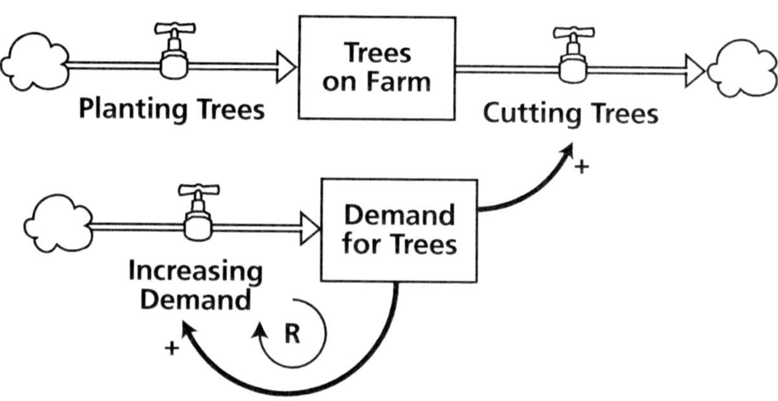

By now students recognize this structure as a reinforcing feedback loop causing exponential growth.

7. Ask students to pair up and practice telling the story of this map, relating it to both the game they played and the graph they drew. Have one or two students share their stories with the class. Here is an example:

> *We have a stock of trees that is growing at a constant rate of four trees per year. In the first year, we cut one tree and sold it. In the second year we could sell two trees, so we cut two trees. People liked our trees and told their friends about them, so each year*

more and more people wanted our trees. As a result, we cut more and more trees. We ran out of trees because we cut them down faster than they could grow back.

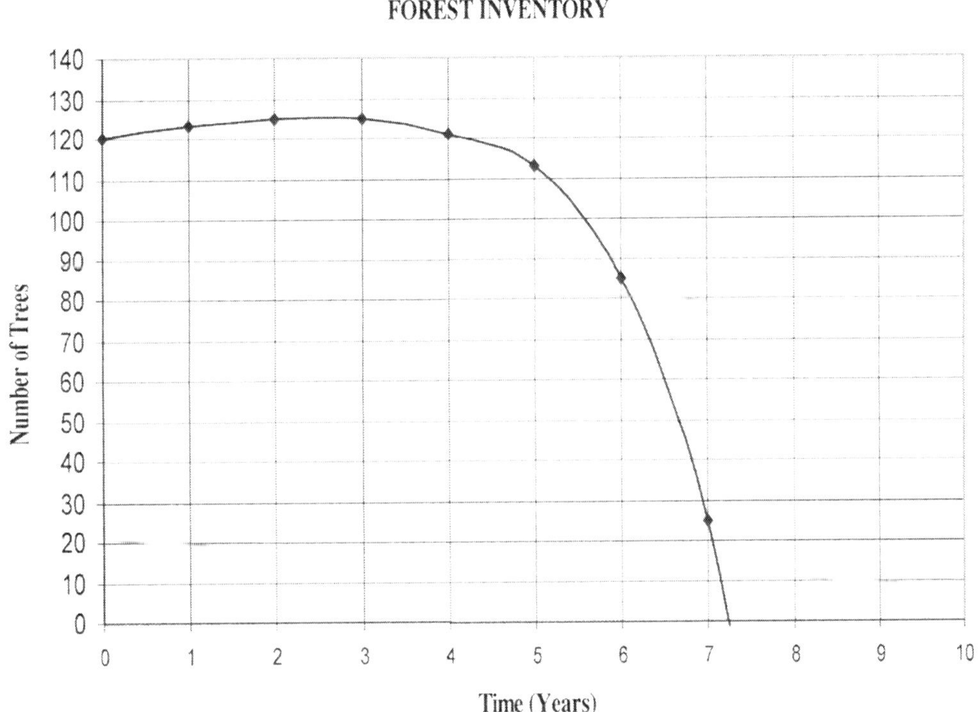

? Why did the stock of trees increase slightly at first?

The stock of trees increased because we were planting more trees than we were harvesting for the first two years.

? Why did we run out of trees? We had plenty of trees in the forest at first.

When the demand for trees increased beyond four trees per year, we were cutting down more trees than we were planting every year. The outflow of trees exceeded the inflow, so the stock of trees decreased. No matter how many trees you start with, if you cut them faster than they can grow back, you will eventually run out of trees.

No matter how many trees you start with, if you cut them faster than they can grow back, you will eventually run out of trees.

? This stock/flow map describes the structure of the Tree Game. Is it a complete reflection of reality?

Our map, like the game, is a greatly simplified version of reality designed to examine how our policies affected the sustainability of our forest. We did not include the concepts of profit and market forces. In the real world, the demand would be influenced by the supply, closing a feedback loop that would cause supply and demand to balance back and forth with delays in the system. These and other elements would make the map more realistic but also much more complex than necessary to examine the basic idea of stocks, flows and sustainability.

? Are there policies that might prevent the depletion of the tree supply?

To keep a sustainable stock of trees in his forest, a forester could either increase the inflow by planting more trees or decrease the outflow by cutting fewer trees. Balancing inflows with outflows is the only way to achieve sustainability.

? Does this apply only to trees in a forest?

Every resource is a stock that is controlled by inflows and outflows, whether it is a stock of fish in the ocean, money in a bank account, or even goodwill with your neighbors.

There are many real-world examples of people using resources faster than they can be replenished. Learning about stocks and flows can help us understand the concept of sustainability.

The Tree Game Puzzle

In Lesson 7 of ***The Shape of Change***, students extended the Tree Game lesson by implementing their own planting and harvesting policies and graphing the results. All the policies and graphs were posted on the wall, and students matched them up. See Pages 73–80 in ***The Shape of Change*** for the complete lesson.

Overview

Developing stock/flow maps for the students' Tree Game puzzles poses a dilemma for the teacher. On one hand, there is a great degree of uncertainty: students come up with all kinds of rules and these rules will require unique maps. On the other hand, this is a great opportunity for students to clarify their own thinking and to experience the power of making stock/flow maps. Students are usually willing to try their hands at this as long as they are given the opportunity to do so in a non-threatening way.

Students will find this exercise easier if they have had more exposure and practice with stocks and flows, so you may want to save this lesson for later. Yet, the best way to get that exposure and practice is to just do it. It is a good way to learn from our own mistakes.

Does This Make Sense?

To help students get started, remind them to always recount the story of their stock/flow maps as they build them. For example:

- "An increase in this causes a decrease in that."
- "This inflow makes the stock grow because..."
- "Tracing the story, this loop causes the stock to grow faster and faster, or decline more and more slowly."

Each link needs to make practical sense and relate directly to what the policies actually do in the game, on the graph and in the real world.

Seeing the Structure

After students have made up their own rules, have matched graphs to rules, and have had a chance to talk about the different rules, ask them to draw stock/flow maps. Student-made rules often fall into the following categories or combinations of them:

Policy	Planting Rule	Cutting Rule
1	Linear increase	Linear increase
2	Constant	Proportion of trees
3	Proportion of trees	Constant
4	Exponential increase	Exponential increase

Policy 1 This policy uses a linear increase in planting and a linear increase in cutting. For example, "Plant 4, 5, 6, … and Cut 3, 5, 7, …"

To show that the flows are increasing at a steady rate, a second set of stocks has to be introduced to represent the policies.

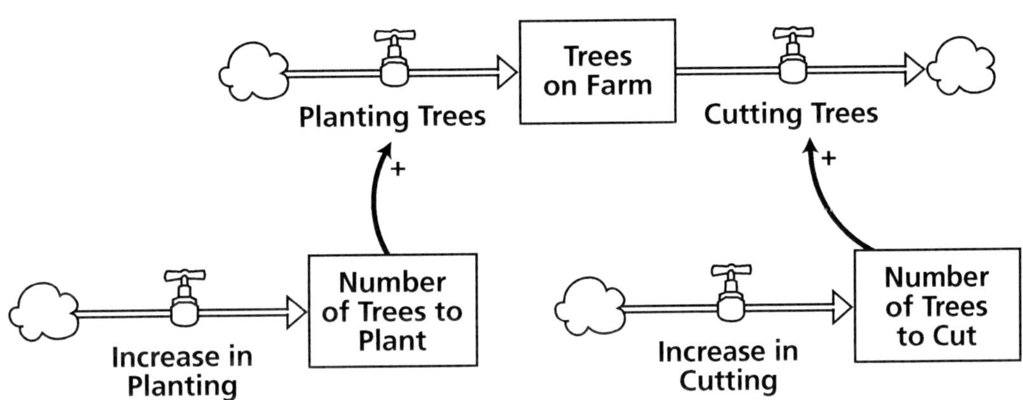

Policy 2 This policy keeps the number of trees planted constant. The number of trees cut is a fraction of the total number of trees.

For example, "Plant 8 trees per year. Cut one-tenth of the trees each year."

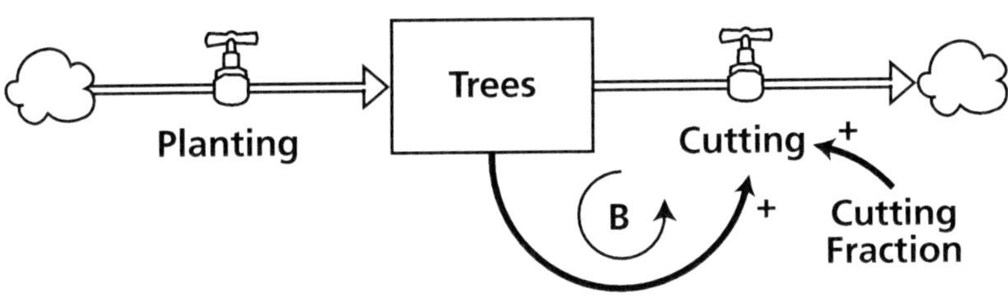

Tell the story of each link as you add it. Does it make sense?

The cutting structure is like deaths in the Mammoth Game. The number of mammoths dying depended on the number of mammoths in the herd times a death fraction. The balancing loop caused the mammoth population to decline to extinction in a pattern of exponential decay, just as it would for the trees.

Policy 3 This is somewhat similar to Policy 2. For example, "Plant 25% more trees every year and cut 5 trees." Students may combine these elements in other ways too.

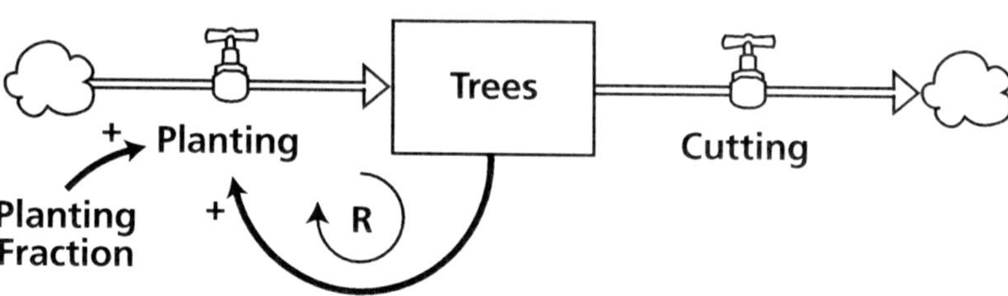

This planting structure is like births in the Mammoth Game. The number of mammoths born depended on the size of the herd and the birth rate. This reinforcing loop caused exponential growth.

Policy 4 Another common rule combines an exponential increase in planting with an exponential increase in cutting (similar to the original tree game).
For example, "Plant 2, 4, 8, 16 ... and Cut 1, 3, 9, 27, ..."

While most policies reflect similar structures seen in earlier lessons, others may require students to stretch their thinking to new situations.

The variables "Planting Fraction" and "Request Fraction" show that the planting/cutting policies do not have to be the same: in the example, the number of plantings doubles every year while the number of cuttings triples.

Notice that although reinforcing feedback loops drive the increased planting and demand for trees, there is no feedback tying these to the number of trees on the farm.

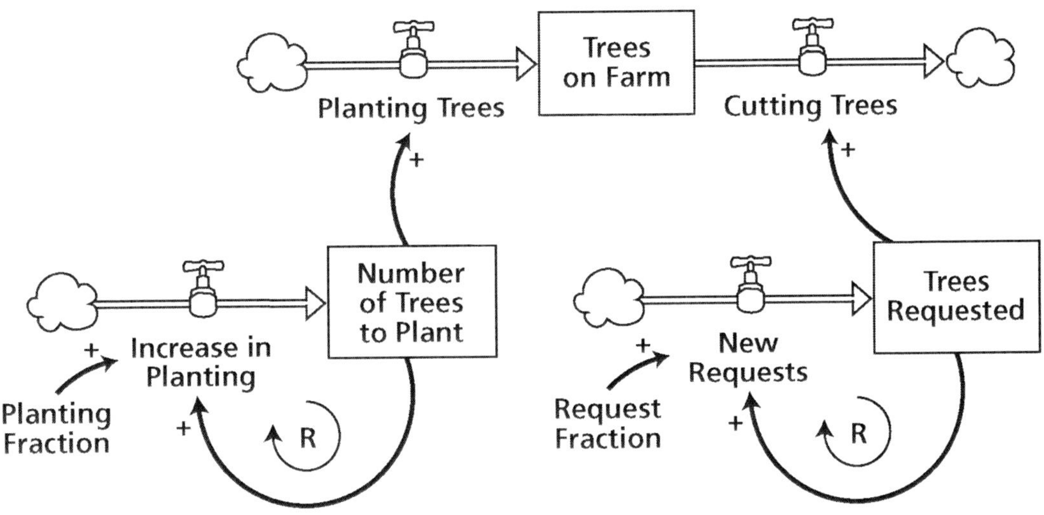

? What stories do your stock/flow maps tell?

After students have matched the graphs with their rules, ask student teams to relate the stories of their stock/flow maps for the class in terms of real trees. This is a good way for students to discuss different ways to view a problem, refine their stock/flow maps, learn from one another and examine their own thinking processes. This is the most important part of the lesson.

After students have presented their maps to the class, turn the discussion back to sustainability. Which policies would maintain the forest for future generations? Which are realistic?

? What about sustainability?

The focus of this lesson has been to help students understand how various inflow and outflow rates cause the stock to change over time. Students have learned how to express different policies in their stock/flow maps. Since students were not asked to consider sustainability when they defined the planting and harvesting policies for their puzzles, their graphs and stock flow maps will show a range of behaviors and structures. (Usually, students are more driven by the challenge to create puzzles that will stump their classmates!)

Ask students to look again at their policies for feasibility and sustainability. Remember from the previous Tree Game lesson that sustainability requires a balancing of inflows and outflows. If you cut more trees than you plant, the forest will eventually disappear.

The Rainforest Game

In Lesson 8 of ***The Shape of Change***, students experienced the effects of delays as they acted out the growth stages of trees in a forest. Following various planting and harvesting policies, they saw their forest grow, reach equilibrium, and decline over time. See Pages 81–96 in ***The Shape of Change*** for the complete lesson.

Overview

The Rainforest Game is a very active classroom activity with students pantomiming the growth of seeds, sprouts, saplings and mature trees, while they are also observing the changes in their forest inventories under three different sets of planting and harvesting decision rules. Students will be surprised to see that the stock/flow map of the game is quite basic, however. The map has four stocks of trees linked together in a chain. Delays arise as the trees grow and move from one stock to the next over time.

Seeing the Structure

1. Review the growth stages of trees in The Rainforest Game. Referring to their Yearly Forest Inventory tables may help students identify each category of tree. Since these stages were accumulations that were changing during the game, they can be represented as stocks.

Seeds in Ground	Sprouts	Saplings	Mature Trees

A Snapshot

One way to identify the stocks in a system is to think of a snapshot. If we could take a picture of the system at the end of any time period, what would we see? In The Rainforest Game, we would see the collections of seeds, sprouts, saplings and mature trees that had accumulated over time. We would see the stocks.

2. Ask students to describe how trees changed during the game. They will recall that seeds were planted and sprouted after one year. The sprouts grew to saplings during the next year, and matured to harvestable size in the following year. Connecting the stocks with flows shows that the trees moved from one stock to the next over time.

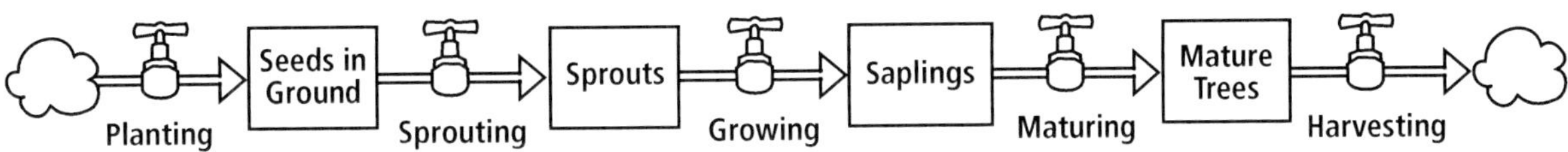

3. Ask students how many trees from each stock moved to the next stage during each turn. Because the simulation is an idealized situation, *all* the seeds sprouted, *all* the sprouts grew, and *all* the saplings matured each year. Show this in the diagram by connecting the stock to the flow, indicating that the number of trees flowing out of the stock is influenced by the number of trees in the stock. In the game, all the trees flowed from one stock to the next until they were mature.

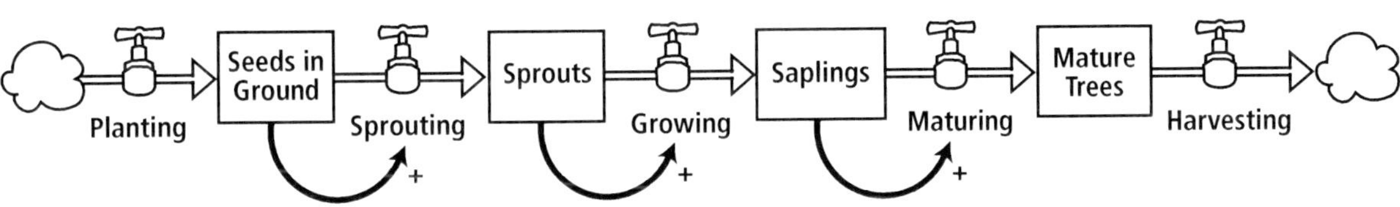

The "+" signs by the arrowheads mean that an **increase** in the stock causes an **increase** in the flow. The more seeds there are in the ground, the more seeds will sprout each year.

4. How many mature trees were harvested each year? That was a policy decision in the game that didn't depend on the number of mature trees. We don't draw a connecting arrow from the "Mature Trees" stock to the "Harvesting" flow.

But the harvesting decision *did* affect another part of the game. Ask students how the harvesting decision affected other parts of the system.

Once a stock of mature trees built up, harvesting began. The harvesting number equaled the number of seeds planted. When harvesting increased, the rate of planting was increased to match it. Ask students how to diagram this relationship.

The "clouds" are the boundaries of the system. For now, we do not care where the seeds came from or where the harvested trees went.

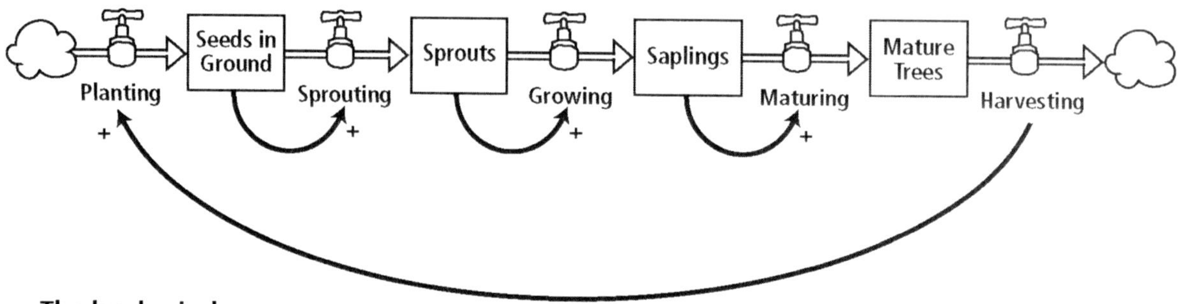

The lumberjack asked the planter to plant a new seed for every tree he cut down.

The arrow means that *information* about the harvesting rate affected the planting rate. An **increase** in the harvesting rate, caused an **increase** in the planting rate.

5. The map is now complete and reflects the structure of the game. The chain of stocks shows the delay as seeds grow into sprouts, saplings and mature trees over time. The connecting arrow from harvesting to planting reflects the policy decision to plant a new seed for every tree cut.

? Can you explain what happened in The Rainforest Game using our stock/flow map?

Every year, we planted a certain number of seeds in the ground. In a year, the seeds all grew into sprouts. After another year, the sprouts all grew into saplings. Finally, after a third year, the saplings grew into mature trees. In our forest inventory we had four stocks of trees, one for each stage of growth; trees flowed from one to the next each year. Our policy was to plant a new tree for every tree that we harvested, as shown by the connecting arrow—the arrow shows that the planting rate was determined by information about the harvesting rate. During the game, we changed the harvesting and planting rates to test different policies, but the structure of the system remained the same.

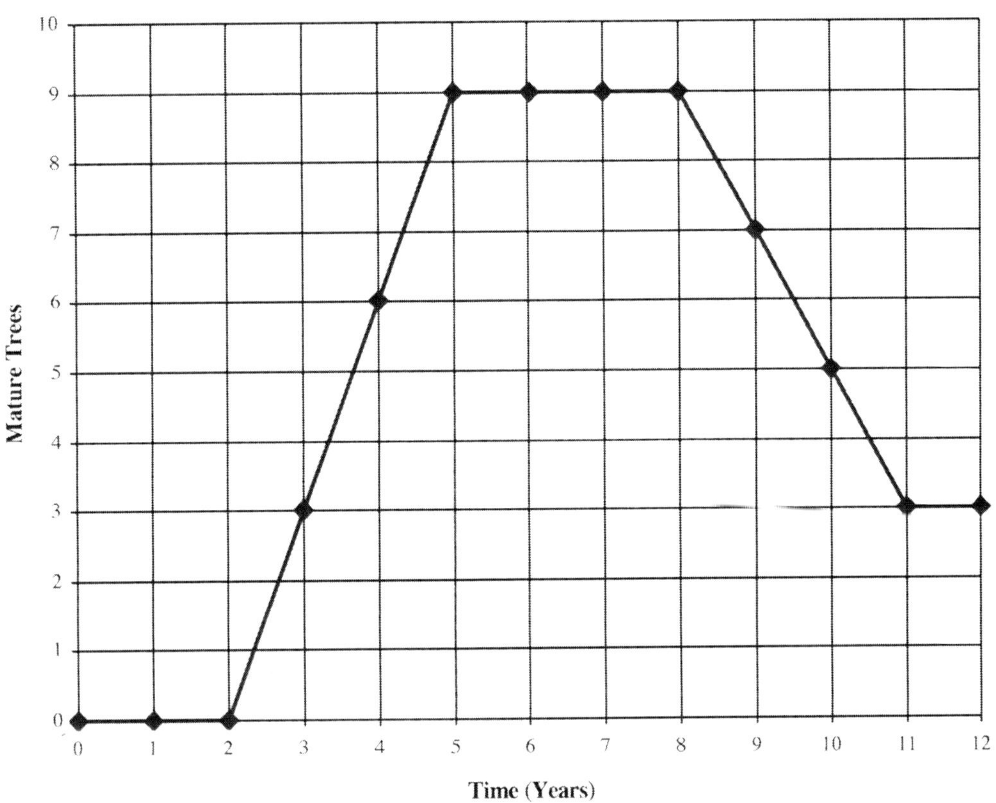

? Looking back at our graph of the Forest Inventory, and relating it to our stock/flow map, why did it take so long to get a stock of nine mature trees?

We started with open land and planted three seeds. It took three years for those seeds to become sprouts, saplings, and finally mature trees. We had a stock of three mature trees in Year 3. Meanwhile, because we continued to plant three seeds every year, those new seeds were also progressing through the growth stages every year, from stock to stock. These new trees kept flowing through the system so that three new trees were added to the stock of mature trees every year. By Year 5, we had nine trees. The stock/flow map shows how it takes time for trees to grow. There was a delay of three years from planting to harvesting our trees.

During the game, we changed the harvesting and planting rates to test different policies, but the structure of the system remained the same.

When students relate their game experience to the graph and the stock/flow map, they begin to grasp the effect of delays on the behavior of a system.

? In Year 9 we increased the harvesting and planting policies. Why did the equilibrium value of the stock of mature trees drop?

As we saw in playing the game, even though the planting rate was increased to match the increased cutting in Year 9, the stocks of sprouts and saplings still contained only three trees which still had to mature through the system. In Years 9–11 we were cutting five trees while only three trees were flowing up into the stock of mature trees. For the stock of mature trees during those years, the outflow exceeded the inflow, so the number of mature trees decreased over time—much like the mammoths dying faster than they were being born in the Mammoth Game.

? Why doesn't the graph reflect a sudden drop in the number of mature trees rather than the gradual decline to three trees?

The graph reflects the total delay of three years during which the trees grew through the growth stages to maturity.

? How is our forest game different from a real-world forest?

In the game, our trees passed from year to year in discrete one-year intervals—every sprout became a sapling at the end of exactly one year, for example. Also, in the game, the growing time for all of the stages was one year.

In the real world, trees grow continuously throughout the year, not in one-year steps. Also, the growing times are not all equal. For example, while it may take a year for a seed to sprout, it may take twenty years for a sapling to mature.

We could specify growing times in our stock flow map.

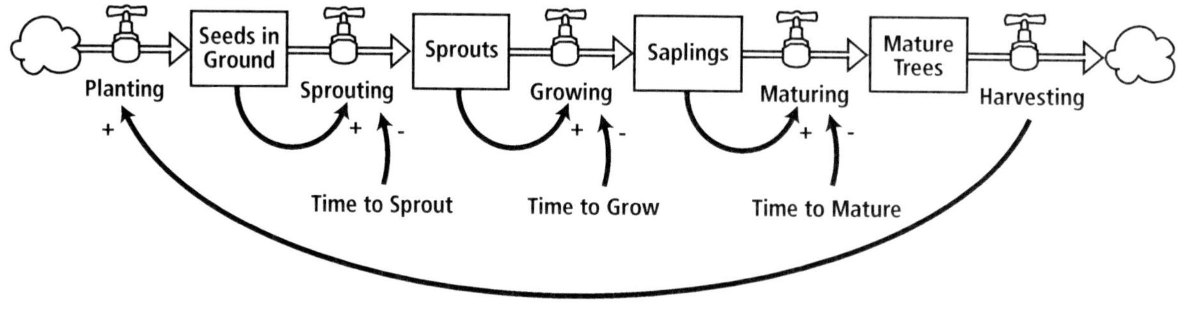

The "-" signs by the arrowheads mean that an ***increase*** *in the delay times causes a* ***decrease*** *in the flows. If it takes longer for seeds to sprout, then fewer seeds will sprout each year.*

Notice that each section of this map is like the deaths structure in the Mammoth Game: a number of trees drains out of each stock each year, depending on the delay times. These are balancing feedback loops; they would produce curved lines on the graph, more like real-world behavior.

It's always a good idea to think about the simplifications we have made in a game or model.

? Can you think of other examples where something moving from stock to stock causes a delay?

- *There is a delay from when students enter kindergarten until they graduate, as they pass from one grade to the next each year.*
- *There is a delay in making school lunches. The food is brought to school, stored, prepared, baked, and finally served to students.*
- *There is a delay from the time you put a letter in the mailbox until it is delivered to your grandmother. The letter is sorted at your post office, put on trucks, sorted again at her post office, and delivered.*
- *There is a delay from the time we burn fossil fuels until greenhouse gases build up in the atmosphere.*

Stocks introduce delays into systems. Accumulations build up and drain *over time.*

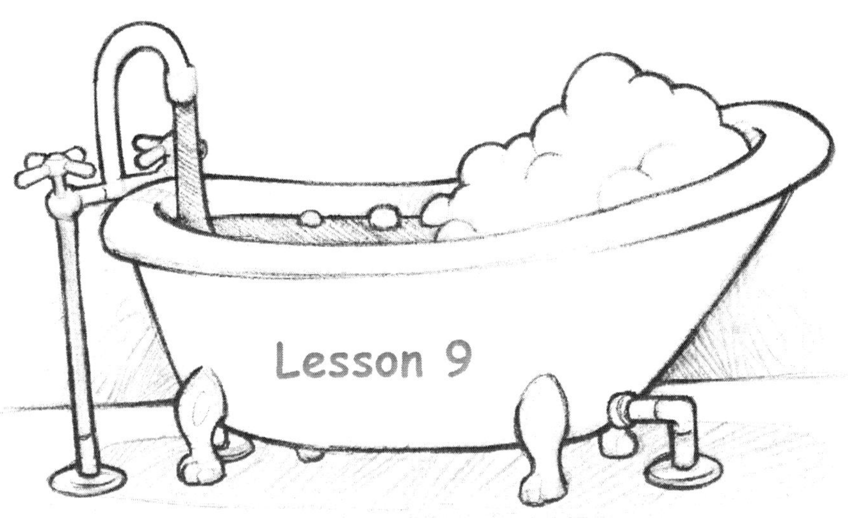

The Connection Game

In Lesson 9 of ***The Shape of Change***, students moved around the classroom trying to maintain an equal distance from two students who were also moving around the room tracking two other students. A small change in the position of one person caused everyone else to move. See Pages 97–102 in ***The Shape of Change*** for the complete lesson.

The Connection Game is a precursor to the next two lessons in ***The Shape of Change*** on drawing causal loop diagrams using connection circles. The game is just an engaging way to experience the complexity of a web of interdependencies. There are no stocks and flows to draw for this lesson.

Do You Want Fries With That?
Learning About Connection Circles

In Lesson 10 of ***The Shape of Change***, students learned how to use a connection circle to analyze an article about rising obesity-related health risks and increased fast food consumption. After identifying key variables and the causal links among them, they traced the causal loops that drive the system. See Pages 103–116 in ***The Shape of Change*** for the complete lesson.

About Connection Circles

A connection circle is a handy graphic organizer that helps students understand the main ideas in their reading. For us, however, the connection circle also has a much broader purpose in our endeavor to heighten students' awareness of the causes of change all around them. We'd like to expand our original explanation to make our purpose more clear.

The purpose of a connection circle is to uncover the causal loops that could be causing the problem we have observed.

The purpose of a connection circle is to uncover the causal loops that could be causing the problem we have observed. That means that there are two essential elements: a problem behavior pattern and the causal loops driving it.

The Behavior: What's the Problem?

After students have read the article, ask them to identify briefly the problem that the author is presenting. In this case, they might say, "People are getting too fat and cardiovascular disease is rising," or, "People are eating more and more French fries."

Try to identify what is increasing or decreasing over time, and if possible, sketch a very rough behavior over time graph of a variable or two. The graph serves to focus attention on the problem behavior, just as we have done in our previous lessons. It is a very quick rough sketch of the pattern of behavior that we are trying to understand. The graph shows us *what* is changing and *how* it is changing.

Focusing attention on a problem helps students find the most relevant variables to place around the circle. Now they are looking for elements in the story that may be contributing to the problem, rather than just listing "important" big words or things that do not change over time.

The Loops: What's Causing the Problem?

Feedback loops are the key to understanding *why* things change over time.

After students have drawn the connecting links across their circles, be sure they follow through with uncovering the causal loops, as we described in ***The Shape of Change*** (Pages 110-116.) When students unfold the causal loops, they extract meaning from their confusing "spaghetti plates" of connections. They get a deeper understanding of the problem and its causes; they find clues to its solutions. The feedback loops explain *why* something is changing. Don't skip this step.

The Fries Connection Circle

The Problem Behavior: Students read in "Eyes on the Fries" by Rene Ebersole[1] that Americans are eating more and more French fries and that cardiovascular disease is rising. They have sketched a behavior over time graph of French fry consumption and the incidence of disease. They could also graph the growing number of restaurants, or rising profits, which also define the problem.

A connection circle is for analyzing a problem: *What* is the author concerned about? *How* is it increasing or decreasing over time? *Why* is it changing?

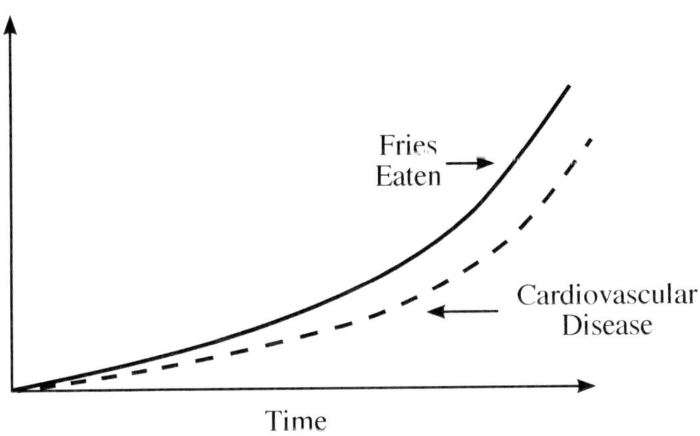

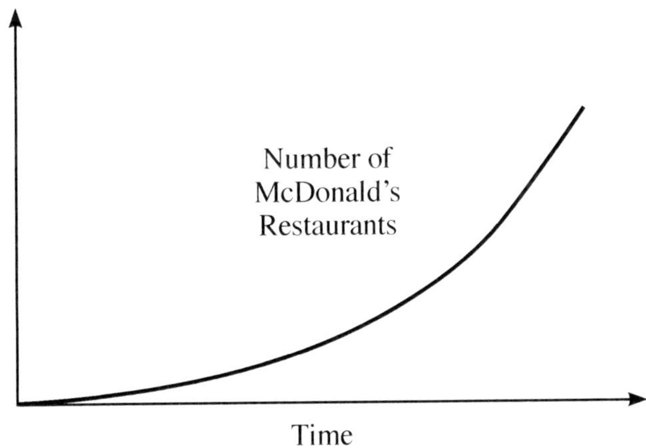

Looking for Causes: What could be causing this rapidly increasing growth in cardiovascular disease, according to the article's author? Students used their connection circles to identify possible causes and placed them around the circle. Remember that each element must be something that can increase or decrease over time and that might somehow be contributing to the problem.

In ***The Shape of Change***, students identified the number of French fries eaten, the growing number of fast food restaurants, and other variables.

The Feedback Loops: After tracing closed loops in their connection circles, students came up with a causal loop diagram something like this one:

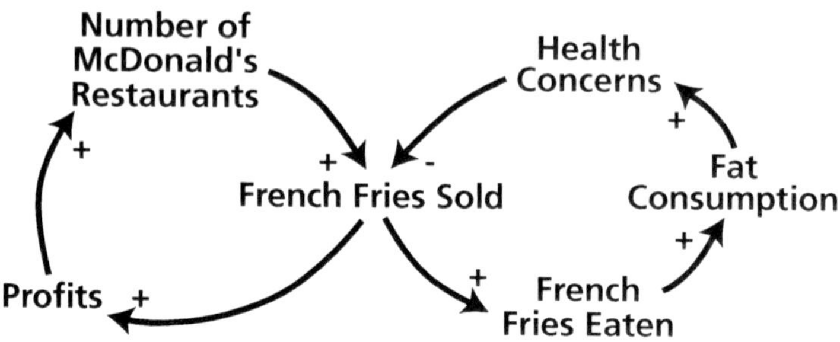

The loop on the left is a *reinforcing feedback loop*: An **increase** in the number of French fries sold produces an **increase** in profits that McDonald's then invests in opening **more** restaurants to sell even **more** French fries. This increasing growth is like the exponential growth we saw in Making Friends. It is also like the exponential growth pattern in our behavior over time sketch of Fries Eaten. It is beginning to look like this loop might be one cause of the problem.

This causal loop drawing is a rough sketch of the feedback processes that might be causing the increases in French fry consumption and cardiovascular disease.

The loop on the right is a *balancing loop*. An **increase** in fries sold leads to an **increase** in fat consumption; however, after a while, increases in obesity **raise** health concerns and people begin to eat **fewer** French fries. The article by Ebersole and our behavior over time sketch describe the first part of the story—the rise in obesity and cardiovascular disease. Our balancing loop could explain what happens when those health concerns get very high.

Stocks and Flows

The connection circle has stimulated a good discussion while helping students examine the article more closely for clues about the causes of the problem. Now, drawing a stock/flow map will help them understand more precisely how the system works.

1. Ask students to name the stocks in the system. Think about the problem we identified, the graphs we drew, and the causal loops we proposed as causes of the problem. Starting with the reinforcing loop, we identify McDonald's Restaurants as our first stock. If we could take a snapshot of the system, we would see the number of restaurants that had accumulated.

McDonald's
Restaurants

2. What caused the number of restaurants to increase? Since a stock can increase only through a flow, add an inflow to increase the number of restaurants.

3. Working backwards from the flow, what caused McDonald's to add new restaurants? According to the article, McDonald's added new restaurants when their profits grew. An increase in profits led to an increase in new restaurants (labeled "+").

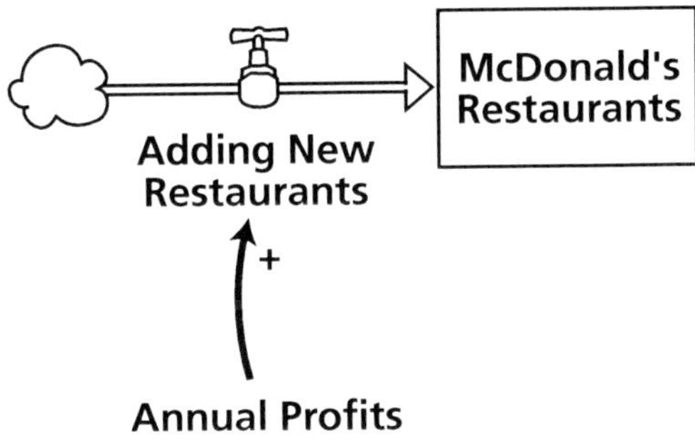

4. What caused the profits to increase? The author says that profits increased as French fry sales increased.

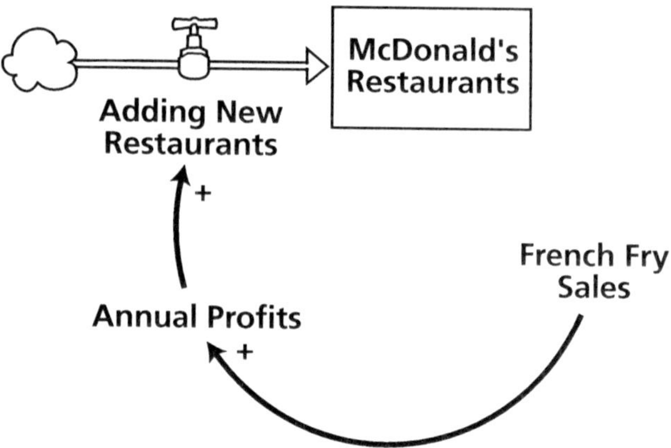

5. What caused the French fry sales to increase? The more restaurants there were, the more French fries they sold.

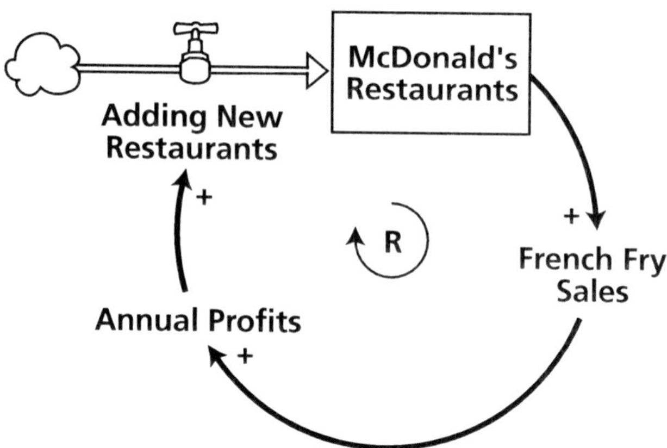

This closes our loop. It is a *reinforcing loop* because an initial **increase** in the number of restaurants works around the loop to further **increase** the number of restaurants. We expect that this reinforcing loop would produce the exponential growth we sketched in our behavior over time graph hypothesis on Page 81.[2]

How to Find the Stocks

- Stocks are accumulations. If you could stop time and take a snapshot of the system, you would see only the stocks. In the fries example, we could count a number of restaurants and a number of overweight people at that moment, but in a snapshot we could not tell whether they were increasing or decreasing. The flows are the rates at which the stocks increase or decrease over time.
- Each feedback loop must have at least one stock to accumulate the increases and decreases that are caused by the feedback processes. Restaurants were increasing. Overweight people were increasing.
- Sometimes we break the flows into parts to make the diagram more understandable and to show the logic of the feedback process. In this case, we show how increased French Fry Sales caused higher Annual Profits which then led to Adding New Restaurants.

6. Are there other stocks in the system? The next loop will take a little more thought. A stock/flow map is not simply a direct translation of a causal loop diagram. While a causal loop diagram is a rough sketch of the feedback loops that may be driving a system, a stock/flow map requires us to look more carefully at how the system actually works—how the accumulations increase and decrease over time.

Try these lines of reasoning:

- Our first loop was about money: French fry sales generated profits that were used to build restaurants to sell more fries and generate even more profits. What is our second loop about? What else does a rise in French fry sales cause? Our second loop is about people eating more French fries and gaining too much weight. Our causal loop diagram listed "Health Concerns," but the problem is more specific than that—the author was worried about too many people getting fat on fast food. Our stock is the growing number of obese people.

A stock/flow map is not simply a direct translation of a causal loop diagram. It must tell more precisely how a system works.

- If we could stop time and take a snapshot of the system, what accumulations would we see? We would see the number of obese people at that point in time.

A stock/flow map traces direct causes. People gain weight because they *eat* more fries, not because sales are rising.

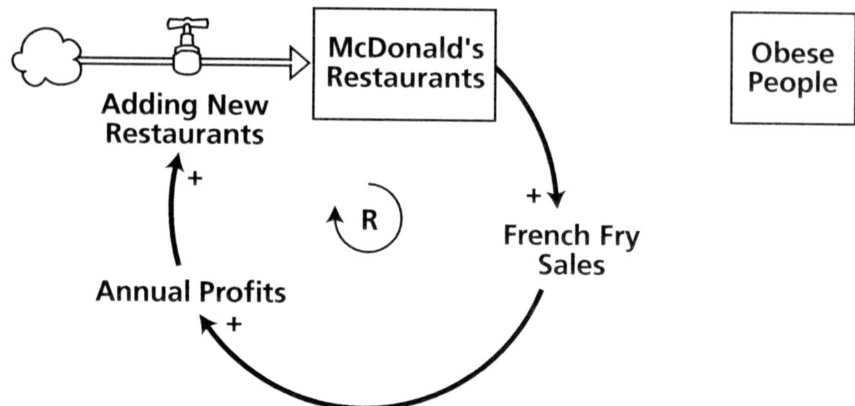

7. How do those people get fat? Follow the causal trail from "French Fry Sales" to tell the story. As French fry sales increase, the number of French fries consumed also increases—people *eat* the French fries that they buy. Since every French fry is loaded with fat, an increase in French fry consumption means an increase in fat consumption. Add these connections.

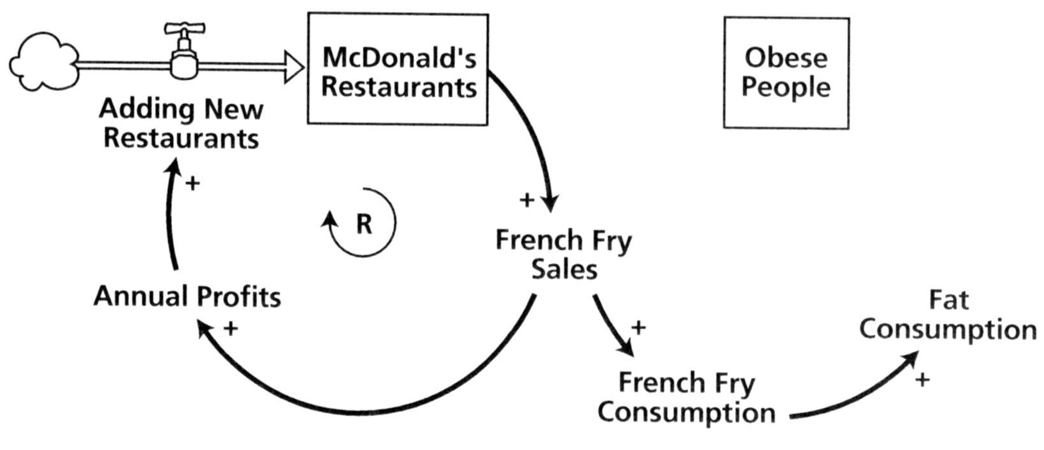

8. Increased fat consumption leads to weight gain. "Fat Consumption," therefore, influences the flow of people gaining weight. Stocks can change only through flows.

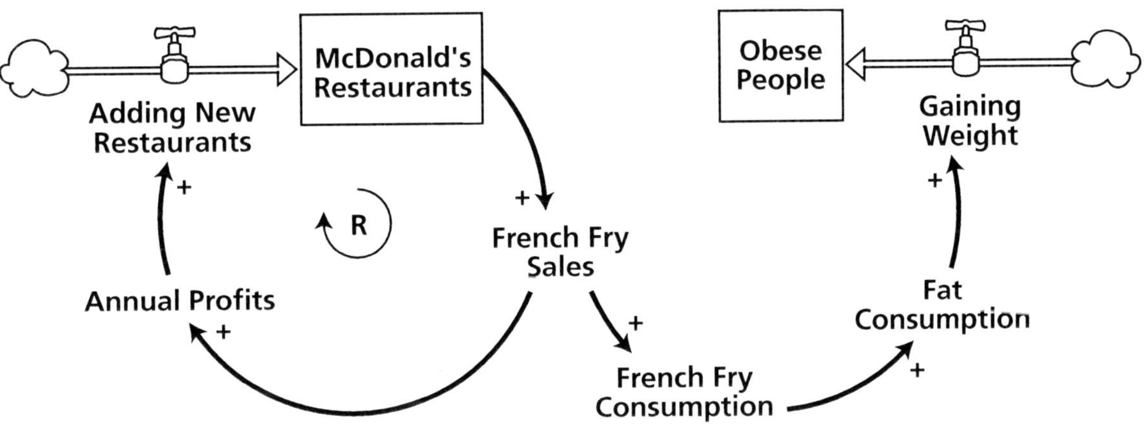

9. In our causal loop hypothesis, we said that rising numbers of obese people raised concerns about cardiovascular disease and other weight-related health problems. Because there are so many obese people now, the author hopes that public concern about the health risks will rise (labeled "+"), and that a rise in health concerns will lead people to consume fewer French fries (labeled "-").

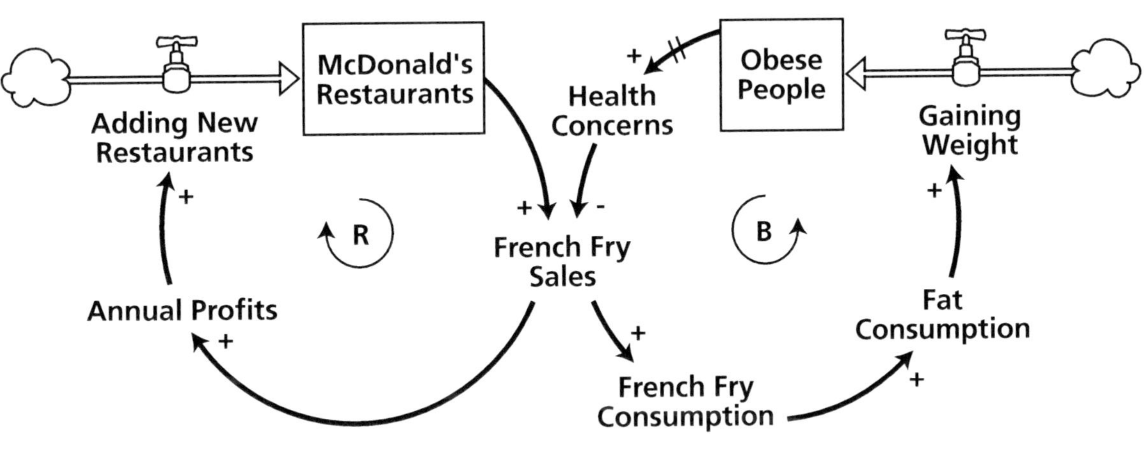

Our balancing loop is now complete. It works to bring fat consumption down to healthier levels when rising obesity numbers raise health concerns.

This stock/flow map represents the problem described in "Eyes on the Fries." It explains how rising French fry sales spur both an increase in restaurants and an increase in obesity in the population.[3]

A Delay

Notice the two little lines on the link to "Health Concerns." This is the symbol for a delay. Health concerns do not rise immediately with an increase in obesity levels. It takes a while for people to notice the change, acknowledge it, and raise the alarm about health risks. (You might argue that there is also a delay before people respond to that alarm and eat less.)

? How does our stock/flow map explain the rising number of obese people? Use the map to tell the story.

In "Eyes on the Fries," Ebersole links the growing obesity and cardiovascular disease epidemic to the increased consumption of French fries. Our map makes the connection more clear. As people buy more and more French fries, McDonald's earns increased profits that it can use to build even more restaurants. This positive loop causes the number of restaurants, fries sales and profits to escalate. The increase in sales of French fries means people are eating more fries, consuming more fat, and gaining more weight.

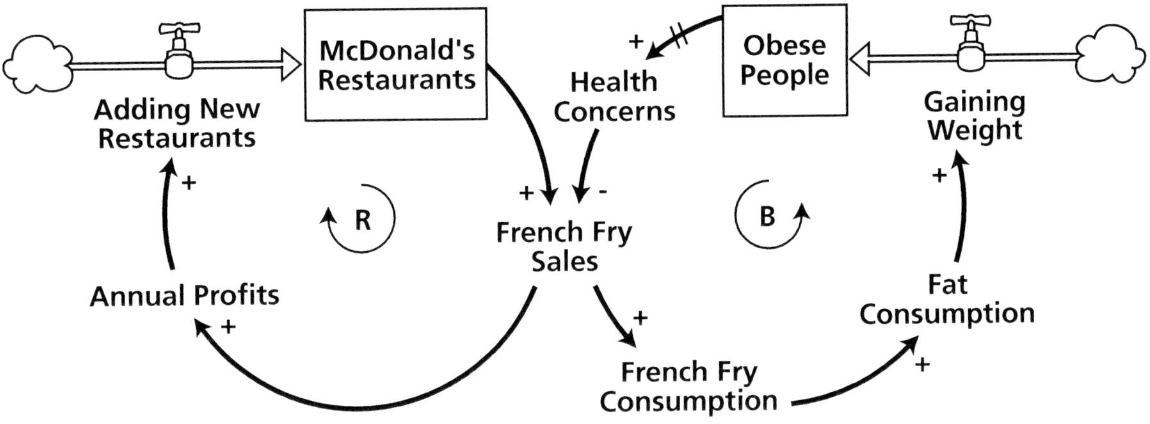

? How does the balancing loop affect the sales of French fries?

After a while, when the number of obese people gets very high, public health concerns rise about cardiovascular disease and other weight-related health problems. This publicity makes people cut back on eating fries (which also reduces French fry profits and the number of new restaurants).

The goal of the balancing loop is to have healthy people. When too many people are obese, health concerns rise to limit the sales and consumption of fries.

Unfortunately, however, a balancing loop "balances" back and forth. After people have abstained from fries for a while, the health concerns fade and people once again indulge their insatiable appetite for fries. The cycle begins again.

? Does the article suggest any solutions to the problem?

Yes, Ebersole explains that the fast food industry, in response to health concerns about saturated fats, will use "healthier" unsaturated oils in making fries. In our map, that change would alter the type of fat consumed, but would that solve the problem? If the change lowers cholesterol levels but not obesity levels, would that allay health concerns? Our map helps us raise good questions about a very complex issue.

While the reinforcing loop causes growth in French fry sales, the balancing loop tends to temper that growth over time when fatter people eventually decide to eat fewer fries.

? Does our stock/flow map tell the whole story? What else is missing?

Ask students to think about how this story and map relate to their own real-world experience.

- *What drives our "humongous appetite for French fries?" Is it more than just their easy availability?*
- *Is increased French fry consumption the only cause of our widening waistlines?*
- *What about exercise, or portion sizes, or changing family mealtime habits?*
- *Do public health warnings about the risks of obesity really reduce fat consumption?*
- *Where does the responsibility lie for the problem of obesity?*
- *What can we do about it?*

Building a stock/flow map can help students think carefully about a problem. What is changing, how is it changing, why is it changing, and what can we do about it?

? Our stock/flow map presents one mental model of the problem. Can there be other views?

Certainly! If students have come up with different maps, use the opportunity to discuss the differences and similarities. A stock/flow map can help students surface their assumptions and examine the causes of problems in objective way. It can also help them be explicit and internally consistent in their reasoning. A stock/flow map is not an "answer;" it represents a thinking and problem-solving process.

NOTES

1 "Eyes on the Fries," by Rene Ebersole, appeared in the student magazine *Current Science,* March 1, 2002. It is reproduced by permission beginning on page 18 in ***The Shape of Change*** (2004). The book is available from The Creative Learning Exchange at www.clexchange.org.

2 A stock/flow diagram "lays out the plumbing" for the next step—building a system dynamics computer model of the system. Here, we would use equations to specify the relationships between the variables. Then, we would run the simulation to see if this loop actually produces exponential growth before adding more to the model.

3 If we wanted to keep going, we would carefully specify the relationships with equations and run a simulation to see if our balancing loop can eventually curtail the consumption of fries. Then, we would use and expand the model to experiment with policy alternatives that might solve the problem of rising obesity rates.

Keystone Species in an Ecosystem

In Lesson 11 of ***The Shape of Change***, students read "The Case of the Twin Islands" by Susan E. Quinlan.[1] They used connection circles to examine why the ecosystems surrounding two neighboring islands are so different. See Pages 117–127 in ***The Shape of Change*** for the complete lesson.

Overview

Ecosystems are built on a complex web of interconnections among many organisms. Each organism can be considered a stock, a population that can increase and decrease. Over time, nature tends to achieve a delicate balance among the stocks: Reinforcing feedback loops drive accelerating growth and decline, while balancing loops work to maintain the balance by keeping the reinforcing loops in check. Drawing a stock/flow map of the ecosystem will help students understand this balance. When the balance is upset, students will be able to trace the causes and the consequences.

Behavior over time graphs are rough sketches of the patterns of behavior we have observed.

In this lesson, students will build the stock/flow map from the ground up, rather than converting the feedback loop as they did in the previous lesson.

What's the Problem?

What problem has Quinlan presented to us in "The Case of the Twin Islands?" Can we capture the problem in a behavior over time graph to look at it more closely? We learned from the story that sea otters were once plentiful in the waters off two neighboring islands until hunters killed them off for their furs. The otter population rebounded around Amchitka Island where kelp forests also flourish, but there are no otters in the barren waters around Shemya today. Why are the two ecosystems so different?

Ask students to sketch important changes over time in the story. Drawing graphs helps students focus on the problem and its causes.

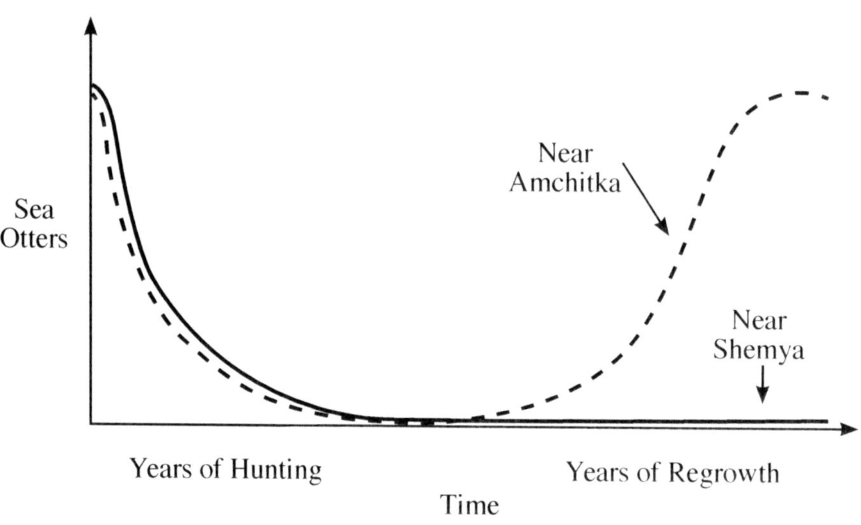

Students may also draw graphs of the changes observed in numbers of seals, eagles, sea urchins, and kelp plants. Some of these patterns will be similar to the pattern for the sea otter population. Sea urchins, however, increased as the otters decreased near Shemya.

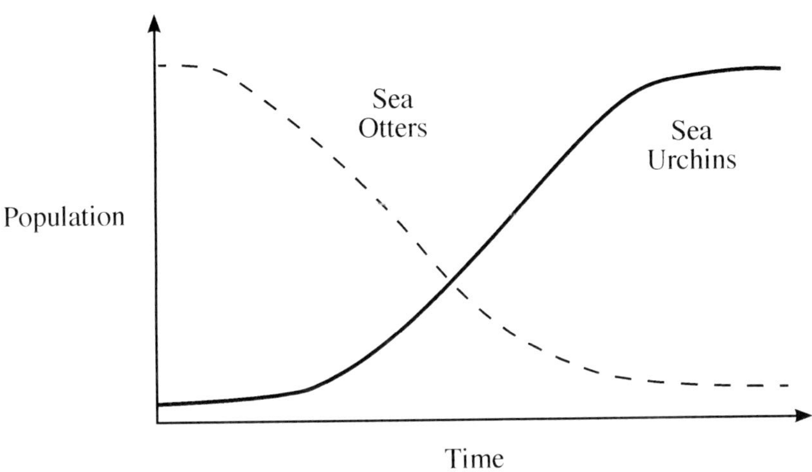

Seeing the Structure

1. The sea otter is one of the key species in the story. Students should be able to construct a simple stock/flow map of otter population.

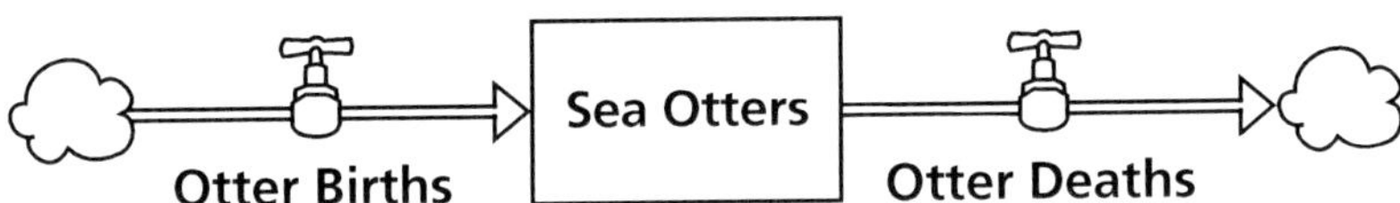

In population stock/flow maps, the size of the population affects the number of births and deaths each year. In the Mammoth Game lesson, for example, births were determined by the number of mammoths in the stock and the rate at which they had babies. Deaths could be seen in a similar way. The reinforcing loop spurred exponential growth, while the balancing loop caused the population to approach zero.

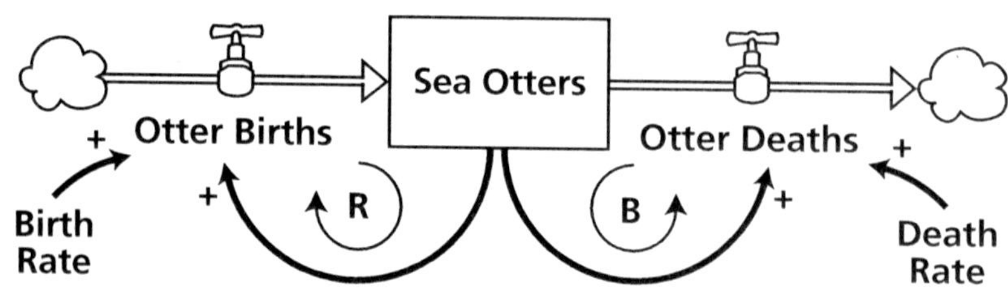

The Twin Islands story has so many population stocks that it is clearer to use the simplified structure of the first diagram. All of the animals and plants in the system increase and decrease according to their own birth (regeneration) and death rates, driven by the feedback processes shown above. Recognizing that these processes are still at work in the background, we will leave these details out of the drawing for now while we focus on the bigger picture—the broader ecological balance among the species.[2]

2. Quinlan tells us that although sea otters eat many kinds of marine animals, sea urchins are their favorite food. Sea otters prey on sea urchins. We can add a stock for sea urchins, since that is another population that increases and decreases over time in our story.

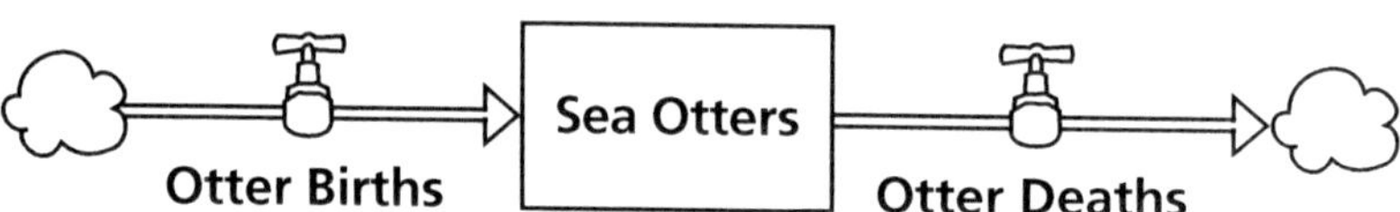

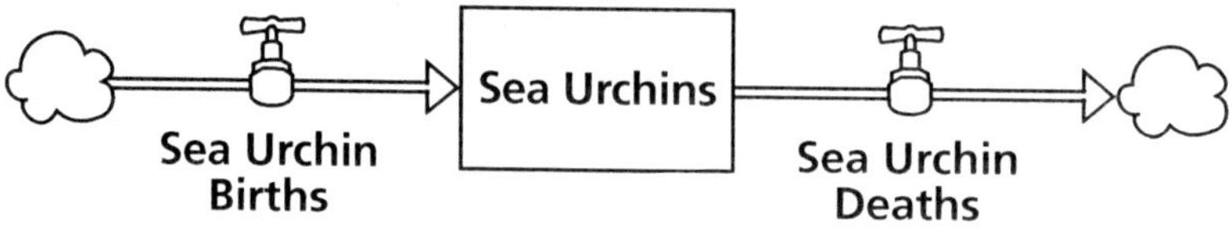

3. Sea urchins are "born" when females release many eggs into the water and some are fertilized and grow into adults. But, what causes sea urchin deaths? Ask students to think about how the populations of sea otters and sea urchins are linked, as told in the story. Sea otters eat the sea urchins. The more sea otters there are, the more sea urchins they eat, reducing the stock of sea urchins.

Sea otters deplete the sea urchin population, but sea otters have other food sources that are not represented in the story and the diagram.

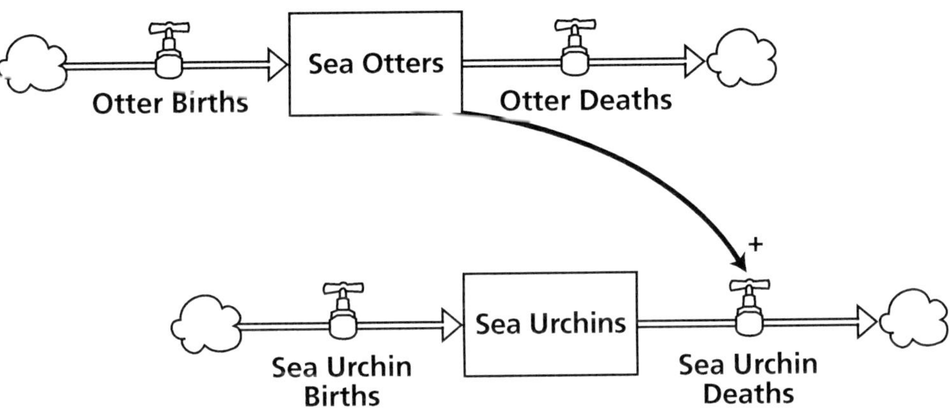

4. Is there more to the relationship between sea otters and sea urchins? Do the sea urchins affect the size of the sea otter population? Yes, when there are plenty of sea urchins to eat, the sea otter population can flourish.

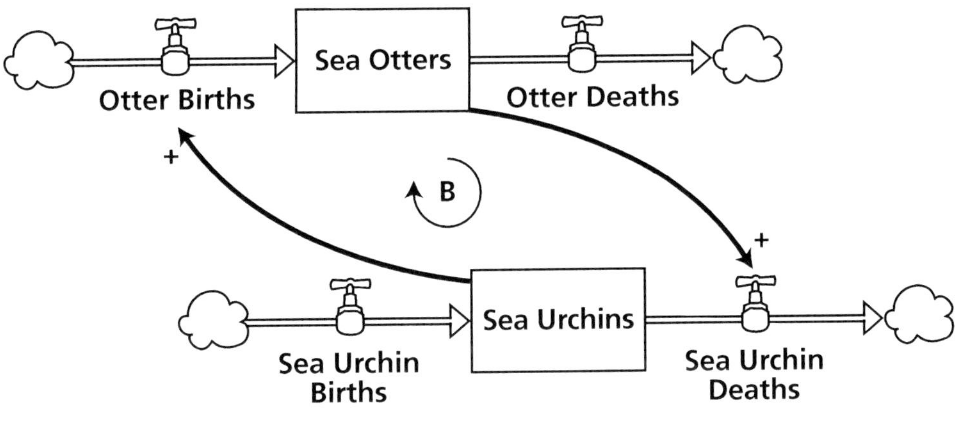

Predator and Prey

Can you tell the story of the relationship between predators and their prey from our stock/flow map of sea otters and sea urchins (Page 95, bottom drawing)?

1. When there are plenty of sea otters, they eat many sea urchins. If sea urchins are eaten faster than they can be "born," then their population declines.
2. When there are few urchins left, the otters do not have enough to eat so their birth rates decline. (Students may notice that a shortage of urchins may also increase the sea otter death rate by starvation.) Eventually there are fewer sea otters around.
3. With fewer otters preying on them, the sea urchin population can grow again to its earlier abundance.
4. But eventually, with plenty of sea urchins to eat, the reduced population of sea otters can once again feast and grow.
5. The cycle repeats again.

This balancing back and forth explains our behavior over time sketch of otters and sea urchins—before hunters upset the delicate predator/prey balance.

5. What else affected the population of sea otters? The author tells us that human hunters nearly drove sea otters to extinction. Show this by constructing a stock/flow diagram of hunters and indicating that the hunters killed the sea otters. The more hunters there were, the more sea otters they caught.

The "clouds" are the boundaries of the system. We are concerned with the number of hunters in our waters, not where they came from or where they go after they leave.

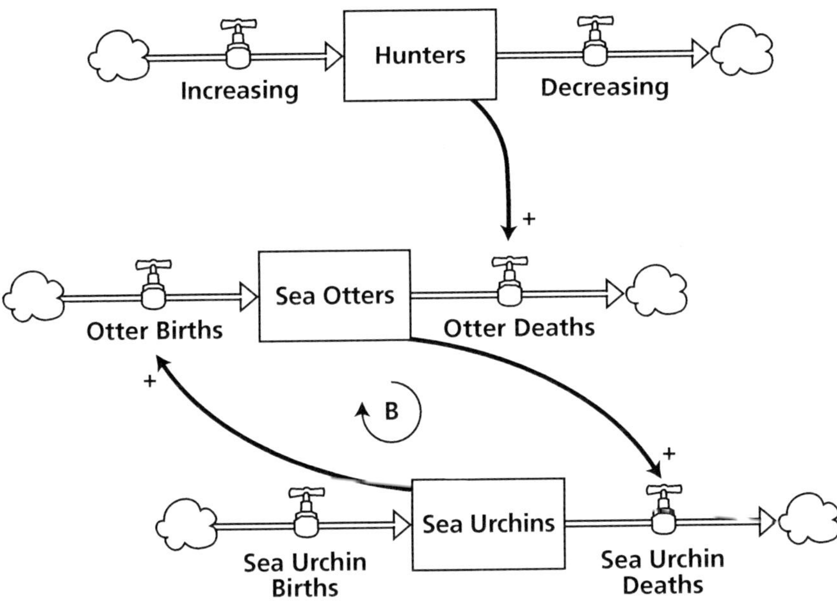

6. How did the sea otters influence the number of hunters? Hunters were attracted to places where otters were originally plentiful. Connect the sea otter stock to the flow that increases the number of hunters.

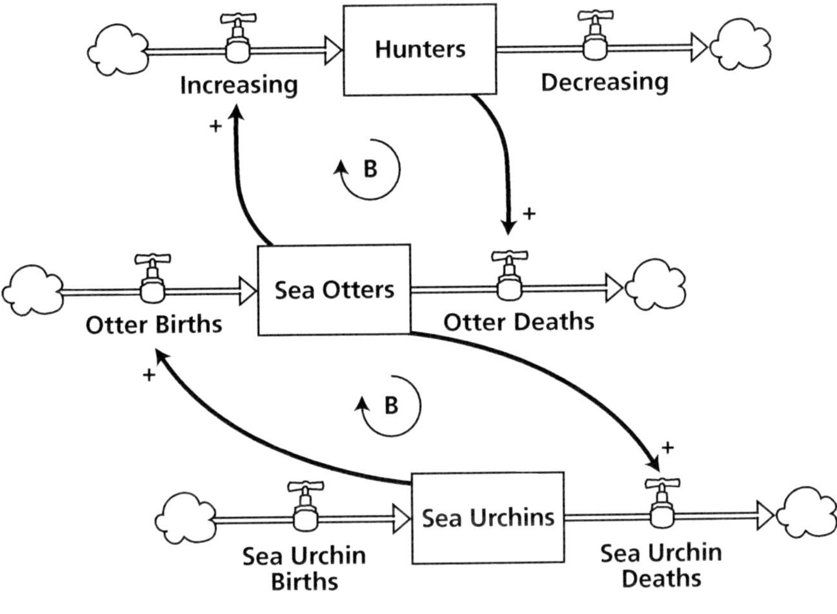

? Does the added structure look familiar? Trace the story of the loops to describe the predator/prey relationship between hunters and sea otters.

When there were many sea otters, many hunters came. As hunters killed off the sea otters in our waters, there were fewer sea otters for hunters to catch, so they went hunting elsewhere. Without hunters, the sea otter population could grow again. If there were not laws against hunting now, hunters would be drawn back to catch their plentiful prey again.

7. What else can affect the population of sea urchins? What does the author tell us about the relationship between sea urchins and kelp plants? The sea urchins graze on the kelp, while the sediments deposited in the calm kelp forests keep the urchin population from growing too fast. When there were "hordes of sea urchins," however, they ate so much that they even gnawed through the bases of the kelp fronds, killing them all.

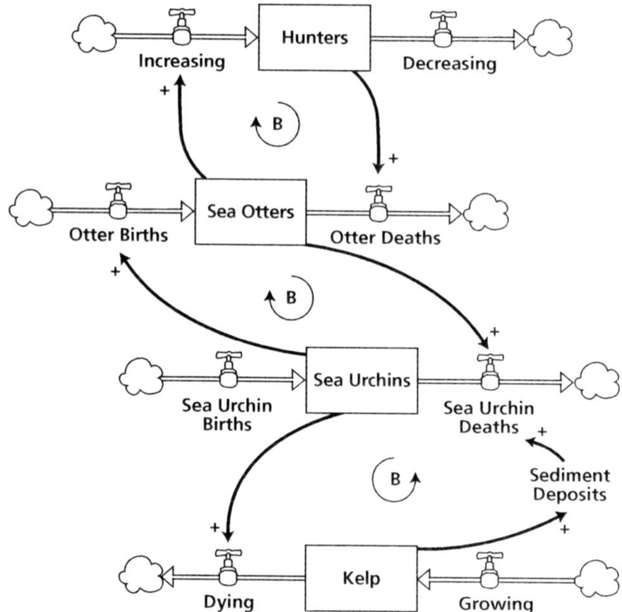

? Can you tell the story of the new loop to explain nature's delicate balance between sea urchins and kelp forests?

When the ecosystem is in balance, the sea urchins eat the kelp, while the kelp allows sediment deposits that limit the sea urchin population. We saw this balance in the lush kelp forests near Amchitka Island.

However, if something causes a very big increase in the sea urchin population (like a decrease in sea otters), the sea urchins eat more and kill all the kelp plants. Without the smothering sediments, the sea urchin death rate slows. If the sea urchin deaths fall below their "births," the population will grow exponentially (remember those population birth and death feedback loops that are still active although not shown). This is what happened around Shemya Island.

If you could take a snapshot of the ecosystem at one moment in time, what accumulations would you see?

8. What else changed when kelp forests were lost? Using the causal loop diagrams students developed after reading "The Case of the Twin Islands," identify the other important stocks in the ecosystem.

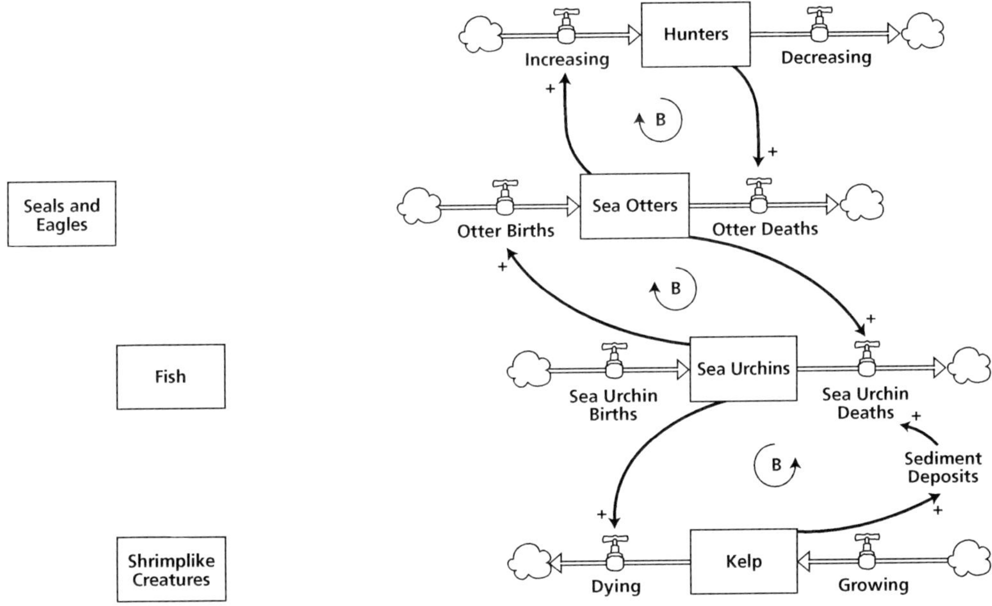

9. Each of the new stocks can increase and decrease depending on the rates of their flows. See if students can create original names for inflows and outflows to the stocks. We use the term "births" loosely here, knowing that these species have very different reproductive systems.

Although not shown in detail here, each population has a reinforcing loop for births and a balancing loop for deaths, just like our earlier otter population diagram.

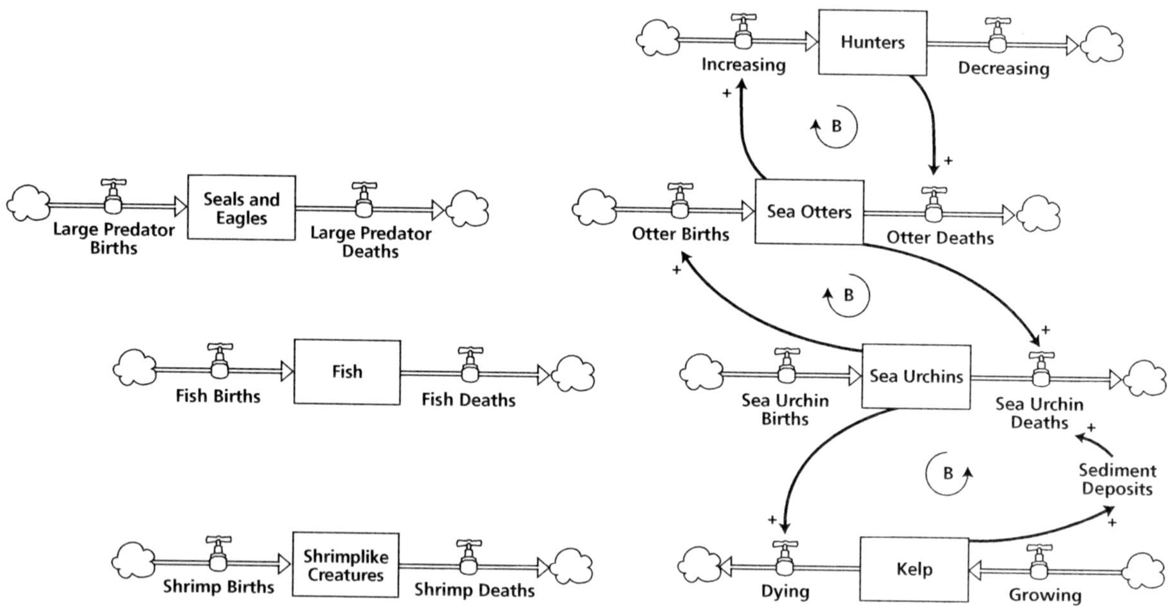

10. Referring back to "The Case of the Twin Islands" and their causal loop diagrams, ask students to draw the connections among these population stocks. Tell the story of each connection.

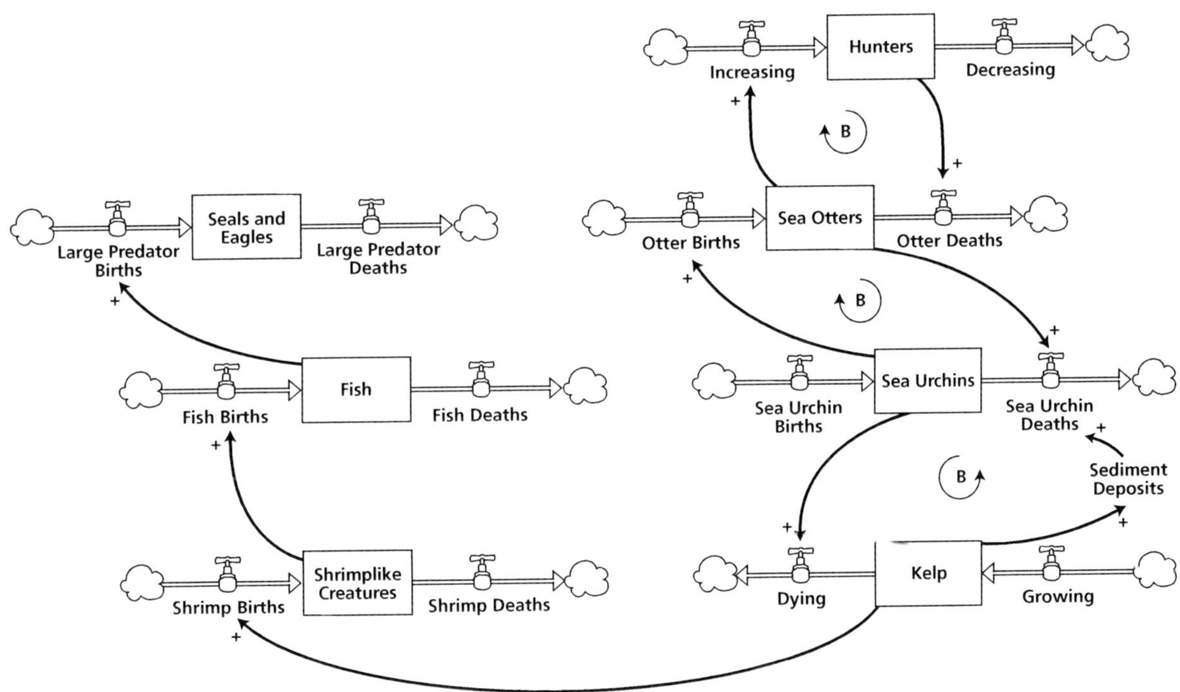

A healthy kelp forest provides a safe habitat for shrimplike amphipods and isopods, so the more kelp plants there are, the more of these creatures there are. The shrimplike creatures provide food for fish—the more food, the more fish. Fish provide food for seals, bald eagles and other large predators.

? Are there more predator/prey relationships in our ecosystem?

Yes, fish prey on the shrimplike creatures, and the large predators prey on the fish. Their relationships are similar to the delicate predator/prey balance we saw between sea otters and sea urchins.

Although students may draw and discuss these additional predator/prey connections, we do not need to include them to address our original problem—the increase in sea urchins and the absence of kelp around Shemya Island—because the shrimp population does not cause an increase or decrease in kelp. An absence of shrimp would not disturb the sea urchin/kelp balance, our problem focus.

Our goal is to understand what is causing the problem—the sea urchin barrens—not to include everything we might know about the system. Keep a sharp focus on the problem.

A stock is not always an accumulation of tangible things. Environmental concerns about biodiversity can increase and decrease over time too.

11. What is missing to finish the story? Quinlan tells us that the ecosystems of sea otters, sea urchins and kelp were originally in balance around both islands. However, when the hunters moved in and caused a drastic outflow, draining the stock of sea otters, the number of otters who were eating sea urchins declined. The stock of urchins grew as their outflow rate slowed, leaving more of the creatures to eat the kelp. The kelp had provided an environment supporting a strong population of shrimp, who in turn were prey for fish. Fish had their place in the food web, feeding seals and eagles.

Eventually, environmentalists began to notice the decline of "popular" species such as sea otters, seals and bald eagles. They became alarmed by the decreasing biodiversity in the area and raised concerns about the ecological consequences of hunting sea otters. When the environmental concerns got high enough, people supported laws to limit or ban hunting and changed their buying habits to use fewer products derived from sea otters.

We can show this rising environmental awareness as a stock (recognizing that it is a simplification for our purposes). Notice that there is a delay in the time it takes people to recognize and acknowledge the problem.

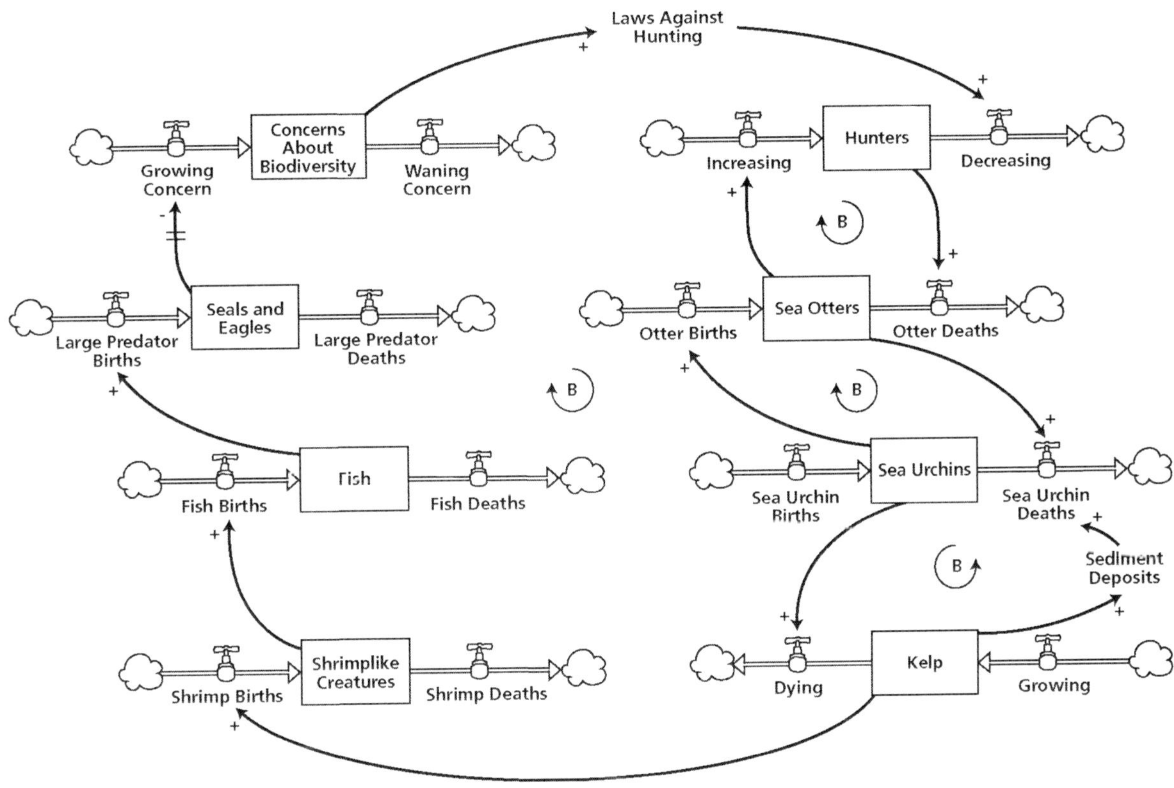

This stock/flow diagram completes our story. As the number of large predators decreased, the environmental concerns eventually grew (a change in the opposite direction labeled "-") until people passed laws to curtail hunting.

? How does our stock/flow map help us see the web of relationships within an ecosystem?

Each stock influences at least one flow that is connected to another stock. Normally, nature maintains a balance. When one stock, or population, reaches a level so high or low that changes begin to ripple through the system, the connections to other flows help stabilize the ecosystem. For example, if the sea urchin population grows beyond a certain level, the kelp forest may be damaged by them. In a healthy ecosystem, the sea otters would feast on the abundance of urchins, and the kelp would have a chance to regenerate.

If an initial change reverses direction around the loop, it is a balancing loop.

? Why is our major feedback loop a balancing loop? From any starting point, trace the increases and decreases around the loop (or use the up and down arrows we introduced in Lesson 2).

An initial increase in hunters causes a decrease in sea otters which then causes an increase in sea urchins. An increase in sea urchins causes a decrease in kelp. Fewer kelp plants means fewer shrimplike creatures which causes fewer fish and then fewer large predators. As seals and eagles decline, environmental awareness rises, which leads to laws banning hunting, and therefore fewer hunters. So, an initial ***increase*** *in hunters caused a* ***decrease*** *in hunters. Around the loop again, this* ***decrease*** *in hunters would lead to more sea otters, relaxed concerns and eventually an* ***increase*** *in hunters again. The change balances back and forth.*

? If the balancing loops tend to balance the ecosystem, what causes growth or decline in the species?

Reinforcing loops cause exponential growth. Remember that each of our population inflows is determined by the size of the population and its growth rate, just like the Mammoth births in Lesson 3 and our earlier sea otter diagram.

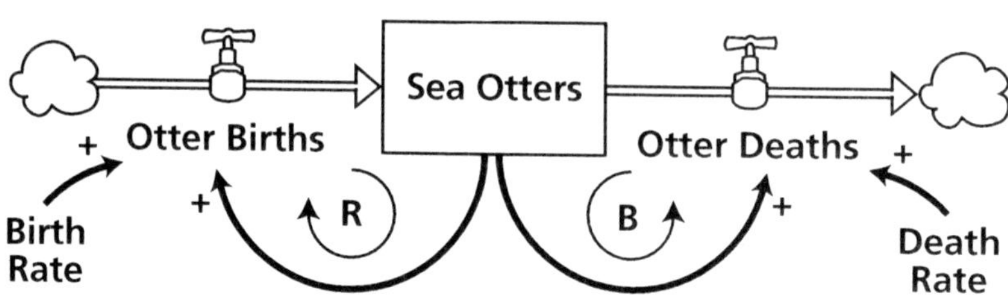

Whenever something causes births to exceed deaths, any population will begin to grow exponentially. In nature, balancing loops in the system work to limit this unrestrained growth.

? Why did the sea otters come back to Amchitka and not to Shemya?

As we read in ***The Shape of Change****, scientists have many theories including differences in coastal currents, algae levels, predator relationships, and environmental contamination. Because sea otters are a keystone species, their presence holds together the diverse ecosystem around Amchitka.*

? Could a vibrant kelp forest come back to Shemya? Look at our stock/flow map for clues.

The stock of kelp plants is controlled by the number of sea urchins eating them. If a big storm or disease decimates the sea urchin population, the kelp can grow back. Scientists have found that sea urchin/kelp ecosystems alternate between relatively stable luxuriant kelp forests and sea urchin barrens.[3] *Our stock/flow map shows us how a disruption in one part of the feedback system can tip the balance from one state to the other.*

Drawing a stock/flow map has helped us understand a complex web of interdependencies. It is not an "answer." It is a process of raising better and better questions about how systems work.

NOTES

1 "The Case of the Twin Islands" is a chapter from *The Case of the Mummified Pigs and Other Mysteries of Nature*, by Susan E. Quinlan, illustrated by Jennifer Owens Dewey, published by Caroline House, Boyds Mills Press, Inc., 1995. The chapter is reprinted with permission in ***The Shape of Change***, Page 133.

2 To build a system dynamics computer simulation model of the system, we would include all the birth, regeneration and death rates (and many other details) to specify explicitly how the stocks increase and decrease over time.

3 For more information, see "Ecological Role of Purple Sea Urchins," by John S. Pearse, *Science* 314, (2006). Also at *www.sciencemag.org*.

About Us

About the Authors

Rob Quaden and Alan Ticotsky are teachers in the Carlisle Public Schools, Carlisle, Massachusetts. Quaden teaches eighth grade math. Ticotsky teaches science and social studies and has written a series of books titled *Science Giants.* For many years, they were also systems mentors generously supported by the Waters Foundation, affording them the time to learn, collaborate, and develop lessons infusing system dynamics into the K-8 curriculum. Debra Lyneis was a Carlisle parent and school board member who now works at the Creative Learning Exchange helping teachers publish system dynamics curriculum materials.

The Creative Learning Exchange

The Creative Learning Exchange is a non-profit organization in Acton, Massachusetts dedicated to promoting learner-centered learning and system dynamics in K-12 education. The CLE disseminates classroom curriculum materials developed by teachers, publishes a quarterly newsletter, hosts a biennial conference for teachers, sponsors an annual student exposition, maintains a listserv, and provides system dynamics training materials and programs for teachers. Information is available at *www.clexchange.org.*

System Dynamics

System dynamics is a field of study and a perspective for understanding change. Using computer simulation and other tools, system dynamics looks at how the feedback structure of systems causes the change we observe all around us. System dynamics was developed fifty years ago by Professor Jay W. Forrester at MIT and is used to address problems in areas ranging from ecology, to business management, economics, and psychology. Under Forrester's guidance, system dynamics is helping teachers make K-12 education more learner-centered, engaging, challenging and relevant to our rapidly changing world. ***The Shape of Change*** and ***The Shape of Change: Stocks and Flows*** introduce young students and their teachers to some of the basic ideas of system dynamics as a way to observe and think about change.

MORE COPIES

The Shape of Change and
The Shape of Change: Stocks and Flows

can be purchased from the
Creative Learning Exchange at:

www.clexchange.org
978-635-9797
milleras@clexchange.org

These and other lessons can be downloaded
for free from the CLE website in PDF format.